W9-BBD-878

The Charm Is Broken

THE CHARM IS BROKEN

*Readings in Arkansas and
Missouri Folklore*

Edited by W. K. McNeil

August House / Little Rock

Library of Congress Cataloging in Publication Data
Main entry under title:

The Charm is broken.

1. Folklore — Arkansas — Addresses, essays, lectures.
2. Folklore — Missouri — Addresses, essays, lectures.
3. Arkansas — Social life and customs — Addresses, essays,
lectures. 4. Missouri — Social life and customs — Addresses,
essays, lectures. I. McNeil, W. K.
GR110.A8C43   1984   398'.09767   83-71902
ISBN 0-935304-66-5
ISBN 0-935304-67-3 (pbk.)

Published 1984 by August House, Inc., 1010 West Third
   Street, Little Rock, Arkansas 72201
   (501) 376-4516
Printed in the United States of America.

Cover design by Madeline Collins
Book design by Ira Hocut

*To my mother
who always encouraged me
in my reading*

CONTENTS

Preface

The following book is compiled with a number of specific goals in mind. First, it is intended primarily for Arkansas and Missouri students taking courses in folklore. Several years ago when I first began working with high school teachers I was struck by the fact that there were a large number of schools that offered courses in folklore and also by the fact that there was no textbook, or even a good book of readings, oriented towards these classes. That situation has not changed although there is now a fine volume, *Country Folks*, by Richard and Laurna Tallman that partially fills the void. Good as it is, the Tallmans' book is not adequate since it is solely concerned with the Arkansas Ozarks and was never intended as anything other than a fieldwork guide. Also it is now somewhat dated and in need of revision. While the present book is not a textbook it is an attempt to offer a representative selection of what has been written on Arkansas and Missouri folklore. This, of course, entails including both good and bad examples of folklore work in the two states but, obviously, more of the worthy items appear than do the less worthy.

Another goal has been to emphasize collections since that is what most high school teachers will be concerned with. Also, I think, collections will be generally more interesting to the nonprofessional than lofty theoretical discussions. In choosing this course I do not mean to imply that folklore theory is unimportant and has no place in a volume like this but, rather, that for the present purpose such works come second in the order of priorities. An attempt has been made to provide articles on every area of fieldwork that students are likely to deal with. Thus, articles on myths and mythology are not included while those on riddles and beliefs are. Still, despite my best efforts, there is no pretense that all genres are covered; some of my choices are attributable to what is available. There are few articles on proverbs or folk dance in Missouri and Arkansas but there are many on folk narrative. Those who wish a greater body of material should consult the articles cited in the headnotes or such journals as *MidAmerica Folklore* or the *Missouri Folklore Society Journal*.

Hopefully, this book will shatter some commonly held stereotypes about folklore, in particular the idea that oral tradition exists only in rural areas. For this reason, among others, material on university folklore and folk narratives

9

from the city are included. Another intention is to provide articles that deal with individual folk artists, performers, or craftsmen. Some other concerns include having material by folklorists — professionals or amateurs — that are, or have been, active in the two states. Thus, Vance Randolph, Mary Parler, and Mary Alicia Owen, among others, are represented; in so doing the book offers in a sense a minihistory of folklore scholarship in Missouri and Arkansas. Of course, for a number of reasons, it has not been possible to include something by every single folklorist or scholar active in the two states. The ever-present and necessary limitations of space partially account for this shortcoming but equally important is the fact that some articles are simply inappropriate, given the intended audience.

Considering the nature of the preceding remarks it seems necessary to add that while this book is intended for students, it will hopefully have some appeal to a more general audience. Undoubtedly there are readers in Missouri, Arkansas, and elsewhere who may wish to learn something about the traditions of the two states but who don't wish to take the time to attend formal classes. It is hoped that this book will fill their needs.

A rite of passage in putting a book together is for the author to state that his work could not have been produced without the help of many other persons. Though well worn, the cliché is true. All of the persons cited below contributed invaluable help or advice or both to the production of this manuscript and their efforts are greatly appreciated and hereby acknowledged: William Clements, Debbie Cochran, Nana Farris, Gordon McCann, Mary Sue Price, Dolf and Becky Schroeder, and Diane Tebbetts.

W. K. McNeil

The Ozark Folk Center
Mountain View, Arkansas

Introduction

In most academic disciplines there is no uniform agreement among scholars on the limits of their field of inquiry. Ask two historians to define history and you will likely get two slightly differing definitions. Probably the same result will occur if two political scientists, two sociologists, two biologists, or two practitioners in any other field of systematic investigation are surveyed. The same situation applies to folklore, for it is a complex area of intellectual study that does not easily lend itself to a brief description. Yet, there are certain points that most authorities would include in any definition of folklore: these are (1) an item of folklore is passed on orally and, usually, informally; (2) it is traditional; (3) it exists in variants and versions; (4) it is generally anonymous; and (5) it is frequently formulaic.

These five parts need further explanation. An item of folklore is oral in the sense that its existence depends on being passed from one person to another or one generation to the next by word of mouth. Some folklorists refer to this as aural transmission because the materials of folklore reach the ear either from voices or musical instruments or by customary demonstration or imitation. An equally important part of this definition is that folklore is never transmitted entirely in a formal manner. This explains why songs of singers such as Joan Baez or Bob Dylan are not folksongs even though some of their numbers are derived from traditional sources.

Folklore is traditional in that it is passed on repeatedly in relatively fixed forms and circulates among members of a particular group. Mere tradition, however, doesn't make an item folklore. It is only when it is passed on orally and informally that traditional material becomes folklore. Such oral transmission inevitably leads to changes over space and time, and this brings up a third defining characteristic of folklore — it must exist in variants and versions. This is one reason why most of the songs of Woody Guthrie, for example, are not folksongs — they are mostly passed on just as they are found in print.

It is, of course, possible for a song, proverb, tale, etc., to be folklore at one point in time and then cease to be at a later era. This seems to be the case with "Home On The Range," which was collected around the turn of the century as a folksong but now, after wide reprinting, is primarily known only in printed form.[1]

11

A fourth feature of folklore is that it is anonymous. This statement is not intended to imply that no one knows who originally authored a ballad, a folktale or a proverb (although that frequently is the case). It merely means that the authorship is not really of significance to the people who pass the item of folklore on because their concern is with the text, not the creator. Some writers carry the trait of anonymity to extremes. For example, Mary D. Hudgins suggests in an article in *Mid-South Folklore* that anonymity is the sole defining characteristic of folklore.[2] Taking as examples two songs, "My Happy Little Home In Arkansas" and "Gambler's Blues," she says that, despite the assertions of many people, these songs are not folksongs. As proof of her argument she cites the fact that "My Happy Little Home In Arkansas" was written in 1893 by Henry DeMoss and "Gambler's Blues" was written in 1925 by Phil Baxter. Thus, because the authors are known, she reasons, these are not folksongs. Actually, Hudgins is right but for the wrong reasons. The songs are not items of folklore because they show no evidence of having undergone the process of oral transmission: they show no textual variation from the original printing. The fact that DeMoss and Baxter wrote them is of little importance in determining whether or not they are folksongs.[3] After all, it is doubtful that most of the people singing these songs are aware of who the original authors were and, in any case, all songs are written by someone. For example, "Little Rosewood Casket" is accurately called a folksong even though it is known that the piece was written in 1870 by Charles White. In folk tradition it has varied far from the original piece and has become part of oral tradition in the United States.

The fifth defining characteristic of folklore — that of formularization — results from being passed on orally. People who keep materials in circulation without mass-media aids such as print or records must rely on other mnemonic (memory) devices. This is where formulas, or clichés, figure, for they are employed mainly as a means of remembering passages. An enormous range of formulas is found in American folklore and varies in complexity from simple phrases to elaborate opening or closing devices for songs and narratives. Perhaps most readers will be familiar with the older British ballads where "milk white steeds," "lily white hands," and like phrases abound.

Complicating the task of defining folklore for a general audience are certain erroneous ideas about the subject that are commonly accepted. At least four faulty assumptions concerning folklore thrive in the popular mind. First is the concept that folklore thrives only in a few areas, and second is the coinciding belief that it exists solely in isolated areas among backward and primitive people. Third is the mistaken assumption that the Southern mountains, meaning the Southern Appalachians and the Ozarks, are the archetypal nonprogressive American area. Finally, it is popularly believed that folklore consists only of survivals from past ages. But folklore exists everywhere, among all peoples, rich or poor, young or old, of all racial backgrounds. It is true that more folklore has been collected from such areas as the Appalachians and the Ozarks than from Cleveland, New York, or Chicago, but that merely reflects greater emphasis on collecting in those areas and is no indication of comparative wealth of folklore. All regions, like the Ozarks and the Appalachians, are rich in the various genres of oral tradition.

Some might argue that a valid case can be made that folklore consists of survivals from past ages. Certainly no one can deny that much folklore is quite ancient. For example, some of the jokes told in recent decades concerning the Little Moron date back to ancient Egypt. Similarly, a legend usually called The Vanishing Hitchhiker, which is periodically popular and has even served as the basis for two popular songs and a movie, can actually be traced back several hundred years to a European origin. However, to say that all folklore comes from ancient or bygone times is to ignore the fact that folklore is constantly changing, always in a state of flux, ever adapting to changing modes of thought, value systems, and the like; it is, in short, a flexible aspect of culture. One relatively recent legend, which also served as the basis for a very popular movie, is sometimes called "The Babysitter and the Man Upstairs"[4] and, since much of the action involves a modern invention, the telephone, it could not very well predate the invention. Likewise, some items of folk speech may be coined, thrive as folklore, and then disappear from oral tradition within a relatively short space of years.

Having dealt with defining folklore it remains to ask and answer the question: who is a folklorist? Often someone who knows some old songs or plays a musical instrument or who writes songs in a traditional style is called a folklorist but the designation is incorrect. A folklorist is not a hobbyist or an entertainer but rather a serious scholar who has a professional interest in folklore. He is a person with training in folklore who does comparative studies in the field. This definition does not mean that only professional folklorists can make substantive contributions to folklore studies. Indeed, much important work can, and has been, done by knowledgeable amateurs. One of the most significant figures in the history of American folklore scholarship was Vance Randolph, an amateur in the best sense of that word. Due to his untiring efforts the Ozark region is better documented from a folklore viewpoint than any region in the United States. Yet, even in this fairly well-covered area it can honestly be said that no genre of oral tradition has been thoroughly collected or studied. Fortunately, contrary to some doomsayers, the time to record this material is not past. True, some informants are dying but other people carry on their traditions.

Now, for the inevitable question: how does one go about collecting folklore? Regardless of whether a person is an amateur or a professional with extensive experience, his fieldwork will benefit from considerable advance planning. Although the gathering of raw data, i.e. texts, is essential for the continued existence of folklore as a discipline it cannot be overemphasized that the recording of any folklore items should not be undertaken until much prior background research has been undertaken. Any type of research project involving fieldwork, i.e. the actual collection of data, consists of at least five stages, each of which is equally important. These stages are:

1. Problem statement: that is, establishing a problem to be solved.
2. Problem analysis.
3. Collection of data.

4. Presentation of research findings.
5. Formulation of theories based on analysis.

All fieldwork does not proceed to the final step. When the problem is one of description, as it will be in most high school projects, step four will be the end product. Here, of course, we will be primarily concerned with the first three steps.

PROBLEM STATEMENT

There was a time when it was fashionable for folklorists to go into the field without having formalized what they wanted to know. The great scholar Franz Boas, for example, believed that any person with a knowledge of folklore merely had to go into the field and after collecting enormous amounts of data would, more or less by osmosis, discover the correct clues for "understanding" the specific culture he was dealing with. This type of fieldwork is no longer seriously advocated by any folklorist. Contemporary scholars support the idea of planning ahead before doing any fieldwork. In fact as much time needs to be spent in planning the fieldwork as in actually doing it, and a person who thinks that the actual interviewing is the initial stage of a field project rather than a later phase is truly an amateur. It is also true of many amateurs that they slough off the initial stages of fieldwork, and particularly the very first — the problem statement. Before proceeding to the interview it is essential that you first decide what it is you want to know. To do otherwise will simply result in a great deal of wasted time, and time is something few of us have in sufficient abundance to be able to afford to waste any. Each stage of your field research must be pursued with equal vigor. Applying the strictest methods during the later stages of investigation will not create a useful end product if the problem statement itself is poorly defined.

It is unlikely that a person will know what folklore problems need solving in a community or region without some knowledge of the area's history. Probably most school students do have some awareness of their community's past but it may be sketchy. The problem does not have to be anything elaborate; often it involves simply recording information about crafts that are or once were prominent in the community or region. Most high school students will, by virtue of their lack of transportation, probably be confined to doing a project that can be done entirely in their hometown. Possibly they can undertake a project that will lead to a program in addition to their collection. For example, if the problem consists of determining to what extent there is a folk music tradition in the immediate vicinity of the school or town this might lead to a program of traditional music in the school. Such a feature could be both entertaining and informative.

Every community has individuals who can provide useful information about local folklore that might not otherwise be preserved. The community's elder members, who have had many experiences that can illuminate aspects of the past, are usually the first individuals selected for interviews. However, it should be remembered that other persons have folklore and may also be good informants. In fact the nonelderly may be the best informants. In the nineteenth century William Wells Newell produced what is still a highly regarded work, *Games and Songs of American Children,* that was based entirely on "memory culture." By neglecting the ongoing tradition bearers and seeking out merely elderly informants who remembered the lore but no longer actually practiced it Newell missed much valuable information about the way games then functioned and how those functions may have changed over the years. It should be kept in mind that elderly people sometimes make poor informants because of senility or even possibly a desire to put all of that old stuff (which oftentimes is their view of folklore) out of their minds. In other words, just because someone is old does not make him a good informant.

Some attention should be paid to the type of folklore one is seeking, for the methodology will vary somewhat according to the kind of material one is looking for. In other words you probably will not use the same techniques for seeking out ballad singers that you will use for finding legend tellers or users of proverbs. I have always found it much easier to turn up musicians and singers than legend bearers because the former type of lore is viewed by informants as primarily entertainment (which is a frequently encountered popular idea of folklore) whereas the latter is viewed in a different light. Musicians and singers may often perform for someone other than just their circle of acquaintances whereas this is not the case with legend tellers. It is possible that a person will sit and sing himself a song but very doubtful that anyone will go sit in a corner of his house and tell himself a tale. Such things must be taken into account by anyone planning on doing a fieldwork project in folklore.

PROBLEM ANALYSIS

Having formulated his plan the person conducting a folklore project can then proceed to the second stage of inquiry: the problem analysis. Doing folklore, or any other kind of fieldwork, one should not simply proceed from the statement of the problem to the interview. First, he should plan to do some background research — his "homework." An unprepared interviewer will not know what questions to ask, when he has thoroughly covered the subject, or whether the material gathered from the informant is unusual or generally in accord with local traditions. Thorough background research is essential for a successful interview and its importance cannot be exaggerated. To fail in this responsibility could result in as great a waste of time as would an arbitrary treatment of the problem statement.

Analysis of the problem involves investigating all accessible materials relevant to the problem. This includes perusal of artifacts, documents, books, and any other materials that may be pertinent to the subject. Those who may not know where to begin finding printed material on folklore are advised to look into one or all of several helpful bibliographies. The oldest and least significant of those available in book form is Charles Haywood's *A Bibliography of North American Folklore and Folksong,* but it may be useful for comparative purposes because it is broken down along state lines and cultural groups as well as generically. Another important folklore bibliography compiled annually appeared in *Southern Folklore Quarterly* during the years 1942-1972, and the issues that have appeared since have been either part of the Indiana University Folklore Institute Monograph Series or part of the folklore publications of the Institute for the Study of Human Issues, an organization located in Philadelphia, Pennsylvania. This bibliography is extensive and is arranged generically, as most older folklore bibliographies are. This particular bibliography is especially useful for those dealing with Hispanic traditions, for it has always been compiled by folklorists primarily concerned with Mexican-American traditions. Because of their budgets and special interests they have opted to confine the bibliography to a relatively limited geographic region that could be more thoroughly covered than a bibliography dealing with the entire world. So at present this bibliography is focused upon the American continent, Spain, Portugal, and other areas in the world where Spanish or Portuguese is spoken.

There are a few folklore bibliographies for specific regions of the country. The best and most extensive of this type is Vance Randolph's *Ozark Folklore: A Bibliography* which appeared in 1972. Soon a supplement to this mammoth work will be available. Most of the more than two thousand references are to works dealing with Missouri or Arkansas folklore. At the present time there is no bibliography devoted to Missouri folklore but there is my *Arkansas Folklore: A Bibliography* which is available from the Regional Resource Center at Arkansas College in Batesville. For titles from both states one might consult the book review section of *MidAmerica Folklore,* a journal devoted to folklore from the Ozark states, or the book review section of the *Missouri Folklore Society Journal*. Another useful source which is unfortunately now defunct is *Folklore Abstracts*. This quarterly bulletin was commenced in 1963 by the American Folklore Society and was devoted to summarizing the contents of articles in folklore journals and periodicals of related interest. Most of these research aids will be available in big city or university libraries but if you do not have access to such sources then you might begin locating folklore works relevant to your region by writing the American Folklore Society, 1703 New Hampshire Avenue NW, Washington, D.C., 20009 or, if you live in Arkansas, state folklorist Stephen Poyser, Arkansas Arts Council, The Heritage Center, Suite 200, 225 East Markham, Little Rock, Arkansas, 72201, will be able to help you. Unfortunately, Missouri does not have a state folklorist, but there are a number of organizations that will be helpful, one of these being the Missouri Friends of the Folk Arts, Jefferson National Expansion Historical Association, 11 North 4th Street, St. Louis, Missouri, 63102.

Besides the obvious folklore publications, the person doing a thorough analysis of his problem may profitably consult such other sources as:

1. General cultural studies.
2. Local antiquarian publications.
3. Miscellanea of local societies.
4. Travel journals and reminiscences.
5. Health, census, and economic reports.
6. Local histories.

7. Popular magazines.
8. Local newspapers.
9. Published diaries, biographies, and reminiscences of local inhabitants.
10. Novels by local authors based on local life.
11. Dictionaries, especially dialect dictionaries.

A careful analysis of the problem will assist the interviewer in determining the probable time necessary for an effective and useful folklore collecting project. He will also be able to converse more intelligently with his informants because he will be familiar with various aspects of the topic. This added knowledge will result in a more informative and useful interview.

After analyzing the problem the next procedure is making up a questionnaire, for I think it is best for inexperienced fieldworkers to have a list of questions in hand. A great deal of time should be spent on this because it is important that the questions really ask what you think they ask. Sometimes the wording of a query can lead an informant astray. Even though the interviewer thinks he has a good question, it may actually be one that can be interpreted in several ways. Make sure that your questions can only be interpreted the way you meant them to be. To test your questions it is a good idea to try them out on someone before actually conducting interviews.

It is best to keep questions short and precise. This makes them understandable and less likely to be confusing. If several closely allied points should be covered, then it is best to group these related queries as subnumbered questions under the main question. Thus, a person might ask question number 1 and have related queries numbered 1a, 1b, and 1c. When the interviewer has had some experience he should proceed from reading the questions to using them merely as guidelines. This approach will be more useful because it allows for some flexibility. Each interview situation differs somewhat and therefore some on-the-spot adaptation will perhaps result in a more useful end product. The person with some fieldwork experience may opt for the finding list in place of the questionnaire. By this I mean that from your research into the lore of a particular town or region you can compile a list of materials in specific genres that you might logically expect to recover in interviews and use this search list as a springboard for your interviews.

After making your questionnaire comes the all-important matter of determining who you should interview. Of course the best way to turn up good informants is through prolonged contact with a large number of people in a community or region. For most high school students it is probably easiest to begin doing fieldwork in their own family. They already know these people well and thus don't have to begin by establishing contacts. Also because they are intimately acquainted with family members, they are probably going to have an easier time getting them to talk and may be able to elicit much more information than an outsider could. Furthermore, the novice interviewer will probably be more at ease and gain a greater feeling of success from interviewing persons he knows intimately.

There are many situations where extensive contact may not be possible and it will be necessary to accomplish a great deal in a short amount of time. For collectors in this kind of hurry some shortcuts to finding informants are necessary. Personally, I have always found newspapermen good sources of information about certain types of folklore bearers, particularly craftsmen, musicians, and singers. It is the newspaperman's responsibility to keep up on his community and he is often likely to know about those people carrying on traditions that may involve public performance or exhibition. There is also another reason why contacting newspapers is a good idea, particularly for collectors from outside the community. Most editors are looking for story material and they will often welcome the chance to print a story about your project and explain it in general terms. This may even result in people calling *you*, wishing to be interviewed, and will almost certainly help your project since it will make local residents aware of some of your goals.

Another fruitful contact, particularly when seeking musicians, is the local radio station or stations. Frequently, they put on programs featuring local musicians and singers and can probably supply you with many good leads. Also, like the newspaper, they may help in publicizing your quest. The Chamber of Commerce secretary, the county agricultural agent, and any other individuals who have to know a wide variety of people may all prove good sources for building up a list of possible informants. However, the collector doesn't have to rely solely on others for leads; he can make his own breaks. One means of doing this is by hanging around gathering places for congenial groups, such as boardinghouse parlors, barber shops, a favorite café. I have been able to uncover a number of traditional tale tellers by frequenting such places. Another good idea is to attend as many local functions as possible. While attending a community musical presentation in Cave City, Arkansas, I happened to sit down next to Hubert Wilkes, a local resident who also happens to be an excellent tale teller and the featured performer in *They Tell It For The Truth: Storytellers of the Ozarks*, a film about tall tale narrators from the Arkansas Ozarks. Some of his texts can also be heard on the double album *Not Far From Here: Traditional Tales and Songs Recorded in the Arkansas Ozarks*.

My fieldwork experience is now largely confined to rural communities and there is, of course, a difference doing fieldwork in an urban setting. It is not, however, an insurmountable difference and any good fieldworker should be able to work in both environments. There is one advantage the person doing fieldwork in cities has over anyone working in rural areas and that is that cities have many more private and public municipal agencies that may well be sources of potential informants. These include nationality clubs and societies, ethnic lodges of international organizations, settlement houses, recreation centers, labor unions, and any other agency that penetrates the supposedly impersonal life of the metropolis. Newspaper notices announce ethnic conventions, festivals, holidays, picnics, school programs, and other occasions where anyone interested in seeking out potential tradition bearers may observe and mingle. In the city as in the country, informants are a good source of leads to other informants. Quite often one person knows others who keep alive the same type of lore he does and your first good informant may well turn out to be your best source for other leads.

Having carefully stated and analyzed the problem, an incipient collector is at last ready to begin actually collecting material. Each collecting situation differs from every other and because the success of a collecting venture depends to a great extent on personality, no specific rules can be set down as universally applicable guidelines. However, there are certain rules of thumb that should be kept in mind although you probably will not be able to follow them always. Arrangements for an interview should be made at least three or four days in advance. The interviewer should describe the purpose of the interview, mentioning the specific topics to be covered and the sort of information he is seeking. One word that should not be mentioned is folklore as it has too many potentially erroneous connotations, thanks to many mass-media misuses of the term. One way of broaching the subject is to simply say, "Several people have told me you know a lot of the kinds of tales people used to tell in the old days. I'm interested in any of these stories that don't come from books." Some people prefer to approach a potential informant with an introduction such as "James Johnston over in Marshall told me that you are a good singer of the old-time songs [once again avoid using the word folk in your initial encounter with an informant]." Often the answer comes back, "I would like to help you out, but you wouldn't want the stories I know." Immediately the collector goes on to focus more sharply his request, perhaps by illustrating with a sample song, tale, etc. To achieve the best results one should avoid performing unless it is absolutely essential because there are too many pitfalls to this approach. The collector who is a poor performer may find his informant losing some of the respect he otherwise might have had for him. On the other hand the collector who is a good performer may make the informant overly self-conscious about his own abilities. In either case the collector is the loser. Keep in mind that your informant knows more about his traditions than you do and anything that makes your gaining access to that information more difficult should be avoided.

Just as one should avoid performing he should also avoid talking except when necessary. There is usually only a limited amount of time available for interviews, and each second taken up by your own talking is that much less time for your informant to talk; in every situation what he has to say is more important than what you have to say. You will have other opportunities to talk, but you may never see him again.

The place and length of an interview are of considerable importance. If possible, the interview should take place at a time when there will be no interruptions — telephone calls, visitors, or anything that would disturb the session. There should be only two persons present. Interviewing two informants can produce arguments hampering the conversation and can complicate establishing the essential feeling of mutual trust. Much of the success of an interview depends on the collector being sensitive to his informants, and one way he can be very insensitive is by allowing the interview to go on too long. Under the best conditions, two hours should be the maximum length of an interview. A number of short sessions is generally preferable to one long one.

Just prior to the interview, the following information should be taped: informant's name, interviewer's name, date, time and place of the interview and possibly the place where the interview will be filed. It is advisable to do this in the room with the informant. Besides giving him time to relax before being questioned, it lends an air of importance to the entire venture. The interviewer should aim to obtain complete and accurate information during the interview, striving constantly to obtain an easy flow of conversation. An interviewer must be a good listener and must focus all of his attention on the speaker, but he must be sympathetic and noncommital at the same time. A little flattery can help to establish the necessary rapport between the two partners for the interview. One should not go so far as to be dishonest, for a prime consideration is that one should above all be himself. Sham, hypocrisy, and condescension have a way of being detected by everyone.

What is it that the amateur folklore collector is going to seek out? The academic folklorist generally looks for six types of data. These are:

1. Personal history of informants.
2. Aesthetics of informants.
3. The informant's knowledge, feelings and meanings regarding the specific items of lore he carries. In other words, the folklorist is interested in determining how folklore functions in a community.
4. Transmission of folklore materials (finding out when, where, and from whom it was learned).
5. Descriptions of folklore situations that the collector is unable to observe.
6. Informants' repertoire.

Usually the amateur collector will be mainly interested in the last of these categories, i.e. the folklore texts, but the other matters are of considerable value to anyone using the collected material. Finding out about the informants' personal history is important because we need to know what kind of person becomes a tradition bearer and the forces that have contributed to his becoming one. Knowing the informants' aesthetics helps in determining why certain items become part of oral tradition and others do not. Getting this information is also a good way of getting to know the person better. Finally one needs to know in what way and why an informant is different from nontradition bearers or from other tradition bearers. It is necessary to find out as much as we possibly can about the transmission of folklore, for it is the method of transmission that determines whether an item is folk or not. We need to know when, where, and from whom the informant learned the items in his repertoire, how they were learned, the circumstances of the first hearing of an item and how often it has been heard since, how often the item is used and under what circumstances.

PRESENTATION OF RESEARCH FINDINGS

After the interview is concluded the most desirable way of preserving the content is to keep the tape and also transcribe it into a permanent written record. When doing this it is also helpful for future researchers using this material if the transcript contains some form indicating what procedures were followed in its preparation. An example of such a form is given below:

_____ Typist instructed to make a verbatim transcript
_____ Transcript reviewed by interviewer for transcription errors
    _____ by comparing transcript with taped record in its entirety
    _____ by comparing transcript with taped record where accuracy of transcription was in doubt
    _____ on basis of recall of content
_____ The oral record has been preserved

If it is financially impossible to make a transcript, then at least preserve the tape, for it preserves not only the content of the interview but also the voice inflections and emphasis by which the informant contributed understanding to the listener. Tapes that are preserved should be accessioned and cataloged. They can also be indexed by referring to specific information or topics by means of the "counter" with which most tape recorders are equipped. The tape should include, or be accompanied by, a description of both the interview setting and the informant, as well as the name of the interviewer.

Tapes that are stored for research purposes should be wound off and rewound at least once every seven years. Tape tends to lose its magnetism, and after many years everything on it will be lost. Tapes should be kept away from any exposure to a strong magnetic field, as in an electric motor, which would erase the tape. A careless user could also erase the tape by improper handling of the recording equipment. With proper care in storage and use, tape should present no greater problems of preservation than other types of cultural documents.

One reason given for transcribing recorded interviews is that researchers are used to obtaining information by reading written words. Transcribing tapes is a time-consuming task, however; typing a one-hour interview takes from eight to fourteen hours. When sending tape to be transcribed it is a good idea for the interviewer to listen to the tape and make a list of words, terms, or phrases that may be confusing or esoteric. In spite of improper grammar or colloquialisms in the interview, any transcription should be made with a minimum of modification.

Typed transcripts should be identified in this way:

informant's name_____
interviewer's name_____
interview date_____
time of interview_____
place interview conducted_____
typist's name_____

Most high-school students undertaking folklore projects will have neither

21

the time nor the opportunity to have typed transcripts made of their interviews. Probably their interviews will not even be taped, but they should strive to get an accurate written account of the material gathered during the interview as well as the context of the interview. Preservation of this data will prove useful to future researchers interested in the folklore or culture of the town or region. If a school does not wish to keep the material collected, it should be donated (for those in Arkansas) to the Arkansas State Folk Arts Coordinator (address given on page 16) and (for those in Missouri) to the Missouri Folklore Society, P. O. Box 1757, Columbia, Missouri, 65205, or to the Ozark States Folklore Society, Arkansas College, Batesville, Arkansas, 72501.

It must be understood that the preceding suggestions on collecting and presenting folklore are merely guidelines. There are no hard and fast rules that always hold for every situation, but generally the recommendations outlined here have been empirically proven successful. Still, in doing fieldwork in folklore, one needs to use common sense and innovate when necessary. The steps given in this introduction will provide a starting point.

NOTES

[1]A thorough discussion of the history of "Home on the Range" is contained in John I. White, *Git Along Little Dogies: Songs and Songmakers of the American West* (Urbana, Illinois: University of Illinois Press, 1975), pp. 153-166.

[2]Mary D. Hudgins," 'Folklore' That Isn't," *Mid-South Folklore* 4:1 (Spring, 1976), pp. 25-29.

[3]Actually, there is considerable reason to doubt that Baxter is the original author-composer of the song "Gambler's Blues," even though he certainly did copyright the piece. Several of the verses are of the type sometimes called "floating verses"; that is, they are found in several songs and seem to fit all of them equally well. Certainly, some of the verses predate the 1920s.

[4]The movie, *When A Stranger Calls*, was released in 1979. This legend has been the subject of several recent studies that are cited in Jan Brunvand, *The Vanishing Hitchhiker: Urban Legends and Their Meanings* (New York: W. W. Norton, 1981).

"THERE WAS NEVER ANE O' MA SANGS PRENTIT TILL YE PRENTIT THEM YOURSEL' AND YE HAE SPOILT THEM A' THEGITHER. THEY WERE MADE FOR SINGING AND NO FOR READING, BUT YE HAE BROKEN THE CHARM NOW AND THEY'LL NEVER BE SUNG MAIR."

James Hogg, *Domestic Manners and Private Life of Sir Walter Scott*, p. 61.

Folklore From The Campus

Mary Celestia Parler

Mary Celestia Parler (1905-1981) is perhaps responsible for teaching more students about folklore than anyone else in either Missouri or Arkansas. For the greater part of three decades, her folklore classes at the University of Arkansas, Fayetteville, were filled with students whom she initiated into the study of oral traditions. Although her academic training was in English, Parler became interested in folklore after moving to Arkansas in the 1940s. In addition to teaching, she published several articles and, along with her future husband, Vance Randolph, and several others, including John Gould Fletcher, established the Arkansas Folklore Society. From 1950 until its demise in 1960 she was the editor of Arkansas Folklore, *the Society's journal.*

In the following article Professor Parler deals with a subject that has only rarely been treated by folklorists — the oral traditions that exist among college students, one of the most educated segments of society. Actually, Parler's article only deals with three genres of folklore: proverbs; stories and anecdotes; and beliefs. One of the better essays on Arkansas proverbs — or more correctly, proverbs used in Arkansas — is Edward Everett Dale's "The Speech of the Pioneers," reprinted elsewhere in this volume. For beliefs, see various chapters in Fred W. Allsopp, Folklore of Romantic Arkansas *(New York: The Grolier Society, 1931); Catherine S. Barker,* Yesterday Today, Life in the Ozarks *(Caldwell, Idaho; Caxton Printers Ltd., 1941), pp. 241-253; Earl Berry,* History of Marion County *(Yellville, Arkansas: Marion County Historical Association, 1977), pp. 40-48; Paul G. Brewster, "An Ozark Superstition and Its World Affinities,"* Arkansas Historical Quarterly *9 (Summer, 1950), pp. 76-86; Rebecca DeArmond,* Old Times Not Forgotten: A History of Drew County *(Little Rock: Rose Publishing Company, 1980), pp. 113-121 and 166-168; and Wayland D. Hand, "A Few Unusual Folk Beliefs from the Ozark Country,"* Mid-South Folklore *3 (Winter, 1975), pp. 105-108. In addition, the volume* Ozark Superstitions *(New York: Columbia University Press, 1947) by Vance Randolph contains a great deal of material on beliefs from the Arkansas Ozarks. This volume was reprinted in 1964 by Dover Publications, Inc., under the title* Ozark Magic and Folklore.

A good account of the folklore that circulates in academe is J. Barre Toelken's "The Folklore of Academe" in Jan Harold Brunvand, The Study of American Folklore: An Introduction *(New York: W. W. Norton & Company, Inc., 1968), pp. 317-337. Much of the folklore discussed in both Toelken's article and the present one by Parler is not exclusively confined to academic circles.*

To most people, a superstition is nonsense that somebody else believes in. Ask anybody to tell you about his superstitions and he will say, "I'm not superstitious; but I do know it's true that ... " He may not believe that it's bad luck to walk under a ladder, sit thirteen at table, or begin something on Friday, but he will call in a *water witch* to tell him where to dig his well. At the University of Arkansas, a folklore student, who had been a semi-professional baseball player, asked if he should report beliefs "even if they are true." To illustrate what he meant, he said that he didn't like for other players to use his bat because "there are just so many good hits in a bat."

Every returning alumnus of the University of Arkansas checks to make sure that his name, along with that of his classmates, is still written in the concrete of Senior Walk. Then he remembers that it's bad luck to step on the Class of 1900, for the story goes that every member of that class died a violent death before the year was out. Although some of the members are yet alive, the superstition is still passed on to every new student. The freshman is also told that the North Tower of Old Main is taller than the South Tower because the architect was a Northern sympathizer in the War between the States. The truth is that Old Main is a replica, taller North Tower and all, of University Hall at the University of Illinois. But who cares? The tradition makes a much better story.

It is widely believed that folklore is transmitted only by the aged, the ignorant, and the indigent. Now, by definition, a university student is none of these. Yet in the past three years, one hundred and twenty students in the course in Arkansas Folklore have reported over forty thousand items of folklore. Songs and tales, riddles and rhymes, games and charms, crafts, and receipts and remedies, dialect and proverbs and sayings are only a few of the categories into which this traditional material falls. The following is but a sampling of the folklore collected in the University classroom.

To return to a house for something you have forgotten is a bad omen. Happily there are a number of ways to take the curse off. Before going back you can *make a cross-mark in the road* and spit in it, or cross your fingers and spit through them. When you return to the house, you can take a seat, then sit a minute, count to ten, make a wish, lift both feet, or spit on the floor. To avoid the appearance of returning, back into the house. Some say it is enough to turn your hat around, so that your hat goes into the house backward. There are those who think it's best to return by a different route.

A black cat crossing the path will bring a momentary shudder to most anybody. Some people believe that to cross a black cat's trail will bring bad luck not only to you but also to the first house you enter. It is such an evil omen that there are those who think you had better turn around and go straight back home. Maybe it's not enough just to give up your trip; Bill Bann of Texarkana, Arkansas, says that before you turn back you should close one eye and spit. Since it is not always feasible to postpone your journey, it is lucky that there are ways to break the spell. You can avoid the contaminated spot by taking another route. If this is impossible, you can keep your fingers crossed, turn your pockets inside-out, turn your hat backwards, or make a cross-mark in the road or in your palm. Against an ill-omen of such potency, many folks use more complicated counter-charms. Some spit in a hat and throw it over the left shoulder. Some spit over the left shoulder thirteen times. Some say, "How do you do, Mr. Cat," three times. Bud Jones' mother told him that in Chicago they used to throw a coin after the cat and say, "Here, kitty, buy yourself some cream." According to Carole Anne Evans, Fort Smith, Arkansas:

> If a black cat crosses your path,
> Turn around and spit in your hat,
> Wear it backward wherever you go,
> Or you'll have bad luck the whole day through.

If you are in a car when a black cat crosses in front of you, mark an "X" on the windshield, or spit out of the window several times. Better still, stop the car, go around behind it, and spit three times. One lady summed up the whole business: "When a black cat runs in front of you — SPIT!"

Everybody knows that it is good luck to *find a horseshoe*, but there is considerable disagreement as to what you should do with one when you find it. Some folks hang it on a fence, while others nail it over a door with the prongs up so that the luck will not run out. Many people spit on it and throw it over the left shoulder without looking back. A girl from northeast Arkansas told Virginia Heinze that the number of nails in a horseshoe designates the number of years of good luck the finder may expect.

At all times and places, human beings have believed in the magical prop-erties of talismans and amulets. In Arkansas today many objects are carried or worn to ward off evil or bring good luck, such as acorns, bat hearts, silver bobby pins, buttons found or received as gifts, coon bones, four-leaf clovers, chicken legs, locks of hair, rattlesnake rattles, and rocks with holes in them. Any rabbit's foot is lucky; but the left hind foot of a graveyard rabbit, killed on Friday, the 13th, at midnight in the dark of the moon, is especially efficacious. A buckeye makes an excellent pocket piece, for it will not only bring good luck, but it will ward off rheumatism and piles as well. Some people believe that you should find a buckeye and face the east while you make a hole in it, then at sundown face the west and put the buckeye in your stocking.

The talisman is frequently a piece of money, such as an Indianhead penny or a dime with a hole in it. Silver dollars are considered lucky, especially one minted in the year of your birth. A few people carry two-dollar bills, but most Southerners think such a bill is extremely bad luck unless you tear a corner off. Because of this mutilation, the United States mint has quit circulating two-dollar bills in the South.

27

The father of one University of Arkansas student never concludes a business deal unless he has a certain black leather notebook in his pocket. Another student always wears a cheap, bright red felt hat while taking a test. A member of the University faculty took to the oral examination for the Master's degree her own left hind foot of a graveyard rabbit and the following lucky pieces lent for the occasion by her friends: a holy medal, a rosary, a lavalliere, a Mexican coin, and a buckeye. She passed.

Many omens refer to specific future events. The arrival of company, for instance, is foretold by a redbird, a bluebird, or a robin, by a cat washing its face, a dog rolling over in the grass, a lightning-bug in the house, food boiling over, scissors dropped, a broom falling across a door, a rocking chair "traveling," or an extra place accidentally set at table. Silverware dropped portends a guest — a fork for a woman, a knife for a man, a spoon for a child — and points in the direction from which the visitor will come. If you drop the dishrag, "somebody's coming dirtier than you are." If you take a second helping of some food which you already have on your plate, or if you drop any food on the floor, "somebody's coming hungry." For a visitor to leave by a door other than the one he entered means more company.

What a sneeze portends depends upon the day of the week:

Sneeze on Monday, sneeze for danger,
Sneeze on Tuesday, kiss a stranger,
Sneeze on Wednesday, get a letter,
Sneeze on Thursday, something better,
Sneeze on Friday, sneeze for sorrow,
Sneeze on Saturday, see your lover tomorrow,
Sneeze on Sunday, your safety seek,
Or the Devil will have you the rest of the week.

When you sneeze all of a sudden, it means somebody is thinking about you. If you sneeze before breakfast, you will have company for supper, and if you sneeze at the table, there will be a guest at the next meal. If you sneeze four times in succession, you will die suddenly. Trying to sneeze and not being able to do so is a sign of loss.

Facial or bodily characteristics are clues to a person's character or to his future:

Mole on the neck, Money by the peck.
Mole above breath, Money before death.

Cold hands, warm heart; dirty feet, no sweetheart.

Ugly baby, pretty adult; pretty baby, ugly adult.

Dimple in the chin, the devil's within.

If your eyebrows meet across your nose,
You'll never wear your wedding clothes.

There are many rhyming proverbs. Here are some examples:

A whistling girl and a crowing hen
Always come to some bad end.

Man works from sun to sun,
Woman's work is never done.

Courting and wooing
Takes dallying and doing.

You'll never find a beau
Where cobwebs grow.

Lazy folks work the best
When the sun is in the west.

A good horse never stumbles,
And a good wife never grumbles.

Maxims from the common store are frequently twisted into wisecracks. Love is blind, but the neighbors ain't. If at first you don't succeed — quit. Early to bed and early to rise makes girls go out with other guys. Old soldiers never die, they just smell that way. Two wrongs never make a right, but maybe three will. Often wisecracks thus derived from proverbs have themselves become proverbial; for instance, absence makes the heart grow fonder — of somebody else. Live and learn, die and forget it all.

This article originally appeared in Arkansas Folklore, *a publication of the Arkansas Folklore Society, 8:1 (February, 1958), pp. 4-9 and is reprinted here with the permission of the late Mary Celestia Parler and the late Vance Randolph.*

Folklore In Arkansas

Octave Thanet

Octave Thanet was the pen name used by Alice French (1850-1934), a well-known nineteenth century local-color writer who spent time at Clover Bend in northeastern Arkansas each year from 1883 to 1909. Although her article is as bad as anything ever written on Arkansas folklore, it is included here for a number of reasons. First, it is one of the earliest publications of Arkansas folklore that presents material collected as folklore. For example, Henry Rowe Schoolcraft, Thomas Nuttall, and some other early writers unintentionally recorded oral traditions in the course of their travels in Arkansas, but Thanet specifically gathered material that she considered folklore. Her essay is also of interest as a typical example of the survivalistic, nostalgic view of folklore held by many collectors of her day. This attitude still exists as attested by the widespread popularity of the Foxfire *books. Thanet's article epitomizes as well as any other the state of knowledge about folklore found among the general public in the later years of the nineteenth century. Folklore was thought to exist only among quaint and curious people who lived in isolated places away from the mainstream of civilized humanity. Modern scholars recognize that folklore exists everywhere, among all peoples, in all economic and age groups.*

But the main reason for including Thanet's paper is as a negative example. Her theoretical biases aside, the article is full of erroneous and misleading statements and reveals that Thanet was not a perceptive collector. For example, her statement that "the whites of this region have no songs" was patently untrue and clearly indicates the narrowness of Thanet's scope. Her characterization of the Br'er Rabbit tales as legends is likewise erroneous. Legends are believable narratives that often call for some statement of belief or disbelief, situations that at no time have held for the Br'er Rabbit stories. For more information about Thanet's life and work, read Michael B. and Carol W. Dougan, By The Cypress Swamp: The Arkansas Stories of Octave Thanet *(Little Rock: Rose Publishing Company, 1980) and George McMichael,* Journey to Obscurity, The Life of Octave Thanet *(Lincoln, Nebraska: University of Nebraska Press, 1965).*

Despite its all-inclusive title, Thanet's paper deals with only three types of folklore: dialect, songs and beliefs. These subjects also appealed to many later collectors of Arkansas folklore. Some of these subsequent dialect studies include Bethany K. Dumas, "The Morphology of Newton County, Arkansas: An Exercise in Studying Ozark Dialect," *Mid-South Folklore 3 (Winter, 1975), pp. 115-125; G. L. Hanford,* "Metaphor and Simile in American Folk-Speech," *Dialect Notes 5 (1922), pp. 159-180; Allen Walker Read,* "The Basis of Correctness in the Pronunciation of Place Names," *American Speech 8 (February, 1933), pp. 42-46; a nonacademic collection is Roy Edwin Thomas,* Popular Dictionary of Ozarks Folk Talk *(Little Rock: Dox Books, 1972).*

There is no better collection of Arkansas folksongs than Vance Randolph's, Ozark Folksongs *(Columbia: University of Missouri Press, 1980; a reissue and revision of a work originally published 1946-1950), a four-volume set that also includes much material from Missouri. The major Missouri collection remains Henry M. Belden's,* Ballads and Songs Collected by the Missouri Folklore Society *(Columbia; University of Missouri Press, 1973; reprint of a work originally issued in 1940). Many of the publications on belief are cited in the headnotes to the Parler article immediately preceding this one.*

For a more complete list of works dealing with dialect, belief, and folksongs, see Vance Randolph, Ozark Folklore: A Bibliography *(Bloomington, Indiana: Indiana University Research Center for the Language Sciences, 1972) and W. K. McNeil,* Arkansas Folklore: A Bibliography *(Batesville, Arkansas: Arkansas College, 1980).*

Every one recalls the famous sentence of Sainte-Beuve, "I define a dialect," says he, "as an ancient language that has seen better days."

The fascination that the Arkansas dialect has always exercised over me comes from this very trait. In the speech of cow-drivers and plough-boys linger the phrases that once were on the tongues of poets and courtiers. Herr von Rosen, Black's delightful German, learned his English from Pepys' Diary; and don't you remember how unique and charming were his "I did think," "I do want," and the like. The Arkansans use the same form of the verb. "I do plough, I did plough, I done ploughed," is how we conjugate the verb; and it is to be noted that educated Southerners, who not for the world say "I done," habitually use the second form, "I did." "I never did" is an especial favorite; any one familiar with Southern speech will recall the reiterated "I never did see" — always with the emphasis on the "did" — of common conversation. "I been" is good old English, also. It occurs in Shakespeare, and Ben Jonson, and all the earlier English of Latimer, and Jewel, and Bacon, and the others. We pronouce it in the old way, as it is spelled, and we use it in the old way, instead of the past "was."

Our use of "like," in the place of "as," can show ancient warrant, also. They say here, "Looks like I ben so puny I cudn't make out, nohow!" And they say in old English, "Yea, it looketh like we ben made a sport to our enemies!" Our common "mabbe" is probably a contraction of "mayhap" rather than of may be. And "right" instead of "very" is as old as the day of Chaucer, to go back no farther.

I need not multiply instances. The same phenomena, if I may call it so, are to be found in the dialect of New England, and many of the same phrases. For example — to give one out of a score — the expression, "He faulted it," is as much Arkansan as Yankee. It was old English before the Puritans set sail for the New World.

In the selfsame fashion, old forms of superstition, old tales, survive in this raw, new soil, side by side with the lore of the forest and the pioneer's rude and toil-marked philosophy. Take the stories of the transcendent cunning of Br'er Rabbit and compare them with the exploits of the equally clever Reynard, in the famous German medieval version, and you will be surprised at the likeness between the two. To be sure, the rabbit has a religious turn that is not assumed, as it is with our friend Reineke, but quite sincere; although it has not better effect on his morals than the fox's frank wickedness. This is the reflection of the African religion, which interferes less with morals than any I know. Br'er Rabbit, indeed, personifies the obscure ideals of the negro race. He has a sort of futility in his "scheeminess" that is very African; so is the simple-minded vanity that is always getting him in the snare. But the enemy against whom he is pitted is so much stupider than he that the main impression made is of amazing arts and resources. Br'er Rabbit always escapes, no matter how dire and pressing the peril; you can feel as sure of him as of Mr. Archibald Clavering Gunter's heroes. But he is unlike those mighty men with the pistol (and therein the more like the race that has created him), in that he gets "powerful scairt up." Mr. Gunter's "Mr. Barnes of New York" or "Mr. Potter of Texas" never turn a hair, as we say.*
But in all his fright, Br'er Rabbit never loses his head; and that is African, too; and he always can make his cunning go farther than the strength of his enemies. Ever since the world began, the weak have been trying to outwit the strong; Br'er Rabbit typifies the revolt of his race. His successes are just the kind of successes that his race have craved.

All over the South the stories of Br'er Rabbit are told; how were they spread? Everywhere not only ideas and plots are repeated, but the very words often are the same; one gets a new vision of the power of oral tradition.

The glory of Br'er Rabbit of the legends does not seem to cast any sacredness over the real rabbit that nibbles tender green things in gardens; *he* is shot, and snared, and poisoned, as ruthlessly as if his fame was not celebrated by the slayers; but in a queer way he has honor paid him, beyond any of the beasts; alive he may be a pest; but dead he becomes a magician again. The right fore foot of a rabbit is one of the mightiest charms known to man. There is no calculating the number of dried rabbits' feet that are circulating in pockets throughout the South. A rabbit's stomach cures most diseases, especially the awful "conjure

---

*Archibald Clavering Gunter (1847-1907) was a former civil engineer, chemist, and stockbroker who became one of the most popular novelists of the late nineteenth century. Born in Liverpool, England, he came to the United States in the 1850s and turned to writing in the 1870s. He published his first and only play in 1872, but beginning in 1879 he published thirty-nine highly successful novels. Two of his most successful works were *Mr. Barnes of New York* (1879) and *Mr. Potter of Texas* (1888), but perhaps Gunter's most intriguing title is *Miss Nobody of Nowhere* (1890). Gunter's work is very much of his time, and today his books are forgotten by most; even those few who know of them consider them without merit. *(Ed.)*

sickness," of which, as is well known, large numbers of negroes die yearly. You must dry the charm, and powder it, and eat it. Teething children, also, are helped by tying the skin of a rabbit's stomach around its neck.

Charms of all kinds are favored both by whites and blacks; but I observe that the white charms and the black charms are usually quite different. A negro is quite indifferent to the fatal number thirteen, and the whites despise the sinister gifts of the black "conjurers." Our conjurers are a feature of African life. They probably represent the survival of the old fetich worship, brought from Africa. I have known several conjurers. One is renowned in three counties, being supposed to have done to death by his black arts no less than ten men and women. He is a pious man and a deacon in the church, — which used to surprise me until I knew more about the African brand of piety.

Conjurers can work "a power of meanness," as the saying goes; they can blight crops, and kill cattle, and keep hens from laying, and bring mysterious trouble on families. The evil accomplishment that excites terror more than any other, perhaps, is that of throwing lizards into the object of wrath. A bottle in which a lizard has been put is placed on the road; and if the unfortunate victim shall step over that bottle, there is an end of peace for him: the lizard miraculously hops into him, and he ends his days in agony. This is no fable so far as the result is concerned; the negroes seem to have no stamina; they succumb at once, let their superstition be once excited, and the only way to help them is by counter charms.

Between conjurers and "conjure doctors" the sparse savings of the negroes have not much chance of escape. But superstition takes a multitude of other shapes. It is bad luck to kill a cat; consequently the negroes who will scald, worry, torment, and beat cats to any extent cannot be induced to drown kittens or to put a cat torn by the dogs out of its pain. One of our various negro "boys" threw a wretched kitten to the dog, to have its eye torn out and its back broken. The poor brute was crawling about in misery, the next day, and my friend said, "Henry, you must kill that cat." He said "Yes'm," as usual; but he did not kill the cat. Presently I saw him hauling the creature over the grass, grinning at its antics of torture and its mewing. I asked the cook, whose teeth were all showing, as she stood at the window, enjoying the sight, "Is Henry going to kill that cat?" "No, ma'am," was the cheerful answer, "he does jest be playin' wid it."

"Why won't he kill it?"

"Kase he lows it wud *ha'nt* him!"

I got a revolver and shot the cat, myself. It was a sickening business; and by the time the smoke cleared away, I was worked up, past toleration of negro superstition, into a genuine Southern feeling about shooting the negro; and I relentlessly made that man and brother pick up the little mangled thing and throw it into the river, which he did, shaking all over with fear, — for it is the worst of signs to touch a dead cat. I think it was only the ugly looks of what he always called "Miss French's little gun" that overcame his fears.

And strange to say — the negroes still tell how the sign came true — that luckless Henry, the very next month, pulled a pistol out in the store and aimed it at one of the clerks, and blew off the top of his own thumb, besides being arrested and fined for carrying concealed weapons, which is a serious offense in Arkansas;

and he had to spend most of his summer in jail.

Since then, he has married the worst-tempered woman on the plantation, and she beats him unmercifully, it is said, not to mention that she makes up for her severity to her lawful lord by very wrong kindness to other men.

A curious sign is the turning back sign; it is very unlucky to turn back after you have once started. If you must turn back, however, you can avert misfortune by making the sign of the cross in the dust with your heel, and spitting in the cross. This is sure. Why the formula is completed in such a surprising manner I cannot say. But I have seen the colored people make the cross, etc., countless times. The darkies do not make anything like so much of the moon as the whites. *They* are quite as superstitious in their fashion as the darkies; although none of their superstitions have the barbarous taint of the negroes'. They hold the "dark of the moon" to be especially ominous. No planting should be done then; and the meat of anything killed at that season will "cripse up in the pot."

Good Friday is the proper day to plant beans, the only recognition, by the way, that is ever made of the day.

Sassafras wood you never must burn, for if it cracks and sputters, that is a sign of the death of some one present.

The whites of this region have no songs that I know about, but the negroes have many. Whatever of vague poetry, of aspiration and yearning and exaltation there is in the African's nature (and there is more than we sometimes imagine, especially we who know his daily vices best), it has found voice in his strange songs.

They all have the same characteristics, an erratic melody, a formless yet sometimes brilliant imagination, pervading melancholy, and no trace of what we call sense. Here is a sample: —

> *O mourner, give up your heart to die,*
> > *When the rocks and the mountains they all fall away,*
> *Then I shall find a new hiding place,*
> > *I'll go!*

This repeated in different parts, with the weirdest intonations.
Here is another: —

> *The prophet addresses the church*

> *O Ziney, Ziney, Ziney, now,*
> > *I wonders what the matter of Ziney;*
> *Ziney don't mourn like she used to mourn,*
> > *O Lord, give a hist unto Ziney!*

A great favorite is one, the first verse of which runs this wise: —

> *Jestice setting on the sprangles of the sun,*
> > *Jestice done plumb the line!*
> *Hypocrite, hypocrite, I despise,*
> > *Jestice done plumb the line!*
> *Wings is craptid, kin not rise,*
> > *Jestice done plumb the line!*

But the public is too familiar with negro songs to ask for much of this kind. My only reason for giving these is that I have never seen them anywhere else. The whites sing Moody and Sankey, like the rest of the world, out of music-books.

This article originally appeared in the Journal of American Folklore *5 (1892), pp. 121-125 and is reprinted here with the permission of the American Folklore Society.*

Attitudes Toward Missouri Speech

Allen Walker Read

One of the major scholars in the field of American speech is Allen Walker Read, a member of the faculty at Columbia University from 1945 to 1974. He is the author of over 150 works dealing with language usage and linguistic theory. One of his important early works, Lexical Evidence from Folk Epigraphy in Western North America *(1935), has recently been reprinted as* Classic American Graffiti *(Waukesha, Wisconsin: Maledicta Press, 1977). Several of his other studies deal directly with aspects of Missouri and Arkansas folklore. These include "Plans for the Study of Missouri Place-Names,"* Missouri Historical Review *22 (January, 1928), pp. 237-241, which outlines a scheme to gather reliable information on Missouri place names; "The Strategic Position of Missouri in Dialect Study,"* The Missouri Alumnus *20 (April, 1932), pp. 231-232, is a brief survey of the literature of Missouri dialect; "The Basis of Correctness in the Pronunciation of Place-Names,"* American Speech *8 (February, 1933), pp. 42-46, is primarily devoted to pronunciation of the name* Arkansas *while "Pronunciation of the Word Missouri,"* American Speech *8 (December, 1933), pp. 22-36, deals with the pronunciation of the name* Missouri. *Finally, in collaboration with Esther Gladys Leech, Read published* Introduction to a Survey of Missouri Place-Names *(1934), which was an early attempt at providing a handbook on the subject of place-name studies.*

In the present article Read provides a survey of the various publications on Missouri dialect available at the time the article was written. Vance Randolph, whose work is prominently mentioned, completed his work in dialect with Down in the Holler: A Gallery of Ozark Speech *(1953), a volume recently reprinted by the University of Oklahoma Press. Also frequently cited by Read is the work of Robert L. Ramsey (1880-1955), longtime professor at the University of Missouri, who published* Our Storehouse of Missouri Place Names *(1952);* The Place Names of Boone County, Missouri *(1952); and* The Place Names of Franklin County, Missouri *(1954). Despite this prolific record, Ramsey's major work,* Dictionary of Missouri Place Names, *was unfinished at his death and remains unpublished despite his voluminous files which are still housed at the University of Missouri, Columbia.*

Being a linguist, Read's interests are only incidentally those of the folklorist. The linguist is concerned with all aspects of speech, while the folklorist's primary interest is traditional speech. This does not mean that he ignores nontraditional language, for it is only by being aware of the broader range of material that one can achieve any deep understanding of the context and function of dialects. Undoubtedly, such broadly based knowledge will also help in determining what linguistic changes are most likely to occur over time and why some outmoded dialect forms persist while others die. For two excellent recent studies of specialized languages see David W. Maurer, Language of the Underworld *(Lexington: The University Press of Kentucky, 1981) and Gary N. Underwood, "Some Characteristics of Slang Used at the University of Arkansas at Fayetteville,"* Mid-South Folklore *4 (Summer, 1976), pp. 49-54.*

In 1855, during the struggles as to whether or not Kansas would be a free state, guards were stationed at the Kansas border to forbid the passing of any abolitionists. The Missourians were to be allowed to enter but the Yankees were to be turned back, and the guards hit upon a single test that determined their decision. They asked the traveler to say the word *cow*, and anyone who said "keow" in the nasal Yankee fashion was not allowed to cross.[1] Here was a workable linguistic test, like the "Shibboleth" of the Gileadites (Judges xii: 6). This incident tends to show that for practical purposes the speech of the Missourians could be distinguished. Does the student of language admit the existence of a "Missouri dialect"? Far from claiming that there is merely *one* Missouri dialect, he says that each person has his own dialect, and consequently there are — according to the latest census figures — 3,629,367 dialects in Missouri.* It is a relative matter as to whether or not the various speech characteristics have any degree of uniformity throughout the State, and each observer is entitled to his own opinion.

Fortunately we do most of our speaking without a conscious thought as to whether or not we are correct or incorrect; and yet our attitudes towards language form an unconscious background that constantly influences the way we speak. The following statements about Missouri speech seem to the writer to be worth serious consideration.

I. *Missouri speech is the product of intricate and notable forces*. It was an optimistic New York critic who prophesied in 1800 that "the future bards of Potowmax and Messouri shall be said to write English,"[2] for the linguistic future of the Missouri country was then far from certain. Jostling about were the diverse Indian languages, the Spanish, the French, and the English. The traditional hostility of the pioneers to the Indians prevented the Indian languages from having much influence except in river names, and the Spaniards were displaced before the population was large enough to be of importance; but the

---

*This is, of course, according to the census of 1930. *(Ed.)*

French long maintained a rivalry. A geographer of 1832, describing linguistic conditions in the central Mississippi valley, wrote: "The English is by no means the universal language; the French is common in the small French settlements of Illinois and Missouri."[3] The French voyageur gave atmosphere to Missouri. General Catlin recorded his conversation with a "free trapper" somewhere along the Missouri in 1832:

"Ne parlez vous l'Anglais?" he asked.

"Non, Monsieur," the Frenchman answered. "I speaks de French and de Americaine; mais je ne parle pas l'Anglais."

"Well, then, my good fellow, I will speak English, and you may speak Americaine."

"Pardón, pardón, Monsieur."

"Well, then, we will both speak Americaine."

"Val, sare, je suis bien content, pour dat I see dat you speaks putty coot Americaine."[4]

It is doubtful whether even the French constitutes a true "substratum" of linguistic influence, for the influx of population was too rapid to allow of much assimilation. As late as 1914, however, the novelist Julian Street remarked on the influence of the diverse racial elements in St. Louis:

> Then, too, I encountered there men bearing French names (which are pronounced in the French manner, although the city's name has been anglicized, being pronounced "Saint Louiss") who, if they did not speak with a real French accent, had, at least, slight mannerisms of speech which were unmistakably of French origin. I noted down a number of French family names I heard: Chauvenet, Papin, Valle, Desloge, De Menil, Lucas, Pettiss, Guion, Chopin, Janis, Benoist, Cabanne, and Chouteau — the latter family descended, I was told, from Laclede himself. And again, I heard such names as Busch, Lehmann, Faust, and Niedringhaus; and still again such other names as Kilpatrick, Farrell, and O'Fallon — for St. Louis, though a Southern city, and an Eastern city, and a French city, and a German city, by being also Irish, proves herself American.[5]

The character of Missouri speech was determined by the particular mixture of the dialects brought from the east of the Mississippi River. Of these the Southern predominated. Typical of speakers of it was Major Christopher Clark, who was a member of the territorial legislature when Lincoln county was named on December 14th, 1818. Said he:

> Mr. Speaker, I was the first man to drive a wagon across Big Creek, the boundary of the proposed new county, and the first permanent white settler within its limits. I was born, Sir, in *Link-horn* County, North Carolina. I lived for many years in *Link-horn* County, in old Kaintuck. I wish to live the remainder of my days and die in *Link-horn* County, in Missouri; and I move, therefore, that the blank in the bill be filled with the name of *Link-horn*.[6]

The clerk disregarded his frontier pronunciation, however, and wrote down *Lincoln*. The same tradition is apparent in the character of Parson Brooks, whom John Monteith wrote of in 1884: "I'm no poet-like," said the parson, "but I larns the boys a leetle scrap like this:

Thomas Jifferson was a squar' man,
A bawn dimokrat was he,
And him that 'ud be a squar' man
A bawn dimokrat must be.'"[7]

The ubiquitous New Englander also found his way to Missouri. An English traveler named Charles Latrobe, at Independence, Missouri, in 1832, recorded the speech of a Yankee settler named Elisha Pike, who had a horse to sell. After many preliminary bickerings Latrobe asked him, "Doe he trot or break?" Pike answered readily, "Ere a thing what you please." Finally he asked an exorbitant price, and Latrobe exclaimed, "Too much by half, Mr. Pike." But Pike had a prompt answer for this too: "Times ain't now as they used to was."[8] The innumerable dialectal strands have become so interwoven that the pattern (if there is one) is now marvelously intricate. And continually Missouri speech was being nourished from the well-springs of pure English; as Lowell said of Lincoln: "The English of Abraham Lincoln was so good not because he learned it in Illinois, but because he learned it of Shakespeare and Milton and the Bible, the constant companions of his leisure."[9]

II. *The teacher should have respect for Missouri speech as he finds it.* All too often the school teacher has been at odds with the local culture of his region, for he likes to think of himself as a missionary bringing something esoteric and *recherche*. One writer of 1837, in predicting the establishment of the University of Missouri, said that "Provincialisms, and sectional errors of writing and speaking, will be removed by its influence."[10] Indeed, many of the teachers were actually from New England and used the English normal to them. In 1837 an English traveler, Miss Harriet Martineau, recorded the boast of the New Englanders that their section "has furnished almost all the school-masters, professors, and clergy of the country."[11] Many natives of the State were willing to bow before the dictates of other regions, some even in the matter of the pronunciation of the state name. Despite the fact that almost all Missourians used (as they still use) the "z" sound rather than the "s" sound in *Missouri*, the state superintendent of schools in 1897 gave as his position:

I pronounce it Mis-soo-ri. My reasons for so pronouncing it are as follows:...With me it is a pure matter of established and arbitrary rule. I pronounce Greek and Latin according to the lexicons and dictionaries. I follow the same rule in the pronunciation of English. I pronounce the word Missouri as above stated because it as yet seems to be authoritative. The following are the chief authorities:

Webster's International Dictionary, Ed. '95, Mis-oo-ri.
Standard Dictionary, Ed. 1895, Mis-soo-ri.
Lippincott's Pr. Gaz., 1896, Mis-soo-ree.
Century Dictionary, Ed. 1889, Mis-oo-ri.

39

... Provincialism or local pronunciation ought not as I see it to influence a scholarly man or a teacher in what he shall teach.[12]

The tide of opinion has been so strong in Missouri, however, that the pronunciations "Mizzoury" or "Mizzoura" should be considered the "correct" ones.[13]

Language is essentially a body of conventions and is a successful instrument only when both the speaker and the hearer are accustomed to the same conventions. The natural give-and-take of conversation assures that people will be so accustomed, unless some extraneous influence such as a misguided teacher interferes. Missouri has her set of language conventions, and any teacher who should attempt to introduce fantastic, far-fetched elements is surely ill-advised.[14] In 1882 Mark Twain lamented that "Aesthetes in many of our schools are now beginning to teach the pupils to broaden the *a*, and to say 'don't you', in the elegant foreign way."[15] There is a vast enough field for the teacher of English if he attacks the carelessness and slovenliness to be found in any well-established regional speech. Too many people have the idea, as Professor G. P. Krapp points out, "that pronunciation is a kind of fine art, like playing the piano, which one acquires at its best only by following an authorized disciplinary method, by acquiring a system."[16] The linguistic details of accent and intonation, minute as they are in relation to the whole of the language, are intuitively felt as symbols of "belonging," of harmony with one's associates and one's environment. When an individual is inhibited from using them, he loses contact with his environment and becomes unrooted and spiritually homeless. The speech which one acquires from one's associates in the normal contacts of living is likely to be that in which one will speak simply, sincerely, and honestly.

III. *Missouri speech offers a valuable field for study.* Missouri has received more attention than most states in language study, because the Ozarks, which make a "speech-pocket,"[17] contain such rich, rewarding material. In 1903 D. S. Crumb published a paper on "The Dialect of Southeastern Missouri";[18] later J. W. Carr made some studies;[19] J. B. Taylor collected more than 800 words in McDonald County in 1923;[20] and since then Vance Randolph has collected several meaty vocabularies.[21] Some of the words of closely restricted areas may have had their source, he thinks, in the imitation of the type of person known as the "jokey feller."[22] The popularity or "vogue" of words is a difficult matter to determine; but it appears that many words which elsewhere are book-words or "high-brow" words are used in the Ozarks in ordinary popular speech.[23] The "taboo" words differ, also.[24]

Randolph has also dealt with the phases of grammar[25] and pronunciation,[26] and has pointed out that many of the peculiarities are survivals from the Elizabethan and even Chaucerian periods of the language.[27] Very little reflection of Ozark speech can be found in dialect fiction.[28] Missouri is fortunate in having had such a thorough and conscientious investigator as Randolph working in this field.

Fascinating as the Ozark material is, it should not blind the student to the fact that a host of interesting words await the collector in other parts of the state. Raymond L. Weeks made a beginning in 1893 when he collected various usages from Kansas City.[29] He included such words as *butternuts* for overalls, *dumpy,* *gumbo, johnnies* for violets, *kitty-corner* and *sock it to him*. Missouri has yielded rich material in folk ballads, as Professor H. M. Belden's collection[30] shows; and it follows that folk words must be present too. Collections are being made for an "American Dialect Dictionary," under the editorship of Percy W. Long at New York University, and the Missouri material should be made available for it. Even now the language is expanding.[31]

One should be aware that the words collected, interesting and apparently unique as they might be, are probably not confined to Missouri. One speaker before the Missouri Writers' Guild is reported as "Smiling at the expressions, peculiar to Missouri, such as 'allowed,' 'howdy,' 'these molasses,' 'et,' 'you all,' and 'I reckon.'"[32] Yet every one of these expressions is current over the South, from Maryland to Texas; and one of them, "et" as the past tense of *eat*, is the standard form in England, used exclusively by well-spoken people.

The word *Missouri* itself has entered into a number of combinations: of plants, "Missouri breadroot," "Missouri currant," "Missouri flax," "Missouri hyacinth," "Missouri pippin," and "Missouri silver-tree"; of animals, "Missouri antelope," "Missouri chipmunk," "Missouri skylark," "Missouri sucker," and the prehistoric "missourium"; of minerals, "Missouri silica" and "missourite" (found principally in Montana); of implements, "Missouri rifle," "Missouri whip," and "Missouri toothpick" (meaning a long knife); and in politics, "Missouri Compromise" and "Missouri question." In 1821 the aged Thomas Jefferson used the monster word *anti-Missourianism*, meaning opposition to the admission of Missouri as a state.[33] A kind of dance in vogue about 1846 was called "the Missouri," and later in the Far West bread was said to have a "Missouri-bake" when it was burnt on top and at the bottom and raw in the middle. The nickname "Puke" has been traced back to 1835, and its origin was thus explained in 1847 by Thomas Ford in his *History of Illinois*, p. 68: "It had been observed that the lower lead mines in Missouri had sent up to the Galena country whole hoards of uncouth ruffians, from which it was inferred that Missouri had taken a 'Puke,' and had vomited forth to the upper lead mines, all her worst population." And the expression "I'm from Missouri" is a well-established addition to the English language.[34] According to a story from a reputable source, a Canadian colonel remarked to a British general, "My men are from Missouri and have to be shown"; and the literalminded British general almost had a stroke of apoplexy in his effort to comprehend how a Canadian officer's men could come from Missouri.[35]

Other studies of language can be made on the basis of Missouri writings. Early documents and newspapers give rich yield,[36] but the most rewarding of all are the works of Mark Twain. His language was first tackled in a doctoral dissertation at the University of Vienna, Austria, in 1923,[37] then in a study at the University of Chicago in 1924,[38] and since that time in an excellent series of studies at the University of Missouri.[39] The primary aim is not to find new and strange words, but to show how the words found reflect the culture of the time and place and the life of the people. The studies at the University of Missouri are doubly useful, because when the essay is completed the original notes are sent to the office of the *Historical Dictionary of American English*, which is being

41

compiled at the University of Chicago, and are used in tracing out the fortunes of words in the American vocabulary.

We sometimes forget that geographic names are as much a part of our vocabulary as the words that we use in every sentence. They must be learned and remembered like ordinary words, and they are subject to the same laws of language. The place-names of the state, then, form a branch of Missouri speech deserving of study. The commonly accepted explanation of the state name, "Muddy waters," has been shown by students of the Indian languages to be false. Dr. John R. Swanton of the Bureau of American Ethnology has written:

> I think that there can be no doubt the name was not originally applied to the river, but to the tribe and was afterward transferred to the river, just as the Illinois is "the river of the Illinois," etc. On some old cards of the late Dr. Gatschet, who studied the Peoria language for some time, I find the interpretation given "people of the big canoes." The original form of the word was *Missourit*, and Dr. Michelson, our Algonquin specialist, says *Missourit* is composed of *missi*, 'big'; *ouri*, an inseparable stem meaning 'canoe'; and -*t*, 'one who uses,' — provided that the *n* of Chippewa *oni*, or *ouni* changes to *r* in Peoria, a very likely thing. At any rate, it seems pretty certain that the word is from some Algonquian dialect, since the name which the Missouri applied to themselves is Niútachi.[40]

Even the abbreviation of the state name, "Mo.," is a hard nut to crack.[41]

A substantial beginning for the study of Missouri place-names was made by David W. Eaton in 1916 under the title, "How Missouri Counties, Towns, and Streams were Named."[42] Since 1927 an intensive survey of the State has been under way by graduate students of the University of Missouri, under the supervision of Professor R. L. Ramsay. Already over half the state has been covered, and one day Missouri will rank with Minnesota, Nebraska, Washington, and Oregon, as having a complete and thorough treatment of its geographic names.[43]

Finally, the spoken language of Missouri is an important field of study. It is a more difficult task than might be supposed to record the phonetics of a regional speech accurately. A beginning was made in 1891 when Professor C. H. Grandgent of Harvard collected samples of "English Sentences in American Mouths," and R. L. Weeks contributed a specimen from Missouri.[44] Among the phonograph records of American speech at Columbia University are several examples from Missouri.[45] At the present time there is being compiled a "Linguistic Atlas of the United States and Canada," under the auspices of the American Council of Learned Societies, and eventually Missouri will have to be mapped. The most important regions in this project are those where different dialect areas meet, and thus Missouri, which has been under such complex influences, will require special care in mapping.[46]

True research can be done only with original, primary materials. The language of Missouri — in the form of its dialect vocabulary, the writings of its authors, its place-names, or the oral utterance of its inhabitants — can be used as a laboratory for studying linguistic phenomena. Edward Eggleston found that the study of folk-speech allows one to peek "through the chinking at the human mind in its mysterious workshop."[47] By treating intensively a closely defined speech-area, one can do work of genuine significance.

IV. *Folk speech, such as that of Missouri, can be a source of vitality to the language.* The French novelist Daudet once said, in speaking of the Russian Turgenev: "What a luxury it must be to have a great big untrodden barbaric language to wade into! We poor fellows who work in the language of an old civilization, we may sit and chisel our little verbal felicities, only to find in the end that it is a borrowed jewel we are polishing."[48] The stores of Missouri speech may well be this "great big untrodden barbaric language," which yields to the transforming touch of the artist. A spokesman of the "New Regionalism" believes that "in folk speech, including dialect, idiom, and metaphor" writers will find "their most potent sources of regeneration."[49]

There will always be, no doubt, a division between the "standard" literary language and the speech of "plain folks." Yet at the same time there should be a filtration from folk speech into the literary language if the latter is to have vitality and growth. The presence of local elements produces a "regional standard," sufficiently like the general body of English so that ease of communication is not affected and yet sufficiently individual so that the speech has a distinctive character. So fastidious a scholar as Professor Henry van Dyke has said that "Dialect and local accent — brogue and burr — are the spice of talke."[50] Anyone who has the stores of Missouri speech at his command has a wealth to draw from for his writing and his conversation.

NOTES

[1]Todd, John, *Early Settlement and Growth of Western Iowa or Reminiscences* (Des Moines, 1906), p. 111.

[2]*Monthly Magazine and American Review,* Vol. III, p. 2 (July, 1800).

[3]Goodrich, Samuel Griswold, *System of Universal Geography* (Boston, 1832), p. 325. Cf. Holweck, F. G., "The Language Question in the Old Cathedral of St. Louis," in *St. Louis Catholic Historical Review*, Vol. II, pp. 5-17 (January, 1920).

[4]Catlin, George, *The Manners, Customs, and Condition of the North American Indians* (London, 1841), Vol. I, p. 63.

[5]*Abroad at Home* (New York, 1920), p. 222.

[6]Mudd, Joseph A., "History of Lincoln County, Missouri," in *An Illustrated Historical Atlas of Lincoln County, Missouri* (Philadelphia, 1878), p. 11.

[7]*Parson Brooks* (St. Louis, 1884), p. 25, from notes kindly furnished me by Dr. M. M. Brashear.

[8]*The Rambler in North America: 1832-1833* (New York, 1835), Vol. I, pp. 140-41.

[9]Quoted in *Academy Papers* (New York, 1925), p. 136. Dr. Brashear has pointed out that Mark Twain was well acquainted in his youth with the notable English writers of the eighteenth century: *Mark Twain: Son of Missouri* (Chapel Hill, 1934), pp. 196-253. Cf. also Williams, Walter, "Missouri Dialect of Highborn Origin," in *Missouri* (organ of the Missouri State Chamber of Commerce), Vol. I, No. 8, pp. 7, 25 (December, 1928).

[10]Wetmore, Alphonse, *Gazetteer of the State of Missouri* (St. Louis, 1837), p. 19.

[11]*Society in America* (London, 1837), Vol. I, pp. 182-83.

[12]Letter printed in the *Columbia Missouri Herald*, October 22, 1897, p. 1 bc.

[13]Consult the writer's article "Pronunciation of the Word Missouri" in *American Speech*, Vol. VIII, No. 4 (December, 1933), pp. 22-36. The use of the "s" sound is due almost always to external pressure — as state Senator Lon S. Haymes admits: "I give the 's' with the short 'i' ending in pronouncing *Missouri*. I didn't do this in my younger days, but when I was in Washington we Missourians were subject to much razzing, so I began the practice of stressing these letters" (*Springfield Press*, January 1, 1933). The situation is best summarized by an editorial writer in the *St. Louis Globe-Democrat*, December 30, 1932. "Of course, the people who made and who populate this state and pay the taxes have an inalienable right to say how it is to be pronounced, and by an overwhelming majority they have declared that it should be pronounced with a 'z', as in 'zebra.' From this there can be no appeal. To prolong the controversy is futile, and the East should know it. But that final vowel. There is the troublesome question. Is it 'Mizzoury' or 'Mizzourah'? Missourians themselves cannot agree."

[14]A persuasive championing of tolerance for local variation is to be found in Barrett H. Clark's excellent pamphlet *Speak the Speech; Reflections on Good English and the Reformers* (University of Washington Chapbooks, No. 36, 1930). An illustration can be found from my own teaching of English in Missouri. While living some years in England, I had picked up from those around me the pronunciation "neye-ther" for *neither*, and consequently was at a disadvantage in drilling my pupils to use the grammatical concord "neither of them is" rather than "neither of them are." During a certain recitation I asked the question, "What is wrong with this sentence, 'Neye-ther of the men are there'?" — and a pupil answered, "You should say, 'Nee-ther of the men are there.'" I am inclined to grant that the pupil has a sound point. In Missouri and the Middle West "nee-ther" is the traditional and standard form; and a teacher who would recommend the pronunciation "neye-ther" would be altogether in the wrong. It may even be futile to teach the agreement "neither of them is"; but here the counter-demand of tangible logic, in a point observed by well-spoken Missourians, supports the reforming impulse of the teacher.

[15]"Concerning the American Language," in *The Stolen White Elephant* (Boston, 1882), p. 269 (a postscript to writing of 1880).

[16]*The English Language in America* (New York, 1925), Vol. I, p. 354.

[17]Vance Randolph has discussed "Is There an Ozark Dialect?" in *American Speech*, Vol. IV (February, 1929), pp. 203-04. The most notable feature of American speech is its near approach to uniformity from coast to coast; but the exceptions of certain districts like the Ozarks, which have been socially isolated, must be allowed. Charles Morrow Wilson treats of the speech of "Ozarkadia" in "Elizabethan America," *Atlantic Monthly*, Vol. CXLIV (August, 1929), pp. 238-44.

[18]*Dialect Notes*, Vol. II, pp. 304-37.

[19]In his "List of Words from Northwest Arkansas" in *Dialect Notes*, Vol. II (1904), pp. 416-22, he states that "Most of the peculiarities of speech of Kentuckians, Tennesseans, and Missourians are to be found in the dialect of Northwest Arkansas" (p. 416); and in his fourth list (in collaboration with Rupert Taylor), *ibid.*, Vol. III, pp. 205-38 (1907), he has a section "Southernisms Common to Northwest Arkansas and Southeastern Missouri."

[20]"Snake County Talk," *ibid.*, Vol. Vm (1923), pp. 197-225.

[21]"A Word-List from the Ozarks," *ibid.*, Vol. V, pp. 397-405 (1926); "More Words from the Ozarks," *ibid.*, pp. 472-480 (1927); "A Third Ozark Word-List," in *American Speech*, Vol. V (October, 1929), pp. 16-21; and "A Fourth Ozark Word-List," *ibid.*, Vol. VIII, No. 1 (February, 1933), pp. 47-53. The total of words recorded is now well over 1500. Randolph's material is drawn from McDonald, Barry, Stone, and Taney counties in Missouri and Benton, Washington, Carroll and Boone counties in Arkansas. His article in collaboration with Isabel Spradley, "Quilt Names in the Ozarks," *ibid.*, pp. 33-36, shows what a marvelous wealth of nomenclature has developed in a very restricted field.

[22]"A Possible Source of Some Ozark Neologisms," *ibid.*, Vol. IV (December, 1928), pp. 116-17.

[23]Such as *cavil, dilatory, proffer, docile, bemean, rectify, beguile, ponder,* etc. — in his "Literary Words in the Ozarks," *ibid.,* Vol. IV (October, 1928), pp. 56-57. A similar situation has been pointed out in England; cf. the chapter "Archaic Literary Words in the Dialects," in Elizabeth Mary Wright's *Rustic Speech and Folklore* (Oxford, 1913), pp. 36-76.

[24]"Verbal Modesty in the Ozarks," *Dialect Notes,* Vol. VI, pp. 57-64 (1928) — the most readable of all Randolph's studies.

[25]"The Grammar of the Ozark Dialect," *American Speech,* Vol. III (October, 1927), pp. 1-11.

[26]In collaboration with Anna Ingleman, "Pronunciation in the Ozark Dialect," *ibid.,* Vol. III (June, 1928), pp. 401-07. Vernon C. Allison, "On the Ozark Pronunciation of 'It,'" *ibid.,* Vol. IV (February, 1929), pp. 205-06, has made the valid criticism that *hit* is used only in places of stress.

[27]In collaboration with Patti Sankee, "Dialectal Survivals in the Ozarks" in three papers: "I. Archaic Pronunciation," *ibid.,* Vol. V (February, 1930), pp. 198-208; "II. Grammatical Peculiarities," *ibid.,* (April, 1930), pp. 264-69; and "III. Archaic Vocabulary," *ibid.,* (June, 1930), pp. 424-30. A popular resume, consisting of material from his previous studies, is to be found in his book, *The Ozarks: An American Survival of Primitive Society* (New York, 1931), Chap. IV, "The Ozark Dialect," pp. 67-86.

[28]In a survey of Ozark novels up to 1926 ("The Ozark Dialect in Fiction," *American Speech,* Vol. II [March, 1927], pp. 283-89), Randolph deals too harshly with the first of the series, Monteith's *Parson Brooks* of 1884 — not realizing that it has a setting near St. Louis, under strong Southern influence. In a later survey ("Recent Fiction and the Ozark Dialect," *ibid.,* Vol. VI [August, 1931], pp. 425-28), he concludes: "Beginning with Monteith's *Parson Brooks,* published in 1884, I have examined the dialect in every Ozark novel that I have been able to find — twenty-two of them in all. The dialect in most of these novels is, in my opinion, very bad indeed. The worst of all, it seems to me, is found in a novel called *Sally of Missouri,* by Rose Emmet Young. Incomparably the best Ozark dialect ever written in fiction, to my mind, is that of Charles Morrow Wilson. The next best — although far below the Wilson standard — must still be sought in the works of the eminent Harold Bell Wright!" Another treatment may be found in Charles Arnold, *The Missouri Ozarks as a Field for Regionalism,* MS Master's thesis, University of Missouri, 1930, section on Ozark dialect, pp. 130-40. Mr. Randolph has lately embarked upon fictional writing of his own.

[29]"Notes from Missouri," in *Dialect Notes,* Vol. I, pp. 235-42 (1893); in two parts: I. Peculiar Words and Usages, and II. Pronunciation and Grammatical Points.

[30]In manuscript available at the Harvard University Library.

[31]Note Virginia Carter, "University of Missouri Slang," in *American Speech,* Vol. VI (February, 1931), pp. 203-06. Each year classes in English at Christian College, under the supervision of Mrs. Mary Paxton Keeley, make a study of current slang.

[32]*Columbia Missourian,* May 2, 1932, p. 2.

[33]*The Writings of Thomas Jefferson,* Definitive ed. (Washington, 1905), Vol. XV, p. 311.

[34]The widespread newspaper discussion of the phrase is summarized in "Whence Came Those Magic Words 'I'm from Missouri'?," *The Literary Digest,* Vol. LXXII, No. 4 (January 28, 1922), pp. 42-44; reprinted in part in the *Mo. Hist. Review,* Vol. XVI (April, 1922), pp. 422-27. The expression "Gone up Salt River" could be attributed to Missouri (as in the New York *Dispatch* of 1857, quoted in the *Mo. Hist. Rev.,* Vol. XXVI [January, 1932], pp. 218-19), although it more probably refers to the Salt River in Kentucky; cf. also Miss Brashear, op. cit., pp. 44-45. For a story about *Piker* see Julian Street in *Collier's Weekly,* August 29, 1914, p. 34.

[35]Paul Shorey, "The American Language," in *Academy Papers* (New York, 1925), p. 142.

[36]Two such doctoral dissertations at the University of Missouri are announced in *American Literature*, Vol. IV (January, 1933), p. 462: Elijah Harry Criswell, *The Vocabulary of the Lewis and Clark Original Journals, 1804-1806* (the early parts referring to Missouri), and Mary Paxton Keeley, *The Vocabulary of The Missouri Intelligencer from 1819 to 1834.*

[37]Dürrigl, Karl, *Die Abweichungen* [i.e., "deviations"] *vom Standard English in The Adventures of Tom Sawyer von Mark Twain (Samuel Langhorn Clemens)*, single type-written copy in the Universitäts-bibliothek, Vienna, 178 pp.

[38]Buxbaum, Katherine Louis, *An Analysis of the Vernacular in Mark Twain's Mississippi Valley Stories*, MS dissertation for the master's degree, 58 pp., the substantial part of which appeared in an article, "Mark Twain and American Dialect," in *American Speech*, Vol. II (February, 1927), pp. 233-236.

[39]These studies, under the direction of Professor R. L. Ramsay, are as follows (all are master's theses except the one otherwise noted): Alma Borth Martin, *A Vocabulary Study of "The Gilded Age"* (1929), 178 pp., and printed in abridged form by the Mark Twain Society (1930), 55 pp.; Frances Guthrie Emberson, *A Vocabulary Study of "Huckleberry Finn"* (1930), 233 pp.; Emma Orr Woods, *A Vocabulary Study of "Tom Sawyer"* (1932), 108 pp.; Ernestine Ernst, *A Vocabulary Study of "Life on the Mississippi"* (1932), 295 pp.; Florence Potter Stedman, *A Vocabulary Study of "The Prince and the Pauper"* (1932), 163 pp.; Avera Leolin Taylor, *A Vocabulary Study of "A Tramp Abroad"* (1932), 229 pp.; Georgia House Watson, *A Vocabulary Study of "Sketches New and Old"* (1932), 194 pp.; Amelia Madera, *A Vocabulary Study of "The Innocents Abroad"* (1932), 177 pp.; Frances Guthrie Emberson, *The Vocabulary of Samuel L. Clemens from 1852 to 1884*, Ph.D. dissertation (1932), 272 pp.; E. M. Webber, *A Vocabulary Study of "Pudd'n-head Wilson" and "Those Extraordinary Twins"* (1933), 179 pp.; and Donald C. Thompson, *A Vocabulary Study of "A Connecticut Yankee at King Arthur's Court"* (1934), 189 pp.

[40]Quoted by Professor William A. Read in *Englische Studien*, Vol. XLVII, (December, 1913), pp. 169-70. This was first pointed out by Col. William F. Switzler in 1897, as quoted in the *Mo. Hist. Rev.*, Vol. XVII (January, 1923), pp. 231-32, and corroborated by J. Walter Fewkes, *ibid.*, (April, 1923), pp. 377-78. Cf. also J. T. Link, *The Origin of the Place Names of Nebraska* (Lincoln, 1933), pp. 72-76.

[41]See the discussion by Monas N. Squires in the *Mo. Hist. Rev.*, Vol. XXVI, (October, 1931), pp. 84-5.

[42]Printed in the *Mo. Hist. Rev.*, Vol. X (April, 1916), pp.197-213, and the four following issues.

[43]The *University of Missouri Studies*, Vol. IX, No. 1 (January, 1934), is devoted to this project. The theses already completed are listed there on p. 40. The procedure worked out with such admirably systematic detail by Professor Ramsay (pp. 14-25), will undoubtedly have an influence upon the work in other states.

[44]*Dialect Notes*, Vol. I, pp. 198-204 (1891). An excellent model for this kind of work is that by Hans Kurath, "A Specimen of Ohio Speech," in *Curme Volume of Linguistic Studies* (1930), pp. 92-101.

[45]This extensive collection is described by Harry Morgan Ayres and W. Cabell Greet, "American Speech Records at Columbia University," in *American Speech*, Vol. V, (June, 1930), pp. 333-58. Record No. 72B is from Lincoln county, Mo., and No. 121 from St. Louis'. Others have been added recently.

[46]The writer has treated this point in his article, "The Strategic Position of Missouri in Dialect Study" in the *Missouri Alumnus*, Vol. XX (April, 1932), pp. 231-232; reprinted under the title "Folk-Speech in Missouri" in the *Arcadian Magazine*, Vol. II, No. 5 (June, 1932), pp. 13-14, and under the title "Dialect in Missouri," in part, in the *Mo. Hist. Rev.*, Vol. XXVI (July, 1932), pp. 426-27.

[47]*Century Magazine*, Vol. XLII (April, 1894), p. 856.

[48]Quoted in *Harper's New Monthly Magazine*, Vol. LXXII (January, 1886), p. 324b.

[49]B. A. Botkin in *Folk-Say: a Regional Miscellany* (Norman, 1929), p. 10.

[50]Before a conference of American and British Professors of English at Columbia University, quoted in the New York *Times*, June 14, 1923, p. 7b.

This article originally appeared in The Missouri Historical Review *29 (July, 1935), pp. 259-271 and is reprinted here by permission of The State Historical Society of Missouri.*

The Speech of the Pioneers

Edward Everett Dale

Edward Everett Dale (1879-1972) was primarily known for his work in history but was also the author of a number of poems and an occasional article on folklore. Although a native of Texas, Dale's academic career was spent at the University of Oklahoma, and the history of the Sooner State was one of the main subjects of his research. He did, however, produce at least two essays dealing with Arkansas history and folklore. One, "Arkansas, the Myth and the State," (Arkansas Historical Quarterly *12 [Spring, 1953], pp. 8-29), is basically a history article but does include a number of good traditional stories and anecdotes. The second, the present article, is more oriented toward folklore. Here, Dale provides considerable information about folklife — that is, the traditional life style of the pioneers — and also offers one of the few discussions of folk speech that attempts to provide the contextual setting in which this material flourished. It is especially important for the present purposes since it is that rarity — a learned work that can be profitably read and enjoyed by a nonspecialized audience.*

There are many important American proverb collections but very few specifically dealing with the traditional saying as found in Arkansas and Missouri. For an annotated list of the general American collections and studies, see F. A. de Caro and W. K. McNeil, American Proverb Literature: A Bibliography *(Bloomington, Indiana: Folklore Forum, 1971; Bibliographic and Special Series). For specific Arkansas and Missouri examples, see Walter Blair, "Inquisitive Descendants in Arkansas,"* American Speech *14:1 (1939), pp. 11-22; five articles by Joseph William Carr that appeared in* Dialect Notes *under the title "A List of Words From Northwest Arkansas" (see 2 [1904], pp. 416-422; 3 [1905], pp. 68-103; 3 [1906], pp. 124-165; 3 [1907], pp. 205-238; and 3 [1909], pp. 392-406); and J. P. Oevitch, "Proverbial Comparisons of Oklahoma and Missouri,"* Hoosier Folklore Bulletin *3 (1944), p. 37.*

"Out of the abundance of the heart," says the Word of God, "the mouth speaketh." The adventurous pioneer who, from the time of the planting of the first English colonies along the Atlantic seaboard down to the near present, and who settled that ever-changing geographic region known as the American frontier, was no diplomat. He used words to reveal rather than to conceal his thoughts. His speech, moreover, was a reflection of this life which he lived. Through it he expressed the thoughts which had to do with his work and play and all the experiences and incidents of daily life and from it may be gleaned an understanding of the heart and mind of the individual himself.

Our first pioneers were those hardy souls who sailed three thousand miles west to plant the seed of European culture in the American wilderness of Virginia or New England. Here they built their crude little homes, cut down the forest trees, planted little crops, and began the task of the conquest of a continent. They had come here English in speech, manners, customs, and traditions, but in this new environment all of these began slowly at first to be modified. When later groups of settlers came over a generation or more later they discovered that the language of these earlier pioneers, like their food, dress, homes, manners and customs had undergone what might be called a "sea change." Many new words and expressions had crept into their language which must at first have proved puzzling to the newcomers.

The earliest immigrants had found themselves faced by the task of giving names to the new lands occupied as well as to the capes, bays, gulfs, rivers, lakes, and mountains and in addition to the new towns and settlements which they had established. With true British loyalty to king and country, members of the royal family and the towns or subdivisions of the old homeland were given first honors. Capes Charles and Henry; the James, Charles, and York Rivers; Carolina, Charleston, New York, New Jersey, New Hampshire, New London, Salem, Dover, Williamsburg, and Jamestown, as well as a host of other names, all bear witness to this tendency of the early colonists. Also discoverers and early explorers, with true frontier modesty, often gave their own names to rivers and lakes, as Lake Champlain, or the Hudson River. As settlements steadily advanced westward, these same general principles were applied except as the mother country became more remote and memories of royalty faded, the names of our own early leaders, of more recent discoverers, or the homeland or towns of the first settlers, were used instead of these earlier English terms. Washington, Franklin, Jefferson City, Jackson, Lincoln, Vermontville in Michigan, Salem and Portland, both in Oregon; Pike's Peak, Long's Peak, or Fremont's Peak are all familiar examples.

At the very first, however, and throughout the entire period of the settling of America, the pioneers were in close contact with the aboriginal inhabitants of the country and from the Indians were derived a very large proportion of our place names. These include those of more than half of the states extending from Massachusetts to Utah or from Minnesota to Alabama as well as of a large number of the most important rivers as the Mississippi, Ohio, Missouri, Arkansas, and Illinois.

In addition to providing numerous place names, the Indians also added many new words and expressions to our language. From them come such words as potato, tomato, tobacco, calumet, squaw, papoose, hominy, succotash, wam-

49

pum, tomahawk, moccasin, and tepee, as well as many phrases still in common use, though their origin is often almost forgotten. Many persons who have almost never seen an Indian "put on their war paint," "do a war dance," or give the "war whoop," and "go on the warpath" use these expressions. Later they may decide to "hold a pow-wow," "make medicine," "smoke the peace pipe," and "bury the hatchet."

It is not the contributions of these native inhabitants, however, that have made the speech of the pioneers so expressive and colorful so much as have been those words, phrases, and expressions which they themselves coined and which grew out of the incidents and experience of their daily lives. Obviously they must be given as they were spoken since any attempt to put them into correct English would destroy their flavor and make them meaningless or in some cases even ludicrous. They are highly condensed, without a superfluous word and are characterized by their vivid imagery. The pioneer, like the Indian, was a close observer. He noted every detail and in speaking of something, did not seek to describe it but with a few bold strokes to paint a word picture. He did not *tell* the listener but preferred to *show* him and show him he did in one apt and sometimes salty phrase that meant more than could any lengthy description. "Well, parson," said Tom Smith of East Texas to the Reverend Johnson, who had just concluded a morning sermon couched in such simple language that even the unlettered old cowman could not fail to understand its every word, "you shore did put the fodder down where the calves could reach it." The words might have been meaningless to a city-bred person but to the minister familiar with farm and ranch life, they could be considered only as the highest possible praise. "Yes, I know Old Man Winters," said Buck Jones speaking of an elderly, narrow-minded individual in the community. "He's one of these fellers that looks through a knot hole with both eyes!" "And do you know his Cousin Jake?" he continued, referring to a pompous but busy, bustling little man of the neighborhood. "Jake allus reminds me of a little dog in high oats."

Every pioneer settler and all of his sons above the age of ten or twelve years had considerable skill in the use of firearms. This was in some cases due to the danger of Indian attack or the necessity of self protection in a region remote from law enforcing agencies and courts but it was primarily because much of the meat consumed by the family must be obtained by hunting. The commonest type of gun in earlier days was the flintlock rifle loaded from the muzzle or the smooth bore fowling piece or shotgun. The rifle bullet was placed on a small circular bit of cloth called the "patching" and pushed by means of a long, straight ramrod down against the charge of powder that had been poured into the muzzle. In the case of the shotgun a wad of tow or paper was hammered down on top of the powder with the ramrod and a charge of shot poured in and held in place by a second wad pounded lightly down on top of it. A small circular receptacle called the "pan" was affixed to the barrel near the breech and connected with its interior by a small hole. Into the "pan" a few grains of powder were poured and these were ignited when the gun was fired by a spark struck by the falling hammer from a flint just above them.

This mechanism and the universal use of firearms gave rise to a number of pioneer expressions. If the tiny hole leading from the pan to the interior of the gun barrel was clogged, there was merely a flash of powder in the pan when the hammer was snapped but the weapon did not fire. In consequence any abortive action was "only a flash in the pan." A person ready to act was said to be "all cocked and primed to go" while one who stood very erect was said to "look like he had swallered a ramrod." The patching which held the bullet in place was, of course, lighted by the burning powder when the gun was fired. Certainty of a battle or skirmish was indicated by the statement: "We shore will smell th' patchin' before mornin'." A worthless individual was "not worth the powder and lead it 'ud take to kill him" and one whose life work was ended was declared to "have shot his wad." "To give 'em both barrels" meant your best efforts, and a man who disposed of all his property was alleged to have "sold out lock, stock, and barrel." "Wouldn't that cock yer pistol?" meant would it not startle you. Any guarantee of safety in government or business was "a gun behind the door," while a scantily clad girl was declared not "to have on enough clothes to wad a shotgun."

There were many other expressions with respect to guns. A favorite one was sometimes given a name. "Whenever Old Betsy speaks," remarked an old hunter, "you can be shore there'll be meat in th' pot." A lone revolver was called a "hog leg," and buckshot were referred to as "blue whizzers." When an eastern tenderfoot displayed a small nickel plated thirty-two caliber pistol to Ranch Foreman Hank Blevins, the latter snorted contemptuously: "Bud, if you'd ever shoot me with that thing and I ever found it out, I'd beat you half to death!" "Don't worry about my pullin' a gun on you," said a young cowhand, "any time my gun comes out, it'll come out a-smokin'." When Sam Thompson was told he'd better not quarrel with Mike O'Donnell, who was six and a half feet tall and weighed two hundred and fifty pounds, Sam only said: "I don't care how big he is. Colts make all men equal." "But suppose he catches you some time when you don't have your Colts?" someone asked. "Well, in that case," said Sam, "I'll just out with my old knife and whittle him down to my size."

Hunting and its logical partner, fishing, were responsible for a large number of the expressions of the American pioneers. The frontier settler hunted and fished not for sport, as most men do today, but for food. Meat, which was quite rare on the tables of most of the poorer people of Europe, was the staple article of diet of the frontier settler and during the first few years after he had established his home in a new western region, much of it was "wild meat" secured by hunting in the forest. In fact, meat was often easier to obtain than bread until sufficient time had elapsed to enable the settler to clear ground and plant and harvest a crop. One who provided an ample supply of food for his family was said to be "a good provider." "I'll admit ain't been too good a provider," said Old Man Hunt, who lived most of his life on the frontier of Texas, always remaining in the vanguard of settlement. "But in th' whole thirty years I've been married, I hain't let my family git plumb out of bread but twice."

Common similes related to hunting were "gentle as a fawn," "wild as a buck," "squall like a catamount," and "he fit like a pant'er." A "fightin' fool" was said to be able to "lick his weight in wildcats," a drunken boaster sometimes asserted that he was "a wild wolf and it was his night to howl," a speedy penman was able to "write like a deer in a walk," and an individual who was too hasty was warned "not to get ahead of the hounds." A man who was in error was alleged to be "barkin' up the wrong tree," while one who hesitated over a decision was urged "either to fish or cut bait," and one who had "been played for a sucker" was declared to "have swallered it, hook, line, and sinker." "Wouldn't that set yer cork to bobbin'?" meant would it not make you nervous and a man ready for an important event or emergency was said to be "loaded for bear." This latter expression came from the pioneer's habit of loading his gun with a heavy charge of powder and eight to twelve buckshot if he thought there was a possibility of his seeing a bear.

The life of the pioneer, however, was by no means all hunting, fishing, and fighting Indians. Fields must be cleared and plowed, crops tilled, water and wood brought for household use, domestic animals cared for, corn taken to the mill to be ground into meal, and the country store.visited to barter butter and eggs or coonskins for "store tea," sugar, coffee, dry goods, or notions. The system of barter probably gave rise to the expression, "I've got a little tradin' to do at the store" which was used even when only cash purchases were to be made. There were, moreover, all the daily chores of cooking, sweeping, housecleaning, washing, ironing, feeding, milking, and all the other little tasks of daily life. The children must be fed, clothed, taught, and disciplined, and some attention given to the church, school, recreation, social life, and local government. All of these things affected the speech of the people creating many colorful and expressive phrases.

Many of these were connected with food since it is the most fundamental of all human needs. White sauce or cream gravy was a staple article of diet and the pioneer's children were sometimes literally brought up on it. Any left over was fed to the dogs which probably was the reason why it was commonly called "hush puppy gravy." The term, "hush puppies," was also applied in the South to "corn dodgers" made of corn meal which had been scalded and made into round cakes which were fried in deep fat. "Calico gravy" was made by adding a little water to the skillet in which ham had been fried. A plate of large, tough biscuits was said to "look like a gang of terrapins a-comin'"while a bachelor who was a good cook was able to "make biscuits with woman tracks on 'em." "Open face pie with pumpkin movement" is self explanatory and frosted layer cake was crudely referred to as "stair steps cake with calf slobbers on it." Sauce to be poured over pudding was "whippem-whoppem," eggs "hen berries," and rice "moonshine." Syrup and sugar were sometimes referred to respectively as "long sweetenin' and "short sweetenin'," while in the Cow Country syrup was "lick," gravy "sop," and stew, or in some areas a type of bread pudding, was known as "slumgullion."

"That's th' best pie I ever flopped my lip over," said an old Texan noted for his love of good food, "but I've allus been a great eater; guess I'll just dig my grave with my teeth." "But you don't get fat," someone remarked. "Get fat? No, of course I don't," was the reply. "Guess I just eat so much it makes me pore to carry it." A particularly delicious dish was said to be "so good I nearly swallered my tongue," or "it 'ud make a mule colt kick its mammy," or "make a boy push his daddy in the creek."

"Does Mrs. Barker feed pretty well?" someone asked one of a rich widow's hired hands. "No, not too good," was the answer, "generally we has apologies for breakfast, promises for dinner, and disappointments for supper." "Why don't you come to see us?" asked Farmer Taylor, "the latch string always hangs outside th' door and if you'll come, we shore will put th' big pot in th' little one and make soup out of th' skillet."

Other expressions with respect to food were common. Coffee was "so strong it could git up and walk," a certain bachelor always made "good firm biscuits," and steak was "so tough you couldn't stick a fork in th' gravy." "Can you manage to eat th' biscuits, Uncle Billy?" sarcastically asked the cook of a threshing crew, when an old teamster complained that the beans were not done and the meat tough, "or had I better throw 'em out and bake another batch?" "They ain't so bad," was the reply, "if you spread lots of this butter on 'em, you can't taste 'em so much. Course you kin taste th' butter but I'm purty strong too as th' feller said and anyhow yer coffee's weak enough to bring up th' gineral average." "Speakin' of coffee," another one of the crew remarked, "lots of people don't know how little water it takes to make good coffee." "Anyhow," he continued, "there ain't no such thing as strong coffee; only weak people!"

One of the most pronounced characteristics of the pioneer's speech, as is also true of his humor, was exaggeration. The tendency to tell tall tales was common on every frontier and this same quality appears in the language of the pioneer. Many of his expressions were neither classical nor elegant but they were vivid and highly descriptive. The average person today might say that a man's "eyes widened and he turned ashy pale with fright" but Bill Jones used more colorful phraseology. "Old Sam shore wuz skeered," he declared; "why, his eyes looked like fried eggs in a slop bucket." "I seen him," chuckled one of Bill's comrades, "his eyes stuck out till you could have roped them with a grapevine and he run so fast that when he finally stopped, it took his shadder twenty minutes to ketch up with him."

"How are you today?" an old freighter was once asked. "Oh, fat as a match and straight as a fishhook," was the prompt reply. Other inquiries as to a neighbor's health were likely to bring the answer, "All so's to be up," "all so's to be about," "all able to eat our daily allowance," or "all gaily." "How's yer fat" was likely to bring the response, "Just a little bit streaked." Other highly exaggerated expressions were common. A knife was "so dull you could ride to mill on it." A girl's hair hung down her face until "she looked like a steer a-peekin' through a brush fence," and she was "so pore she had to stand twice in th' same place to make a shadder." The ground was "so muddy it'd bog th' shadder of a buzzard," while a man with projecting front teeth "looked like he could bite a pun'kin through th' fence," and one convalescing from a serious illness "looked like he had been pulled through a knot hole" or "had been chewed up and spit out." A tall, lean individual was "tall as a telegraph pole but not quite so heavy set" and a horse was "so pore you had to tie a knot in his tail to keep him from slippin' through th' collar."

There was an alliterative quality about many pioneer phrases and in some a rhythm that was almost poetic. A dejected appearing individual "looked like he'd supped sorrow out of a big spoon." An unfortunate one "had th' luck of a lousy calf — live all winter and die in th' spring." A man was so ignorant that "he didn't know B from a bull's foot," and determination to accomplish something was expressed by saying, "I'll make a spoon or spile a horn." It was said that "he took to tall timber" or "came out of there like a bat out of a burnin' stump." Mary White's beau was very small and slender but when twitted about it, Mary only remarked, "Well, maw, I've allus heerd that precious goods is put up in small packages."

The homespun philosophy of the pioneer settler was responsible for some phrases that were almost proverbs. "Even a blind sow will find an acorn once in a while"; "it seems that th' world is gettin' weaker and wiser"; and "it's a mighty dry year when th' crabgrass fails" are all familiar examples. The chagrin or embarrassment of an individual were sometimes expressed in apt terms. "Old Wes looked down his nose like a pore sow." He "took th' dry grins," or "Sam wuz like th' little boy th' calf run over — he didn't have much to say." A man "stumbled around like a blind dog in a meat house" or "like a blind horse in a pawpaw patch."

Sneers and jeers or terms of reproach were often expressed in curious fashion as in the following expressions: "He's so contrary that if he ever gets drowned, I'll shore hunt upstream for him"; "if I could buy him for what he's worth and sell him for what he thinks he's worth, I shore would git mighty rich"; "I wouldn't trust that feller as fur as I could throw a steer by th' tail — why he'd ruther lie on ninety days time than tell th' truth for cash." All these are self-explanatory as is the saying: "Why, I could lick a whole cow pen full like you and mind th' gate." To say that a man who would do that "would pull up young corn," or that "he ort to be shot, hung, and snake bit" was to refer to the activity of the crows that were often a pest and to the three most common causes of sudden death in some frontier communities. The pioneer usually chose his words carefully. When Old Man Carter, who was notoriously stingy and disagreeable, died, a group of neighbors came in "to sit up with the corpse." Under the time honored rule that no evil must be spoken of the dead, conversation with respect to the deceased languished until Ab Walker suddenly spoke up with considerable enthusiasm. "Well, there's one thing you kin say fer Mr. Carter; he wuzn't as mean *all* of th' time as he wuz *some* of th' time."

Words were often used in curious fashion as they still are in certain remote hill regions where the customs and traditions of a century ago still exist as "fossil remains" of a way of life that elsewhere has gone forever. It often became "hit," whip "whup," fire "fahr," James "Jeems," and the plural you became "you-uns." A bag was a "poke" and in alliterative fashion, one was warned not to "buy a pig in a poke." People were likely to "pack in some wood" or "tote a bucket of water from the spring" or "carry the cow to the pasture." Nouns were doubled as "ham meat," "hound dog," "man person," or "biscuit bread." Nouns were turned into verbs. A man "neighbored his meals" and did not mind work but "hated to be muled around." Hospitable and generous persons were "mighty clever people" and an irritable one was said to be "ill as a cat." The frontiersman, moreover, defended his use of words quite ably at times. "Why do you say that you 'are satisfied' that this corn will make forty bushels to the acre?" an old Arkansas farmer was once asked. "Satisfied means the same as contented." "No such thing," was the prompt response, "I'm satisfied that Nigger Sam over here is stealin' my chickens but I shore ain't contented about it." The questioner made no answer. Like the little boy the calf ran over, he didn't have much to say!

Social life and especially courtship and marriage brought out a great number of interesting expressions. A young girl who seemed to be interested in a certain young man was said to have "set her cap for him," while a young chap diligently wooing a girl was said to be "waitin' on her," surely a very apt phrase! A man who had evidently made up his mind to get married was alleged to have "set out" and a young woman who had just married was reported to "have jumped the broom." "I saw Henry and Ruth settin' on a bench and you just couldn't see daylight between 'em," an old lady once remarked. Boys were said to have "gone a gallin'," and a bunch of flowers "smelled like girls a-goin' to meetin'." Frank and Ed called so frequently on the Armstrong sisters that "Miz Armstrong says she can't throw out a pan o' water without throwin' it on one of them boys." "Why didn't you come to the party Saturday night?" someone asked Besse Blevins. "Just couldn't make it," was the reply, "it 'uz too fur and snaky." "I told my wife I'd be home by five o'clock," remarked Tom Burton to his cronies sitting around the country store, "and here it is after six." "Well, when you do git there," one of his friends remarked, "you'll probably git all beat up and have yer tobaccer took away from you."

There were many smart sayings of children or adolescents and a host of miscellaneous phrases and expressions which require little or no explanation. "Don't let that take up with you," a boy was warned when he picked up his friend's knife or some other bit of property to examine it. To "carry water on both shoulders" meant to refuse to take a stand on any question, while "he's any man's dog that will hunt with him" had about the same connotation. A coat or other garment too small for the wearer looked like it "had been pulled too soon" and a balky horse "wouldn't pull th' hat off yer head." "If Jenny likes that feller, she shore must have a taste for roughness," an elderly livestock man once remarked when his niece had manifested an interest in an uncouth and disreputable young fellow in the community. "That's right," said his companion, "believe me, if she marries him, she shore will drive her ducks to a pore market." The phrase, "take a turn of corn to mill," probably originated with someone who had to wait his turn to have the corn ground. "If he wuz my boy, I'd tie him up and whup him till he broke loose," said Old Man Richey referring to a bad boy in the community. "Yes, sirree," said a backwoods school teacher, "there's a whole lot of new ideas bobbin' up these days about education and any time one comes out, it ain't three days till most all the teachers in our county are whuppin' theirselves with their hats to git in on it."

"You'd better let me alone," said a boy to a bullying companion, "if you don't, in about three minutes you'll be goin' around with yer hand on yer head and a knot under it." "If I win that prize, I'll cut my galluses and go straight up," needs no comment, nor does the saying that "if you bored a hole in that feller's head, you wouldn't find brains enough to grease the gimlet." To become angry was to "fly off the handle," evidently referring to an axe which was likely to hurt someone if it flew off the handle. "If it had been a snake, it would a-bit me" meant that the sought-for object had at last been discovered within easy reach of the hand, while "polite as a whipped nigger" was a common phrase on the Southwestern frontier. Similes had to do with objects or incidents common to daily

55

life. An individual was "tall as a tree," "big as a barn," "thin as a rail," "dirty as a pig," "pretty as a spotted pup," "fat as a hog," "bright as a dollar," "sharp as a briar," or "ugly as a mud fence." One who fiercely attacked an antagonist "went after him like a bitin' shoat," and another who fled in terror was alleged to have "run like a skeered Injun."

Some pioneer settlers had a real flair for language and used words that were meaningless or absurd with studied deliberation. "I'd shore like to sell you that cow," said Walt Maxwell. "She's a good cow and she's been sold lots of times and always with a good many extrys. A pitchfork, a log chain, and shotgun always goes with her. She never had a calf. Her mother before her never had one. She was raised by her grandmother." "What luck did you have fishin'?" a settler once asked his neighbor. "Oh, I caught a good many," was the response, "some of 'em wuz all of three inches long and the rest of 'em little bitty fellers." The term "suffer" was often used. People "suffered" from heat or cold and crops "suffered" from lack of rain. "I just got in last night after dark," said a man who had been away from home for a month, "and it seems pretty dry to me. I guess th' corn ain't re'ly a-sufferin', though, is it, Jim?" "Law no," Jim replied, "mine ain't. It did suffer a great deal, though, before it died."

The extension of settlement to the prairie plains and the development of the Cow Country brought in many new phrases and expressions, but the older ones brought from the hills and woods of the East still persisted in spite of the new environment. "I hope you don't churndasher the calves," said an old ranchman to a homesteader to whom he had loaned some cows to milk. A man was so poor a marksman that "he couldn't hit a barn door" and moreover "couldn't rope a pile of buckhorns." Spurs were "flesh diggers," a saddle a "kack" or "hull" and cartridges were universally called "catteridges." "Slim," an ill featured cowhand who slept in a shed room of the ranchhouse with an old man hired to build fence remarked the second day: "No, th' old man don't kick none but he allus seems to want to take his hundred and sixty right in the middle of the bed and give me eighty acres on each side." There were other exaggerated and quaint phrases and sayings. "She nearly shook th' bark off th' trees with chills"; "shut th' door — Arkansas!" "He'll do to tie to"; or "He'll do to throw in with"; "he had th' gall of a government mule," or "was all swelled up like a pizened pup," are typical. Shakespeare's "something rotten in Denmark" had its frontier equivalent of "there's something dead up the creek," or "there's a bug under the chip." "Well, this ain't buyin' th' baby a new dress nor payin' for th' one it's already wore out" meant that it was time to get to work as did also the phrase, "We're burnin' daylight, boys." "You can't find that between th' lids of th' Bible," an old fellow well versed in the Scriptures would sometimes exclaim. Or "that must be either on th' left hand side of Genesis or th' right hand side of Revelation." Before matches were in common use, a neighbor sometimes hurried over to borrow a shovel full of coals which was the origin of the query: "Did you come to borry fire?" when someone stopped in for only a minute or two.

A drunken man walked "like he'd lost his rudder." Liquor was variously referred to as "squirrel whiskey," "tanglefoot," "busthead," "red eye," or "kill devil." Old English words appeared at times. Help became "holp" and a man could not move a boulder or a log because "a fellow just can't get no purchase on it." Visitors were asked to "alight and tarry awhile," to pet a dog was to "much" him. A half sick individual was likely to remark that he felt like he "had been sent for and couldn't go"; a man who was so carried away by delusions of grandeur as to seek to exceed his limitations was "too big for his britches," while a fervent kiss "sounded like a cow a-pullin' her foot out of th' mud."

Such phrases and expressions of the American pioneers might be continued indefinitely but enough and more than enough have been given to reveal that the speech of long ago was vivid, colorful, and filled with meaning. It is plain, too, that it was a reflection of a life now gone forever except in a few remote localities where something close kin to the customs of past generations still survives. Yet the quaint phrases are still sometimes used by a people who never knew the conditions out of which they have grown. Persons born and bred in a great city still refer to the "grapevine telegraph" or hospitably remark that "the latchstring always hangs outside the door" though they know nothing of rural life in the wooded hills and have never occupied a log cabin. For, though the frontier has gone, it still exists as a "state of mind" to give flavor to the words of those who never stop to think of the origin of the phrases they use or of the history which they might reveal.

In recent years there has been a revival, amounting almost to a renaissance, of many of those things which grew in pioneer soil. One who travels through the Appalachian Mountains, or the Ozark Mountains, may frequently find offered for sale beside the road the old fashioned hooked rugs and hand woven coverlets, as well as the ladder backed chairs, and other articles that belong to the handicrafts of a century ago. One can tune in on the radio any evening and get hillbilly orchestras, old fiddlers' contests, and quartets that sing the songs of long ago. Wealthy men often build log cabins far back in the hills to which they retire at times for a few days to live again the life of their great grandfathers. We have developed almost a mania for cowboy songs, dude ranches, rodeos, square dances, and pioneer celebrations. College students wear overalls, cowboy boots, plaid shirts, and sombreros, and there is some indication that the styles of half a century ago may be coming back even in more formal clothing. Collectors comb the hills seeking for old glass, furniture, china, and cooking utensils, and once they are found, bear them home in triumph to be proudly displayed to their envious friends who may be financially able to buy the finest articles of modern manufacture.

It may be that all this is merely a passing fad but some talented artists and able scholars believe that the old time arts and crafts, music, and even the earlier ways of life have something to contribute to the culture and civilization of modern society that will be not only permanent in its nature but will serve to make that society richer and more attractive. If this is true, may it not also be true that the salty, picturesque phraseology of our early pioneer settlers has something to contribute to our language which will make it stronger, richer, and more expressive? Is it not possible that teachers of English or of speech may learn by a study of the apt, condensed expressions of the frontier settlers, which reveal so much in so few words and bring to the mind such vivid pictures, something which they can use to develop more forceful and colorful writing and speaking by their students? May it not also be possible that students and teachers of history will gain from a study of the language of the American pioneers a better understanding of the life, manners, and customs, which that language must unquestionably reflect? Perhaps no one can say, but these questions may be worthy of consideration.

This article originally appeared in the Arkansas Historical Quarterly *6 (Summer, 1951), pp. 117-131 and is reprinted here with the permission of the Arkansas Historical Association and the editor of the* Arkansas Historical Quarterly.

Ozark Mountain Riddles

Vance Randolph and Isabel Spradley

One of the most significant personalities in the history of American folklore studies is Vance Randolph (1892-1980). A native of Pittsburg, Kansas, Randolph spent the greater part of his life in the Ozarks of Missouri, Arkansas, and Oklahoma and wrote about the region in more than two hundred articles and two dozen books. Most of his writing was in the field of folklore but he also produced several publications on outdoors life, science, philosophy and religion, as well as a number of poems and works of fiction. His extensive writings on Ozark folklore are catalogued in Robert Cochran and Michael Luster, For Love and For Money: the Writings of Vance Randolph, an annotated bibliography (Batesville, Arkansas: Arkansas College, 1979).

To cite all of Randolph's accomplishments in folklore would take up too much space, but some of his major achievements must be mentioned. He was an excellent writer who, as Richard Dorson noted in 1953, "knows best how to avoid commercial shoddiness and scholarly dullness" and was an early proponent of the folklife approach. At the time he began his work, most folklorists specialized in a single genre or genres, but Randolph's efforts were more broad-ranging, dealing with most of the folklore genres found in America. In the 1920s, when Randolph did his first collecting, the idea of working with Ozark folklore was a ground-breaking action. Most academics of the time were not concerned with Anglo-American lore but instead occupied themselves with Native American lore and the traditions of other "exotic" groups generally considered to be outside mainstream society. The few who did vary from this pattern focused mainly on Appalachia, where they sought out "contemporary ancestors" (i.e. people who essentially lived what the outside collectors perceived as an archaic life style). Randolph, more than anyone else, helped change that popular image, and he did it not by showing "quaint and colorful characters" but by presenting the traditions of Ozark Mountain people with respect. This attitude was atypical at the time: most scholars of the day regarded their informants as social and intellectual inferiors.

But Randolph's greatest accomplishment is probably the compilation of the most complete collection from a single region of the United States. The word "collection" is deliberate, for, in a sense, all of Randolph's folklore publications can be accurately viewed as a single mammoth work on Ozark folklore.

Randolph's collaborator on the present article is Isabel Spradley of Van Buren, Arkansas, who also published under the name Isabel France. In addition to the present collection, Randolph also collaborated with Archer Taylor on "Riddles in the Ozarks," Southern Folklore Quarterly 8 (1944), pp. 1-10. Besides Randolph's writings there are few other detailed examinations of Arkansas or Missouri riddles. One exception is W. K. McNeil, "Folklore From Big Flat, Arkansas, Part 1: Rhymes and Riddles," MidAmerica Folklore 9:1 (Spring, 1981), pp. 9-21. The most detailed work on the riddle is Archer Taylor's, English Riddles from Oral Tradition (Berkeley: University of California Press, 1951), which established the basic corpus of English and Anglo-American "true" riddles (i.e. those riddles consisting of a comparison between the unstated answer and something else that is described in the question). For a brief consideration of other types of traditional riddles, see Jan Harold Brunvand, The Study of American Folklore: An Introduction (New York:. W. W. Norton and Company, 1968), pp. 48-60.

The people who live in the more islolated sections of the Ozarks have changed little since their ancestors wandered west from the Southern Appalachians more than a century ago. They have preserved many old ballads, obsolete expressions, outworn folk-beliefs and the like which have long been forgotten by educated folk in other parts of the United States. Some attempt has been made to record the hillman's dialect and folk-songs and superstitions, but students of these matters seem to have overlooked another class of folk material — the old-time conundrums, enigmas, charades, puns, puzzles and bucolic wisecracks which the hillman lumps together under the name "riddles."

The old-time Ozarkers are all agreed that riddles were formerly very much more in favor than they are today. Young folks used to sit around the fireplace and "riddle theirselves" through long winter evenings. Riddles served the purpose of the modern intelligence-tests, and the ability to solve puzzles was often taken as an index of general mental development. "Workin' out riddles" was supposed to be an excellent intellectual discipline, too, and many people put riddles to their children in order to train their minds, just as more sophisticated parents used to urge their children to study Latin and mathematics. "But seems like folks don't keer nothin' 'bout riddles no more," said one old man sadly. "I reckon maybe they *was* kinder durgen," he added. *Durgen* is a dialect word meaning countrified or old-fashioned.

Since no study of riddles has ever been made in the Ozark country, and as much of this material will certainly be lost forever with the passing of the present generation, it seems worth while to publish our fragmentary collection at this time. Some of the following items were collected in McDonald, Barry, Stone and Taney counties, in southwest Missouri; others came from Benton, Carroll, Boone, and Washington counties in Arkansas.

Whut is it walks up hills an' down, hollers all day, an' sets under a bed all night?

A pair of boots

Whut is it goes when th' wagon goes, stops when th' wagon stops, aint no good, but you caint git along without it?

The squeak

Whut is it gallops down th' road on its head?

A horse-shoe nail

Runs an' runs an' never walks,
Great long tongue an' never talks.

A wagon

Two heads, caint talk,
Four legs, caint walk,
Five ribs an' a backbone.

A flax-break

Riddledy, riddledy, riddledy rout,
Whut does a leetle boy hold in his hand
When he goes out?

The door-pin

One time thar was a feller sentenced t' be hung, but if he could make a riddle whut nobody couldn't unriddle th' jedge was goin' t' let him off. He had a leetle dawg name of Love, so he jest cut off Love's ear an' put one piece in his shoe, helt 'nother piece in his hand, an' hung th' rest of it up in a tree close by th' gallows. Then when they fetched him out he says:

On Love I stand, on Love I stand,
Love I hold in my right hand;
Love I see in yon green tree,
If you riddle this riddle you kin hang me!

Nobody couldn't figger out th' riddle, so they had t' turn him loose.

Down in th' dark dungeon
Thar sets a brave knight,
All bridled, all saddled,
All ready t' fight;
Call me his name for th' brass o' my bow,
I've told you three times now
An' still you don't know!

The knight's name is *All*.

White all over, black all over,
Red all over — whut is it?

A newspaper

My face is marked,
My hands a-movin',
No time t' play,
Got t' run all day!

A clock

Whut is it goes round th' house an' round th' house, an' leaves a white glove in
th' winder?

Snow

Which would you ruther have, a silver dollar or a dollar bill?

Th' bill is worth more, 'cause ever' time you take it out o' your pocket you
kin see it in-creases!

Crooked as a rainbow,
Teeth like a cat,
I bet a gold fiddle
You caint guess that!

A green brier

Whut won't go up th' chimney up,
But will go up th' chimney down?
Whut won't go down th' chimney up,
But will go down th' chimney down?

An umbrella

In a big red cave thar's a leetle white fence. It don't never rain on th' leetle white
fence, but still it's allus wet. Whut is it?

A feller's teeth

Whut do folks call leetle gray cats back in Tennessee?

Kittens — haw, haw, haw!

Whut's th' difference between a purty gal an' a mouse?

One charms he's an' t'other harms cheese!

As I walked over London Bridge
I met five barrows,
But they all went off sows!

Barrows are castrated male pigs. These were not suddenly transformed into females, however — they simply jumped off the bridge and "went souse" in the water.

Round as a sasser,
Shaller as a cup,
Mississippi River
Couldn't fill it up.

A sieve

Round as a biscuit,
Deeper than a cup,
All th' king's horses
Cain't pull it up.

A well

Hickamore hackamore
On th' king's kitchen door.
All th' king's horses an' all th' king's men
Cain't pull hickamore hackamore
Off'n th' king's kitchen door.

The sunlight

Riddledum riddledum rideo,
Guess whut I seen last Frideo!
How th' wind did blow,
How th' leaves did shake,
An' look whut a hole th' fox did make!

This rhyme is somehow concerned with an old story about a woman who saw her lover digging a grave to bury her in.

Whut's round at both ends an' high in th' middle?

The word OHIO

Not on th' land, not in th' sea,
An' I swear t' Gawd it's not on a tree!

A knot on a tree

The ol' woman turned it down,
Th' ol' man jumped in it.

The bed

Gold is my fiddle, silver is my bow,
I done told you my name three times

An' still you don't know!

The name is *My*.

Jim Damper rid acrost th' bridge,
Bow, bow she bent t' me,
Jim Damper rid acrost th' bridge,
An' yit he walked — how kin it be?

Yit was the name of Jim Damper's horse.

As I was goin' t' Saint Ives
I met a feller with fifty wives,
Ever' wife she had a sack,
Ever' sack it had a cat,
Ever' cat it had a kit.
Kits, cats, sacks an' wives,
How many was goin' t' Saint Ives?

One, naturally

Adam an' Eve an' Pinchme
All fell spang in th' creek;
Adam an' Eve was. drownded,
Who got out?

The chump says "Pinchme" and the jokers certainly do pinch him.

Round as a biscuit,
Busy as a bee,
Purtiest leetle thing
You ever did see.

A watch

Crooked as a ram's horn,
Flat as a plate,
All King George's men
Couldn't git it straight.

A river

Seven big pears was hangin' high,
Seven big men come a-ridin' by,
Each lit down an' tuck him a pear,
How many pears was left a-hangin' there?

Five. One of the men was named "Each," and *he* took a *pair*.

As I was walkin' down th' road
I met up with my very best friend,

I pulled off his head an' drinked his blood
And left his body stand!

A bottle of whiskey

Whut has got eyes but never sees?
Whut has got a tongue but never talks?
Whut has got a soul that caint be saved?

A shoe

What is it goes through th' pasture all day, an' sets in th' water at night?

Milk

Wooden belly, iron back,
Fire in th' hole, goes off with a crack.

A rifle

As I went over Heepo Steeple
I met up with a heap o' people,
Some was nicky, some was nacky,
Some was th' color o' brown tobacky.

An anthill full of ants

House full, barn full,
But you caint git a spoonful.

Air

Corn et corn in a high oak tree,
If you guess this riddle you kin hang me!

This derives from an old tale about a man named Corn, who deserted from the Confederate infantry. As the men searching for him passed, the fugitive sat in a tree, eating parched corn from his pockets.

I got up one mornin' an' I seen a unicle unicle corn,
Settin' under a prictical, practical present.
I called for my fiddle, my feather, my fan,
To ketch th' unicle cunicle corn
That set under th' prictical practical present.

A man planted an evergreen tree, which was given to him as a present. One morning he saw a rabbit sitting under this tree and called his three hounds to catch it.

Twenty-four white cows a-standin' in a stall,
In come a red cow an' licked 'em over all.

Teeth and tongue

There was a room with eight corners,
In each corner set a cat,
On each cat's tail set a cat,
Before each cat set seven cats,
How many cats was in th' room?

Eight

Once there was a leetle green house,
In th' leetle green house was a leetle white house,
In th' leetle white house was a leetle red house,
In th' leetle red house was a lot o' leetle black niggers,
Whut was it?

A watermelon

Whut's th' difference between a watermelon an' a sweet pea?

Th' watermelon allus comes first.

Whut is it that's got a good eye, but caint see?

A needle

As I set in my tintle-tontle
I seen a findle carryin' a fondle over th' hingle-jingle;
I hollered t' my whirly-burly t' fetch me my humble-bumble,
T' kill th' findle carryin' a fondle over th' hingle-jingle.

A tintle-tontle is a house, a findle is a fox, a fondle is a goose, a whirly-burly is a woman, a humble-bumble is a shotgun, and a hingle-jingle is a hill.

Riddle my riddle my riddle my rocket,
Two in my mouth an' one in my pocket!

Boy had three loose teeth, but has pulled out one and carries it in his pocket.

Eliza, Elizabeth, Lizzie, Bess,
Went over th' river t' seek a bird's nest,
An' found one with four eggs in it.
Each tuck one egg — how many eggs was left?

Three. There was only one girl, and her name was Elizabeth Each. Eliza, Lizzie and Bess are only her nicknames.

Two lookers, two hookers,
Four down-standers, one switch-about.

A cow

Down she squat,
Out it come,
Up she jumped,
Home she run.

    Girl milking a cow

In it went, out it come,
Saved th' lives of seven sons.

    An old woman has seven sons, and they were to be hanged unless she could spin a riddle that the King couldn't solve. She went into the woods and saw a woodpecker enter a hole in a tree, and then come out again. So she gave the riddle above, the King failed to guess it, and the seven sons were saved.

If it takes a peckerwood eight months t' peck a four-inch hole in a gum-tree that would make 250 bundles o' good shingles, how long would it take a wooden-legged grasshopper t' kick all th' seeds out'n a dill pickle seven inches long an' a inch an' a quarter thick?

    Thar aint no answer, you fool!

East an' West, North an' South,
Ten thousand teeth but no mouth.

    Cotton-cards

All over th' house in th' daytime,
Stands in th' corner at night.

    A broom

Whut's th' difference between a woman an' a umbrella?

    You kin shut a umberella up.

Little red thing on th' hill,
Give it hay, it will live;
Give it water, it will die.

    Fire

Why is it watermelons allus got so much water in 'em?

    'Cause they're planted in th' spring.

As I went over London Bridge I met up with a wagon full o' people, but not a single one in it!

    They was all married folks.

Do you know why ol' man Jinkins allus wears red galluses?
Naw, whut for does he allus wear red galluses?

T' hold up his britches, I reckon!

Why is it them furriners allus draws water out'n th' north side o' th' well? I don't know — why is it?

T' drink, I reckon!

Big at th' bottom an' leetle at the top,
Thing in th' middle goes flippity-flop.

A churn

Three legs up, as hard as stone,
Two legs down, all meat an' bone,
Two ears livin' an' two ears dead,
Riddle me this an' take th' head!

A man with an old-fashioned iron pot on his head

Black upon black come through th' town,
Three legs up an' six legs down.

A Negro on horseback, carrying a three-legged kettle on his head

An old sow had nine starving pigs, an' she had t' pack corn to 'em. If she only carried three ears at a time, how many trips would she have t' make t' give each pig one ear o' corn?

Three? Naw, you're wrong. Hit would take nine trips, 'cause two o' them ears are fast t' her head!

Thar was a pore ol' starvin' mule on one side o' th' river, an' a fine big haystack on t'other side. Th' river was too deep t' ford an' too swift t' swim, an' thar wasn't no bridge. How did th' mule git th' hay?

I caint figger it out. I give up.

Uh-huh, that's jest whut t'other mule done!

Many of the riddles listed above are known in other parts of the Southern hinterland, and many of them can be traced back to their beginnings in England or Scotland. The question of origins, however, is better left to specialists in this field, who have the entire literature of folklore at their fingertips and plenty of time at their disposal. But the work of collecting must be attended to at once, before the whole body of Ozark folklore is driven into hiding by the tourist invasion. It is our hope that this paper, which presents only a small part of the existent material, will attract the attention of some student who can make a more serious and exhaustive study of this matter.

This article originally appeared in the Journal of American Folklore *47 (1934), pp. 81-89 and is reprinted here with permission of the American Folklore Society.*

Some Old French Place Names in the State of Arkansas

John Casper Branner

Onomastics — the study of names — is a field unto itself but one that frequently enters the domain of folklore, particularly where traditional place names and their folk etymologies are involved. The folk imagination can be counted on to concoct some humorous or interesting story to explain how Ink, Peculiar, or Avert in Missouri or Fifty-Six in Arkansas acquired their names. The actual origin may be more mundane — such as, for example, in the case of Fifty-Six, where the name was taken from the number of the school district in the township. These samples are, of course, somewhat unusual names, but even more common place names often acquire traditional explanations for their origin. Here the folklorist can be of help to onomastic scholars, for he is trained to recognize such stories. A frequently recounted episode holds that Hamburg, Arkansas received its name from a hunting incident. According to the legend, one of the commissioners appointed to select a name for the town killed a deer nearby. The animal had a remarkable pair of hams which inspired the name. Certainly, this purported happening is not an impossibility, and the fact that it is in oral tradition does not necessarily transport it into the realm of fiction, but the knowledge that similar stories are told about places widely removed from Arkansas casts doubt on its accuracy. Still, whether the story of Hamburg's naming is fact or fiction is not so important as the fact that it is psychologically true — people believe it to be accurate. Thus, to ignore the story simply because it may be historically false is to bypass an element of history.

John Casper Branner (1850-1922), one-time state geologist of Arkansas, was for most of his adult life associated with Stanford University, where he served on the faculty for more than three decades. Although written over eighty years ago, the article reprinted here still stands as an excellent example of scholarship on place names — the most thoroughly researched aspect of namelore. Some other excellent place name studies include the various works of Robert L. Ramsey which are mentioned on page 36 ; Norman W. Caldwell's "Place Names and Place Name Study," Arkansas Historical Quarterly 3 (Spring, 1944), pp. 28-36; David W. Eaton's "How Missouri Counties, Towns, and Streams Were Named," Missouri Historical Review 10 (1916), pp. 197-213, 263-287; 11 (1917), pp. 164-200, 330-347; 13 (1918), pp. 57-74; George R. Stewart's Names on the Land (1945); and several unpublished master's theses written under the direction of Professor Ramsey at the University of Missouri — Nadine Pace, Place Names in the Central Counties of Missouri (1928); Robert Lee Myers, Place Names in the Southwest Counties of Missouri (1930); Berenice Johnson, Place Names in Six of the West Central Counties of Missouri (1933); Frank T. Weber, Place Names of Six South Central Counties of Missouri (1938); Anna O'Brien, Place Names of Five Central Southern Counties of Missouri (1939); Fauna R. Overlay, Place Names of Five South Central Counties of Missouri (1943); and Cora Ann Pottenger, Places Names of Five Southern Border Counties of Missouri (1945).

To the above titles should be added the unpublished works of Arthur Paul Moser on Missouri place names which are available in manuscript form in the Greene County, Missouri, Public Library. In 1982 Gerald Leonard Cohen of Rolla, Missouri published the first of a planned series of monographs about Missouri place names. This is a very detailed and well documented investigation of twenty-two unusual place names titled Interesting Missouri Place Names.

Anyone seriously interested in onomastics should also be aware of Names, *the journal of the American Name Society which has been in existence since 1953. It is currently edited at North Country Community College, Saranac Lake, New York.*

The southern part of the state of Arkansas was early explored and settled by French traders and trappers. The history of these first settlers is mostly lost already, for they were frontiersmen, who left but few documents or other records by which their history can be traced. The French names given by them to streams and camping grounds have clung to some of the places, while in other instances these names have been so modified and Anglicized as to be almost, if not quite, beyond recognition.

It is worthy of note that the French names are confined chiefly to the southern and eastern parts of the state, and to the valley of the Arkansas. I have no doubt that this is owing to the fact that trappers and traders were the first white men to enter the state in considerable numbers, and that they traveled chiefly along the navigable streams. They did not enter the Ozark-Mountains region because there are no navigable streams entering the Arkansas river from that direction, while the Upper White river is swift, and, in places, difficult of navigation.

During the progress of the Geological Survey of the state, I have had occasion to use these place names on my maps, and I have been puzzled to know how to spell some of them, and have thus been interested in learning their origin. I have here brought together several of them, with such explanations of their origins as are suggested by the words themselves, or by some circumstance connected with the localities. In many instances I have been unable to find what seems to be a rational explanation of the origin of the words. Concerning a certain number of them, I am able to give the opinion of Judge U. M. Rose, of Little Rock, and I have inserted his name in parentheses after the explanations for which he is responsible. Judge Rose remarks, however, that he considers some of his suggestions "exceedingly risky." Indeed but few of the explanations offered in the present paper are to be accepted without question. It is to be hoped that the Arkansas Historical Society will try to trace these words to their sources while yet there is some possibility of its being done: If, for example, *Moro* is from *Moreau*, why was it called *Moureau*? Such a history cannot be deciphered by an inspection of the word alone.

Some of our most valuable records of these old names are to be found in Dunbar and Hunter's *Observations*, written in 1805, during a trip up the Washita to Hot Springs.[1] Unfortunately it contains many typographic errors.

Nuttall, the botanist, who traveled in Arkansas Territory in 1819, makes mention of some of these place names, and as he was on the ground before the French origins of the words were entirely lost sight of, his spellings of them are of interest.[2]

I have looked up the spelling of most of these names on the lithographed copies of the original land plats of the first official surveys of the state. The references given in the present paper under the head of "plats" are to the lithographs, not to the original sheets themselves. The field notes of the surveyors who did this work are preserved in the office of the Land Commissioner at Little Rock. It would be of interest to find how the names are spelled in those notes, for while it is not to be supposed that the names were all properly written down in them, changes are liable to have been made in putting those memoranda upon the original plats, and others may have been made when they were lithographed. It is a remarkable fact that some of the names now in use have originated, not by any process of philological evolution, but simply in clerical errors in copying them. *Bodcaw* seems to be a good illustration of a name of this kind.

No doubt some of the difficulty in tracing these names is due to the fact that travelers in new and unsettled countries often name places from trivial events, or for persons, rather than from some local feature or characteristic.

Certain habits regarding the names have been pretty firmly fixed upon the state by these French settlers. For example, streams having several large branches, generally known in the northern part of the state as "forks" (as Buffalo Fork and North Fork of the White River), in the southern part of the state are often called "fourche," as Fourche a Loup, Fourche a Caddo. We even find the "South Fork of Fourche La Fave."

In some instances the original French names have been preserved intact, as in the case of the Vache Grasse, Petit Jean, Bayou de Roche, Fourche a Loup,[3] Terre Rouge, etc.; in others, one may occasionally see sometimes the French form, and sometimes the Anglicized word, as in the case of the Terre noir or Turnwall.

It is not to be supposed that in the substitution of an English word, or of an English-sounding word, for a French one, the changes are necessarily, or even likely to be, of a kind that would take place among a people using a patois or some provincial form of French, but they are often nothing more nor less than a complete abandonment of the French word for an English word that it seems to resemble, or that strikes the fancy.

Although this region was first explored by the Spaniards, they seem to have left but few Spanish names. In looking over a list of the place names of a state as new as Arkansas, one must of course be on his guard against names of foreign origin but recently bestowed, such as *Bon Air*, *Belmont*, *Barcelona*, *La Belle*, etc.

The words given in the list are far from being the only ones of French origin in the state.

In the following alphabetic list the name, as now used, is given first, then the word from which it is derived. Some words are put down without any suggestion as to their origin or meaning. They are possibly of French origin, but I am unable to make any satisfactory suggestion as to their derivation.

ANTOINE. — L. Page Du Pratz mentions in his *Histoire de la Louisiane*, Vol. i, p. 303, a silver mine in the country of the "Cadodaquioux" or Caddos, located "by a Portuguese named Antoine." Stream in Pike and Clark counties, and town in Pike Co.

ARKANSAS. — Father Marquette, who visited this region in 1673, spelled the word *Akansea* on his map, but in the text it is spelled *Akamsea* and *Akensea*.[4] In both instances it is the name of a village.

Father Membre, who was one of La Salle's party on his voyage down the Mississippi in 1681, speaks of a tribe or nation of Indians called *Akansa*.[5] It was spelled *Akansa* by Tonty in 1682.[6]

Father Anastasius Douay who was with La Salle at the time of his death in this region in 1687, mentions "the famous river of the Achansa, who here form several villages" (p. 219); elsewhere he calls the people and the stream Akansa (pp. 220-1-2-3; 226).

Joutel, the companion of La Salle, spelled it *Accancea's* in 1687.[7] He says there was a nation of Indians of this name, and on the map accompanying his account the river is called "Riviere des Acanssas." Dr. Elliott Coues says:[8] "the name Akansa adopted in some form by the French, is what the Kwapas were called by the Illinois Indians, and the origin of our Arkansas or Arkansaw. The form Acanza is found on Vaugondy's map, 1783."

Joutel, cited above, used the name a century earlier. Du Pratz says (p. 125) "The river of the Arkansas ... is so denominated from the Indians of that name." (See also pp. 60 and 318-319.)

"There are a few villages of the Quawpaws, or Arkansaws and Chocktaws, situated on the south side of the Arkansa river below the high lands" (*Long's Expedition*, vol. ii, p. 347).

In 1811 Brackenridge spoke of these Indians and spelled the word as it is now spelled (p. 83). Sibley[9] spelled it Arkansa in 1805, and Nuttall spelled it so in 1819.

It is frequently assumed that the words Arkansas and Kansas are genetically related. This is erroneous. The word Kansas is also of Indian origin, and it was also the name of a tribe, and in old publications is variously spelled. On Marquette's map made in 1673, it is spelled *Kansa*. Le Page Du Pratz, who lived in old Louisiana territory from 1718 to 1735, makes frequent mention of the Canzas Indians and of Canzas river.[10] On his map this name is Cansez.

Pike makes frequent mention of both the river and the Indians, and calls them both Kans and Kanses. In one place he says: "The Kans are a small nation situated on the river of that name."[11]

In *Long's Expedition*[12] the Konzas nation and river are spoken of, and it is stated that these Indians lived upon the river of that name (Vol. ii, p. 348). In one place the author speaks of "the Konzas or Konzays, as it is pronounced by the Indians." (Vol. ii, p. 354.)

In a foot-note to the new edition of Lewis and Clark, Vol. i, pp. 32-33, Dr. Coues says the early French forms of the word were Quans, Cans, Kances and Kansez. It is, therefore, evident that the words *Kansas* and *Arkansas* are not related in origin, and that the *-kansas* part of the Arkansas was not pronounced like the name of the state of Kansas.

The spelling of Marquette in 1673; by Membre in 1681 (*Akansa*); by Douay in 1687; by Joutel in 1687 (*Accancea's* and *Acanssas*), and the subsequent spelling by Sibley, Dunbar and Hunter, Pike, and Nuttall (*Arkansa*), show as plainly as can be expected that the pronunciation now in vogue in the state is the one originally used.

BARRAQUE. — Featherstonhaugh,[13] who travelled in the state in 1834-5, has much about M. Barraque, who then lived on the Arkansas River near Pine Bluff. Township in Jefferson county.

BAYOU. — This word is in common use in Louisiana, Mississippi, and Arkansas. It is thus defined by Du Pratz:[14] "Bayouc, a stream of dead water, with little or no observable current." The same has been extended in many cases to swift mountain streams in spite of the protests of the people; for example, Polk Bayou at Batesville. The word is a corruption of the French *boyau*, a gut, and by extension, a long narrow passage. Sibley, and Dunbar and Hunter write it "bayau."

BARTHOLOMEW. — Bartholome was the name of a Frenchman who lived near Pine Bluff in 1819 (Nuttall). This name, however, was already in use in 1804, when Dunbar and Hunter ascended the Ouachita. (See their *Observations*, p. 126.) Bayou in Lincoln, Drew, and Ashley counties.

BELLE POINT. — "The site of Fort Smith was selected by Major Long in the fall of 1817, and called Belle Point in allusion to its peculiar beauty."[15] Nuttall calls it by this name.

BODCAW. — The original land map (1824) has it spelled *Bodcau*. This, and the fact that this stream is called *Badeau* in Louisiana, lead me to believe that *Bodcaw* comes from Bodcau, which is from Badeau by a clerical error; mistaking the *a* of *Badeau* for an *o* and the *e* for a *c*, thus turned *Badeau* into *Bodcau*, and later it was spelled as we now have it — *Bodcaw*. One difficulty with this theory is that the lake into which the Badeau flows in Louisiana is called the Bodcau. Another one is that as long ago as 1805 Dr.

John Sibley said this stream was called Badkah by the Indians. Dunbar and Hunter, p. 103. Stream and township in Lafayette county.

BODOCK. — *Bois d'arc* (the Osage orange). This is the name of several small streams in the southwestern part of the state, but these stream-names are always, so far as I know, derived from the "bodock" or *bois d'arc* wood.

BOUFF. — *Boeuf* (beef). Dunbar and Hunter call it "Bayau aux Boeufs" (p. 124), and the old land plat of 19 S. 3 W. has it "Bayou Boeuff," 1839. Stream in Chicot county.

CADDO. — Judge Rose tells me that he has seen an old French manuscript that refers to a tribe of Indians living in Northern Louisiana and Southern Arkansas called *les Caddaux*. The date of the manuscript is not mentioned. This word seems to be of Indian origin. Father Anastasius Douay, who accompanied La Salle in his attempt to ascend the Mississippi in 1687, mentions the Cadodacchos,[16] a tribe of Indians in this part of the country. In Joutel's journal of La Salle's last voyage, mention is made [17] of a village called *Cadodaquio* in what is now Texas or Louisiana. The map in Page Du Pratz shows, north of the Red River, "the country of the Quadodaquious." In the text he calls the "Cadodaquioux" (p. 318) "a great nation." Dunbar and Hunter speak of these people as "Cadadoquis, or Cadaux as the French pronounce the word" (p. 136), while Sibley calls them Caddos and Caddoquies (Dunbar and Hunter, p. 105). Pike's map of Louisiana has this word both "Cadaux" and "Caddo"; and he represents a trail "from Caddos to Arkansaw," showing that these Indians lived southwest of Red River. Brackenridge speaks[18] in one place of the "Cado nation," and in another of the "Caddoquis" Indians, who lived thirty-five miles west of Red River and "one hundred and twenty miles by land above Natchitoches."

CADRON. — Pike calls it "Quatran"; Nuttall says the French hunters called it "Quadrant." Mr. Rose thinks it may come from *cadran*, a sun dial. Stream, old village and township in Faulkner county.

CHAMPAGNOLLE. — Possibly the name or nickname of a person, derived from Champagne. On the old land plats it is spelled "Champagnole" (1818-45). The name was in use in 1805 (Dunbar and Hunter, p. 133). Stream and landing in Calhoun county.

CANADIAN. — *Canada* (Spanish).[19] Diminutive form of *canon*, a steep-sided gorge. A stream in Clark county.

CHICOT. — *Chicot*, a stump. Name of a county on the Mississippi River.

CASH. — *Cache*. Brackenridge (*Op. cit.*, 101) calls this stream *Eaux cache(s)*. Stream and village in Greene county.

CORNIE, or CORNY. — (?) Streams in Union county.

COSSATOT. — *Casse tete*. The stream runs through a very rough country, and the name may have been suggested by the topography along its course. The word *cassetete*, however, was the French for "tomahawk," and the name may have been given the stream, just as a stream in Searcy county is now known as Tomahawk creek. River in Sevier county.

DARDANELLE. — Nuttall says (p. 126) this place was commonly called "Derdanai" by both the French and Americans. I do not know whether the name was imported from Europe, or, as is said of the European name, was derived directly from *dort d'un aille*. A rocky point projects into the river at this place making the navigation a little dangerous. In Long's expedition it is usually given as Dardenai, but in one case it is called "Dardenai Eye" (Vol. ii, 288). Name of a town on the Arkansas River.

DARYSAW, DARISAW, AND DAIRYSAW. — *Des ruisseaux* (streamlets). Mr. Rose tells me that one of the early settlers at Pine Bluff was named Des Ruisseaux. Township and village in Grant county.

DECIPER. — (?) The land plat of 9 S. 19 W. (1819) has it "Decepier"; that of 8 S. 19 W. has it "Deciper." Streams in Clark county.

DE GRAY. — *De gres* (sandstone). The stream of this name is noted for the soft, easily cut, sandstone along its course. This rock was formerly much used for chimneys and foundations. The original land plat, surveyed in 1819, calls it "Bayou Degraff," however, and it may be that it comes from a personal name, and that the sandstone has nothing to do with the case. Stream in Clark county.

DES ARC. — *Des arcs*. See explanation of "Ozark." Stream and town in Prairie county.

DE LUTER. — This is Saluter on the original land plat (1838-1844); possibly from *Salutaire*. In *Long's Expedition* (ii, 301) some of the tributaries of the Washita are spoken of as the "Saluder, Derbane," etc. *Saluda* is a rather common name in South Carolina, North Carolina, and Virginia. Or was it originally *Bayou de loutre*; that is, otter creek? Bayou in Union county.

DEVOE and DEVIEW. — *De veau*. On the old land plat this name is spelled both "Deview" and "Devue." Stream in Craighead, Poinsett, and Woodruff counties.

DORCHEAT. — In *Long's Expedition to the Rocky Mountains* (ii, 307) mention is made of "Bayou Dache" which enters Lake Bistineau in Louisiana. In *Dunbar and Hunter's Observations* (ii, 102), Doctor Sibley mentions *Bayau Daicet*. There is nothing said that suggests the origin of the word.

Dunbar and Hunter mention (p. 133) the "Bayau de Hachis" at a certain place on the west side of the Washita. At the point referred to there is no considerable stream, and I cannot learn that any of the creeks of the vicinity have, or ever had, such a name. Pike's map of the Washita gives a Bayou Hachis and also "Cote de Hachis" in this same region. I infer that Pike took the names from Dunbar and Hunter, and that the latter by mistake put down a stream on the Washita that was reported to them to lie to the west of where they locate it. Another suggestion comes from the mention by Father Anastasius Douay (in 1697) of a tribe of Indians in this part of the world under the name of *Haquis*.[20] Stream and township in Columbia county.

DOTA or DOTY. — *D'eau tiede* (Rose). Doty is so common a name that it might well have come from the name of a Doty family. Stream in Independence county.

ECORE FABRE. — *Ecore* (or *accore*), a shorebank or bluff, and *Fabre*, a proper name. On the land plat of 12 S. 18 W. it is put down "Fabre," "Ecoze a Fabra" and "Ecoze Fabra" (1838). These last are only misspellings by the draftsmen. Stream and township in Ouachita county. The Ecore Fabre is now a stream entering the Ouachita just above the high bluffs at Camden. The name *Ecore Fabre* was originally applied to the bluffs on which the city of Camden is built. Dunbar and Hunter (p. 134) speak of "the Ecor Frabri [*sic*] (Fabri's cliffs). ... and a little distance above, a" smaller cliff called Le Petit Ecor a Fabri.

ELEVEN POINTS. — *Leve pont* (? Rose). River in Randolph county.

FORT SMITH. — See *Belle Point*.

FOURCHE A LOUP. — I supposed this name was correct as it stands, but Dunbar and Hunter call it "Fourche a Luke" (p. 166).

FRANCEWAY. — Francois, a proper name. Creek in Grant county.

FREEO. — *Frio*, cold. (Spanish.) On the land plat (1845) this is spelled "Frio." Creek in Dallas and Ouachita counties.

GALLA or GALLEY ROCK. — *Galets* (pebbles). Landing on the Arkansas River in Pope county.

GLAZYPOOL or GLAZYPEAU. — *Glaise a Paul*, Paul's clay pit. (Dunbar and Hunter, p. 166.) On the land plat of 2 S. 20 W. it is called "Glady pole" (1838); while on 1 S. 20 W. it is "Glazy pole." Mountain and stream near Hot Springs.

GLAISE (GRAND). — *Glaise*, pottery clay. Pike has a "Great Glaise" on his map of Louisiana about where Arkadelphia now stands. Dunbar and Hunter have the following upon the origin of *Glaise*:

> "The salt lick marsh does not derive its name from any brackishness in the water of the lake or marsh, but from its contiguity to some of the licks, sometimes called saline, and sometimes 'glaise,' generally found in a clay compact enough for a potters' ware." (*Observations*, p. 130.)

Name of an old landing and town on the White River in Jackson county.

GULPHA. — *Calfat*, calker, a proper name. On land plat 3 S. 19 W. this is "Gulfer"; on 3 S. 18 W. it is "Sulphur" (1837-8). Creeks near Hot Springs. Dunbar and Hunter call it "Fourche of Calfat" (pp. 143, 157, 159).

LA FAVE. — *La Feve* (Bean). A family of this name formerly lived near the mouth of the stream. (Nuttall, 103.) Dunbar and Hunter (p. 159) mention "a Mr. Le Fevre ... residing at the Arkansas." On land plat 4 N. 18-20 W. it is "La Feve"; on 4 N. 17 W. it is "La Feve" (1839-42), and in *Long's Expedition to the Rocky Mountains* (ii. 345) it is called "Le Fevre." Stream in Perry county.

L'AGLES. — *L'aigle*, an eagle. On the old land plat it is called "Eagle or L'aigle Creek." Streams in Bradley county.

LAGRUE. — *La grue*, a crane. On Pike's map this is called Crane river. Streams in Arkansas county.

L'ANGUILLE. — *L'anguille*, an eel. Stream and township in St. Francis county.

LAPILE. — *La pile*, a pile or pier. Probably a personal name. It is spelled "La Peil" on the original plat of the land survey. Stream and town in Union county.

LOW FREIGHT. — *L'eau froide*. On the land plat 16 S. 17 W. this name is spelled "Low Freight" (1856). Dunbar and Hunter call it "Bayau de l'eau Froide"

(p. 137). Stream in Clark county.

LUFRA. — This name of a post-office in Ouachita is, in all probability, another form derived from "Low Freight" and *l'eau fraiche* or *l'eau froide*. (*Camp de l'or-fraie*, fish-hawk, Rose).

MADDRY. — Possibly *Madre*, of Spanish origin. Post-office in Hot Spring county.

MAGAZINE. — *Magasin*, a barn or warehouse. The name was probably given the mountain on account of its peculiar house-like form, and the town took its name from the mountain. Mountain and town in Logan county.

MARIE SALINE LANDING. — *Marais salin*, salt marsh. Dunbar and Hunter mention the "marais de saline" near this place and state that: "the salt lick marsh does not derive its name from any brackishness in the water of the lake or marsh, but from its contiguity to some of the licks, sometimes called saline" (p. 130). Landing in Ashley county.

MASON. — *Maison*, a proper name.

> "On this part of the river lies a considerable tract of land granted by the Spanish government to the marquis of Maison Rouge, a French emigrant, who bequeathed it with all his property to M. Bouligny." (*Dunbar and Hunter's Observations*, p. 126.)

MASSARD. — This word is variously spelled on the old land plats: on 7 N. 31 W. (1829), and on 8 N. 32 W. it is "Massara" and "Massaras," evidently due to a mistake of the draftsman of the final *d* for an *a*. On 7 N. 32 W. (1827), it is "Massards prairie"; on 8 N. 31 W. (1827), it is "Massard Creek" and "Massards prairie"; Nuttall speaks (p. 121) of the *Mazern* mountains; and this, it seems, was the name formerly applied to what is now called the Massard. The name appears to have originated as suggested below for the Mazarn.

I quote from *Long's Expedition* (ii, 264). On leaving Fort Smith to go to Hot Springs the writer says: — "Our route lay on the south side of the Arkansas, at considerable distance from the river, and led us across two small creeks, one called Massern, or Mount Cerne and the other Vache Grasse."

In a foot-note to this statement it is said:

> "The word Masserne applied by Darby as a name to the hills of the Arkansa territory, near the boundary of Louisiana, by Nuttall to the mountains at the sources of the Kiemesha and the Poteau, is supposed to be a corruption of *Mont Cerne*, the name of a small hill near Belle Point, long used as a look-out post by the French hunters."

Stream and prairie in Sebastian county.

MAUMELLE. — *Mamelle*, breast. It is spelled *Mamelle* in *Long's Expedition*, ii, 345. A conical hill in Pulaski county which has given name to streams also.

MAZARN. — *Mt. Cerne*, round mountain. A mountain in the region southwest of Hot Springs is called Mt. Cerne on the map accompanying Pike's report.[21] This reference is to the streams and mountains southwest of Hot Springs.

METO or METER. — *Bayou mi-terre* (Rose). This stream is about half-way between the White and the Arkansas, and nearly parallel with both. On the land plat of 2 N. 10 W. it is called "Bayou Netto" (1818-19).

MORO. —*Moreau*, feed-bag. Probably a proper name. On the original land plats it is spelled "Moro," "Moroe," and on one sheet "Moreau" (1832). Stream and village in Bradley county.

OSAGE. — Father Membre of La Salle's party in 1680-81 makes mention of the *Ozage river*, while Father Douay speaks of the river of the *Osages* and of tribes of the same name.[22]

> "The name of this nation, agreeably to their own pronunciation is *Waw-sach-e*, but our border inhabitants speak of them under the names of *Huz-zaws* and *O-saw-ses*, as well as *Osages*. The word *Wawsashe* of three syllables has been corrupted by the French traders into *Osage*. ..."[23]

Stream in north Arkansas.

OUACHITA or WASHITA. — Indian origin.

> "Between the Red River and the Arkansas there is at present no nation. Formerly the Ouachites lived upon the Black River and gave their name to it; but at this time there are no remains of that nation."[24]

On the maps accompanying Du Pratz's history the Ouachita is called Black River in the English translation, and Riviere Noire in the original French. Du Pratz tells why the stream was called Black River and adds (English, p. 169; French, ii, 304-5): "It is sometimes called the river of the Wachitas, because its banks were occupied by a nation of that name who are now extinct." Pike spells it Wascheta (appendix to part iii, p. 56).

OZAN. —*Aux anes*. Prairie d'Ane or "De Ann" is near Ozan. The old land plats call the creek Ozan. Town and stream in Hempstead county.

OZARK. — Featherstonhaugh, who traveled in the state in 1834-5, says this word is a corruption of "Aux arcs," the French abbreviation of "Aux Arkansas."[25] Schoolcraft thinks it "to be compounded from Osage and Arkansas."[26]

PALARM. — *Place des alarmes* (Rose). Pike mentions (p. 128, appendix 41) Babtiste Larme, and the place name may have come from a personal name. Town and stream in Faulkner county.

POINT REMOVE. —*Remous*, an eddy. In *Long's Expedition* (ii, 274) mention is made of "*Point Remove* or *Eddy Point* creek, which enters the Arkansa about thirty miles above the Cadron." Nuttall spells it "Remu," which suggests that the word was so pronounced in his time. It is spelled Point Remove on the original land plats. Stream in Conway county.

POTEAU. — *Poteau*, a post, possibly some old land-mark, as Professor Coues suggests. Pike and Nuttall call it "Pottoe." "The Poteau, so called by the French, from the word signifying a post or station."[27] Mountain and stream in Scott county.

QUAPAW. — Kappas and Cappas. (Indian.) In 1687 M. Joutel[28] of La Salle's party spoke of "Cappa," an Indian village. The name of a land line near Little Rock.

SALINE. — This name, of such common occurrence in South Arkansas, is best explained by Dunbar and Hunter in speaking of the Saline River that enters the Ouachita between Ashley and Bradley counties.

> "It has obtained its name from the many buffaloe salt licks which have been discovered in its vicinity. Although most of these licks, by digging, furnish water which holds marine salt in solution there exists no reason for believing that many of them would produce nitre" (p. 131).

See also *Marie Saline*.

SALISAW. — Nuttall (p. 168) has "Salaiseau"; in *Long's Expedition* (ii, 225) reference is made to *"Bayou Salaison,* or meat salting Bayou," which is probably the correct derivation. It might have come, however, from *Sales eaux,* dirty water, or from *Salissant,* that soon gets dirty. Stream in Indian Territory near the Arkansas line.

SMACKOVER. — *Chemin couvert,* covered road. The original land map surveyed between 1838 and 1845 has this spelled "Smack overt": this suggests that the original might have been *Chemin overt,* open road. Dunbar and Hunter, however, speak of it as follows: "A creek called Chemin Couvert, which forms a deep ravine in the highlands, here enters the river." (p. 133.) Stream in Union county.

SPADRA. — (?) Village and stream in Johnson county.

TCHEMANAHAUT. — *Chemin a haut,* or *Chemin a eau.* The old land plat of 19 S. 7 W. spells it "Chimanahaw" (1842). Stream in Ashley county.

TEAGER CREEK. — Probably from a proper name. Dunbar and Hunter (p. 142) say: "'Fourche au Tigree' (Tyger's Creek.)" Stream in Hot Spring county.

TURNWALL. — *Terre noir,* black land. This stream runs through the "Black lands." Featherstonhaugh speaks of it[29] as Tournois, and philologists suggest that Turnwall would not be derived from *Terre noir.* Terre Rouge is the name of a stream in the same region, and this stream flows through the tertiary red lands. The Terre Noir flows through the chalky cretaceous black lands, and I think there can be no doubt about the explanation here given. Some of the maps of the state put it down "Terre noir." The old land plat of 9 S. 19 W. (1819) has it "Terre noire"; others have it "Terre noir." Creek in Clark County.

WASHITA. — See Ouachita.

WAVER LIGHT. — *Wavellite.* The mineral of this name is found in Garland county. Formerly post-office in Garland county west of Hot Springs.

NOTES

[1]*Message from the President of the United States communicating discoveries made in exploring the Missouri, Red River, and Washita, by Captains Lewis and Clark, Doctor Sibley and Mr. Dunbar*. Washington, 1806.

[2]a. *A Journal of Travels into the Arkansas Territory during the Year 1819*. By Thomas Nuttall, Philadelphia, 1821.

b. *Observations on the Geological Structure of the Valley of the Mississippi. Journal of the Acad. Nat. Sci.*, vol. II, pp. 14-52. Philadelphia, 1820.

[3]Dunbar and Hunter in their *Observations* (p. 166) call this stream "Fourche a Luke."

[4]*Discovery and Exploration of the Mississippi Valley:* with the original narratives of Marquette, Allouez, etc. By John G. Shea. New York, 1852, pp. 46, 50, 254, and 257. This work contains a "facsimile of the autograph map of the Mississippi or Conception River, drawn by Father Marquette at the time of his voyage. From the original preserved at St. Mary's College, Montreal."

[5]Op. cit., pp. 168, 170, 172.

[6]*Relation of Henri de Tonty Concerning the Explorations of La Salle from 1678 to 1683*. Translated by M. B. Anderson. Chicago, The Caxton Club, 1898, pp. 73, 77, 95, 105, 106.

[7]*A Journal of the Last Voyage Performed by Monsr. de la Sale to the Gulph of Mexico*. By Monsieur Joutel ... and translated from the edition just published at Paris, London, 1817. Reprinted by the Caxton Club, Chicago, 1896, pp. 155, 158, 159, 162.

[8]*Pike's Expedition*. New ed. by Elliott Coues, N. Y. 1895. Vol. ii, p. 559, foot-note.

[9]*Historical Sketches of the Several Indian Tribes in Louisiana*. By John Sibley. Part of *Message from the President ...Discoveries by Lewis and Clark, Doctor Sibley and Mr. Dunbar*. Washington, 1806, pp. 66-86.

[10]*The History of Louisiana*. Translated from the French of M. Le Page Du Pratz. New ed., London, 1774. The first edition of this work was the *Histoire de la Louisana*, Paris, 1758.

[11]*An Account of Expeditions to the Sources of the Mississippi and Through the Western Parts of Louisana ... in the Year 1807*. By Major Z. M. Pike. Philadelphia, 1810. Appendix to Part ii, p. 17. See also pp. 107, 108, 116, 123, 137, 138, 140, 149, 152, etc.

[12]*An Account of an Expedition from Pittsburgh to the Rocky Mountains Performed in the Years 1819 and '20, by Order of the Hon. J. C. Calhoun, Sec'y of War; under the command of Major Stephen H. Long ...* Compiled by Edwin James. 2 vols. Philadelphia, 1823. Vol. i, chaps. vi and vii; Vol. ii, 245, 346, 348, 354.

[13]*Excursion Through the Slave States*. New York, 1844, pp. 131, 133.

[14]*The History of Louisiana*. Translated from the French of M. Le Page Du Pratz. New ed., London, 1774, page 20.

[15]*Long's Expedition from Pittsburgh to the Rocky Mountains*, Vol. ii, p. 260.

[16]*Discovery and Exploration of the Miss. Valley*, etc. By J. G. Shea. Pp. 217, 221.

[17]*A Journal of the Latest Voyage Perform'd by Monsr. de la Sale*. By Monsieur Joutel. London, 1714. Reprint Chicago, 1896, pages 140, 142.

[18]*Views of Louisiana: Together with a Journal of a Voyage up the Missouri River in 1811*. By H. M. Brackenridge. Pittsburgh, 1814, pp. 63 and 80.

[19]*The Expedition of Z. M. Pike*. By Elliott Coues, New York, 1895. Vol. ii, p. 558, foot-note.

[20]*Discovery and Exploration*, etc. By J. G. Shea, New York, 1852, p. 217.

[21]*An Account of an Expedition to the Sources of the Mississippi*, etc. By Major Z. M. Pike. Philadelphia, 1810.

[22]*Discovery and Exploration of the Mississippi Valley, with the Original Narratives of Marquette, Allouez, Membre, Hennepin and Anastase Douay*. By J. G. Shea, New York, 1852. Pp. 166-7; 222.

[23]*Expedition from Pittsburgh to the Rocky Mountains*. By Stephen H. Long. 2 vols. Philadelphia, 1823, Vol. ii, p. 244.

[24]*The History of Louisiana*. Translated from the French of M. Le Page Du Pratz. A new edition. London, 1774, p. 318. See also Dunbar and Hunter, p. 121.

[25]*Excursions Through the Slave States*, p. 89.

[26]*Scenes and Adventures in the Ozark Mountains*. By H. R. Schoolcraft. Philadelphia, 1853, p. 246.

[27]*Long's Expedition*, Vol. ii, p. 260.

[28]Op. cit., pp. 142, 149, 155, 159, 160.

[29]*Geological Report of an Examination made in 1834*. Washington, 1835, p. 73.

This article originally appeared in Modern Language Notes *14 (February, 1899), pp. 33-40 and is reprinted here with the permission of* Modern Language Notes *and the Johns Hopkins University Press.*

Some Folk Tales of the Big City

Albert Howard Carter

The word folktale *as used by folklorists may be somewhat confusing to nonspecialized readers. Scholars utilize it as a generic term referring to any narrative found in folk tradition, but they also use it as a highly specific term that serves to distinguish between various kinds of folk narratives. In this latter usage folktale refers to complex stories set in an unrealistic world and often featuring supernatural actors.* Fairy tale *is a popular term applied to this type of narrative, but folklorists use the German word* märchen *(pronounced "may-er-shin"), which has no exact English equivalent, to denote such tales. Legends differ from folktales in that they are set in a realistic world, generally in contemporary times or in the relatively recent historic past, are believable and generally call for a statement of belief or disbelief on the narrator's part. Considered in the light of these distinctions, the items related in the following article are folktales only in the broad generic sense and would be classified by folklorists as legends.*

The legends reported by Carter, one-time professor of English at the University of Arkansas, are periodically reported in newspapers as actual happenings. For example, on May 28, 1959, the Bloomington, Indiana Daily Herald-Telephone *printed an account of "The Corpse of the Cat" which supposedly happened in Indianapolis. In 1963, Herb Caen, a* San Francisco Chronicle *reporter, claimed to have printed the story in 1938 and noted that it appeared at least once a year in somebody's column as gospel. A detailed discussion and examination of such items appears in Jan Harold Brunvand,* The Vanishing Hitchhiker: American Urban Legends and Their Meanings *(New York: W. W. Norton and Company, 1981). "The Corpse and the Cat" is treated on pp. 103-112. Also useful for its consideration of these legends, although now dated, is the chapter titled "Modern Folklore" in Richard M. Dorson,* American Folklore *(Chicago: University of Chicago Press, 1959), pp. 244-278.*

Folklore is where you find it. And the big city is the only place I had to hear tales during four-fifths of my life. The tales I know are folk tales in the sense that I learned them from the mouths of friends. I have heard them all from more than one person, with differences of detail of locale, persons, and events. Those I have to relate deal with life in the big city, and the streets, department stores, hotels may change their names as the tale crops up in different cities. Characteristically, they are presented as true accounts of actual happenings (indeed, they sometimes appear in the newspapers years after they have been told around the dinner table), and they are usually told as having happened to a friend of a friend. One of the most widespread is that of the midnight pickup of the girl long since dead, too widely known to need repetition. Perhaps our members have heard variants of it and of those I have to tell which they would like to share. I tell them as I would to a gathering of friends. My first is typical in its setting and in its moral — "You can't be too careful!" It is:

THE STRANGER DISGUISED

A neighbor used to tell of a friend of hers who was doing the breakfast dishes one morning when someone rang the front doorbell. There was a well-dressed woman, largish and polite. She didn't look or act like a door-to-door saleswoman, but then you really can't tell these days. She was obviously distressed, and when the friend appeared, the woman said, "Oh, I beg your pardon, madam, but I wonder if I might use your bathroom. I'm really in embarrassing straits." "You certainly may," the friend replied; "it's just at the top of the stairs. I'd take you up, but I've got something on the stove." Well, the woman went up, and after what seemed an awfully long time, the friend began to feel uneasy; perhaps the woman was ill and needed some help. So the friend went upstairs and knocked at the bathroom door. No reply. She knocked again and said, "You all right?" "Just a minute," came the reply. And with that the door opened, and out rushed a man, downstairs, and out of the house before either could say a word. Well, she phoned the police, but all they did was to take her name and address and say thank-you.

The big city also has its ghost stories, as witness one which involves a department store, a frequent locale for big-city folk tales, a house party, and

THE PHANTOM COACHMAN

The girl — she was a friend of who was it? — was at a house party, and late one night after everyone had gone to bed, she was awakened by the brightness of the moon shining into her room. So she rose to pull the shade further down, but while at the window she

83

looked out to see a coach, of all things, coming up the drive, with a coachman with the most haunting kind of face. She was extremely puzzled, and the more she thought about it the more mysterious it seemed to her, especially the fact that the coach had made no sound whatsoever. The next day, she looked on the gravel drive for horses' hoof prints and wheel tracks, but there were none. At first she thought it was part of the entertainment, a surprise, and so she didn't mention it to her hostess. As a matter of fact she dismissed it as part of a dream. But some time later, she was in Marshall Field's waiting for an elevator. One came, and the operator called out, "Going down?" She gave one look at him and saw that he had the face of the coachman she had seen at the house party. She was so taken aback that she walked away from the elevator and didn't get on. The doors closed, and the elevator crashed to the basement, killing all the occupants.

Some department-store tales have happier endings as does that of

THE UNIQUE COMPACT

My mother-in-law had this friend who was given a beautiful compact. It was marvelously inlaid and made you say "Why, I've never seen anything like it!" As a matter of fact, the donor had replied to such an exclamation that it was an original and that there wasn't another one like it. So when the owner of the compact was going through Marshall Field's one day, she stopped to examine one like it she saw in a showcase. Yes, it was just like hers, and to make sure, she pulled hers from her purse. Yes, it was the same design, and she was shocked to see how much it cost. As she was leaving the store, wondering whether to tell the friend who had given it to her, a detective tapped her on her shoulder. "I beg your pardon, madam," he said, "but would you mind opening your purse?" She showed it to him, and he said he thought she'd better go with him to the store offices. There were several men there, and the detective said, "I'm afraid I'll have to accuse you of trying to steal that compact." "Nonsense," she said, "a friend of mine gave it to me." He looked at the other men, as much as to say, "That's what they all say." They explained to her that it was an exclusive with Marshall Field's and that none of them had been sold so that they could only conclude that she had taken it. Now flustered, she pointed out to them that it showed signs of having been used. And they said that they had been following her all around the store, and she'd plenty of time to use it. "Well, call up my friend, then," she said. They didn't know what good that would do, for she could readily have a confederate. But they called the number she gave them, and the donor verified the fact that she had given her friend a compact of rare design and of such a price.

84

They asked her where she had bought it, and she told them Peacock's. They thanked her and phoned Peacock's. Yes, they had such a compact, but it was unique, and they had sold it to Mrs. So-and-so. They would tell them the name of the maker; perhaps they could order another. They thanked them and turned to the woman and said, "We're terribly sorry that this has happened. You see, it was supposed to be an original, exclusive with Marshall Field's. Peacock's gave us the name of the manufacturer, and the company will certainly hear from us. They'll apologize to you and your friend, we hope. We'd like to do something for you. Won't you accept a gift from us? I'm sure you don't need a compact. What in the store would you like? Name it, and it's yours." "No, really," the woman replied, "I wouldn't think of accepting anything. We all make mistakes, and I'm just glad this happened because I can see that you really watch the store, and I'm glad to know how the detectives work. It's been embarrassing, but it's been a fine experience." "Well, we appreciate that, but you'll want to tell your friends about it, and we'd like you to tell them too that we'd tried to make it up to you. What do you really want more than anything else? What would you buy if you had the money?" The woman replied, "The only thing I can think of — oh, it's out of the question. The only thing I can think of is a grand piano. But just forget it." "Well, perhaps you'd like to think it over. If you think of anything, give us a ring. Here's my card." Well, the woman went home, and when she got there she found some men delivering to her apartment a grand piano.

Like many of Mr. Randolph's Ozark stories, the big-city tales are really extended funny stories. This one is both a funny story and a department-store tale involving shoplifting and

THE CORPSE OF THE CAT

This lady we knew in Washington was working for the Government and living, as so many government girls do, in a rooming house. She had brought her cat with her when she came, and the cat was pretty old. One day it died, and she didn't know how to dispose of it. So she phoned a friend who lived way out North West, and the friend said to bring it out and they'd bury it in her garden. [In some versions, she suggests a pet cemetery.] So that being her day off, the woman got on the bus with the cat in a shoe-box, and went into town. While changing buses, at E Street, she thought she'd stop into Woodward and Lothrop's to get some things she needed. Which she did. She laid the bundle down on the counter and got the things she needed — the store would be closed by the time she was on her way home — and turned to pick up her cat. But no cat. The clerk asked her what was the matter, and she said she'd lost her bundle. Not knowing whether to laugh or cry, the lady stood dazed there while the clerk called the house detective. That, the detective, a woman in plain clothes, said, was a typical shoplifter's trick to take something from a private person rather than from the department store, which would be more likely to prosecute. She said further that there was a woman whom they'd been watching and that if she knew her she'd take it immediately to the ladies' room where she'd examine her loot and do away with the wrappings in order to disguise it — they all did, all the female shoplifters, that is. So they went up, and waited. The matron finally had to open one of the booths with her key, and there was a woman in a faint with a dead cat in her lap!

A version of this tale is sufficiently variant to warrant telling both as amusing and as instructive of the way big-city folk tales crop up with different slants. It is

THE CAT PARCEL

A friend of ours tells this on herself. She is a maiden-lady scholar and was working at the British Museum. Living in a boarding house, she was unable to keep a cat to fend off loneliness, but an English friend offered her one, which, the friend suggested, she might secrete in her room; she would have to tip the maid with some silence money, but the cat was well-behaved — a box in the bathroom with some newspapers would do. So, she brought the cat to her room, under her coat, and had it for company during the winter. But presently the cat died. So she had to dispose of it. She made up a neat little bundle and was about to put it into the incinerator when the proprietress greeted her. "This will never do," she said to herself, and went off to the library. On the way, she passed a likely-looking place to ditch the cat, a culvert or something, but this time a bobby came around the corner just in time to deter her — she thought he might ask questions. On her way to lunch, the guard called to her to tell her that she'd forgotten her parcel. "This is getting to be funny," she said to herself. But she resolved on taking a bus ride and leaving the cat on it. But as she rose to leave, a passenger tipped his hat and handed her her forgotten parcel. She tried to leave it at the restaurant where she ate lunch. But here the waitress prevented her. And again she was foiled on a subway ride. Just about desperate, she phoned the friend who had given her the cat. "Bring it out," the friend said, "and we'll take it to the pet cemetery in the neighborhood." So she did. When she got there, she thought she'd take one last look at her beloved cat and opened the parcel. It was a leg of mutton!

I'd like to tell some more of my big-city folk tales, but our secretary tells me that our space is limited. Besides, some, she thinks, aren't fit for mixed company.

This essay originally appeared in Arkansas Folklore, *a publication of the Arkansas Folklore Society, 4:1 (August 15, 1953), 4-6. It is reprinted here with the permission of the late Mary Celestia Parler and the late Vance Randolph.*

Ralph E. Hughey:
Northwest Arkansas Storyteller

James M. Grover

One persistent popular image holds that bearers of folk traditions must be elderly and uneducated. As the following paper by James M. Grover illustrates this stereotype is erroneous, for his informant is both young and a college graduate. Ralph Hughey is no ordinary informant, as his narrative style demonstrates. He uses no slang and speaks in what seems at times an artificial, stilted manner. Still, there is little reason to doubt its authenticity for, as Grover notes, this idiosyncratic style is largely a result of Hughey's aesthetic sense and his choice of a future career.

Hughey's narratives are what folklorists refer to as memorates — *that is, narratives of actual events, even of happenings personally experienced by the narrator. The term was coined by the Swedish folklorist Carl Wilhelm von Sydow (1878-1952), who also offered many other terminological proposals that have since been adopted by folklorists internationally. Perhaps the most commonly used of these is* oicotype, *which refers to widely traveled items of folklore that take on a distinctive local form, with "local" being defined in a geographical or cultural sense. An example is found in an Arkansas version of the British ballad "Gypsy Davy," which is called "When Carnal First Came to Arkansas."*

Several years ago, I collected a number of Ralph Hughey's stories as a project for a class at John Brown University in Siloam Springs, Arkansas. The project was quite successful. As part of the requirements for a folklore course at Arkansas State University, I decided to deal with the same informant again. One reason for this was that my original project was not handled as a folklore collection should be handled due to my inexperience. Much had been added to Ralph's accounts and much was deleted, thus making them not his own. Ralph's qualities as a storyteller — once he's had a shot or two of his favorite whiskey — require no assistance from a collector to make his narratives interesting and valuable. Another reason that I chose to repeat my original project with Ralph arises out of our close personal relationship. Ralph enjoys telling stories, and I enjoy listening; the collection was worthwhile simply for the pleasure derived from his company.

Every time Ralph and I have traveled through Northwest Arkansas, Ralph has pointed out places of interest along the highway or dirt road. He knows who owns land and houses, when — to the day — that person was born, how much the property is worth, and the facts surrounding memorable incidents happening there. His memory is uncanny. He remembers the dates of most noteworthy events in at least five counties, including the dates of birth of almost anyone he has ever met there. Sometimes I have tried to stump him by pointing out particular mountains or valleys as we have been driving through Madison County. Ralph would tell everything he knows about those properties and astonish me by including names, dates of owner's birth, and even the year in which the land was abstracted.

Ralph has acquired this knowledge through what he would call "the College of Hard Knocks." His parents were divorced when he was quite young. He was an only child and early learned the value of money. When seventeen years old, he left home and invested all the money he could get in land. Any available land that was lost through nonpayment of taxes has been bought up by Ralph. At twenty-five he now owns land in several counties in Northwest Arkansas and one piece in Oklahoma. Ralph enlisted in the United States Marine Corps when he was nineteen, but was discharged six months later because of a foot injury. After his discharge, he spent two years investing in and selling land, buying and selling used cars, and even speculating in junk. He became involved in several court cases concerning the deeds of the land he bought and finally decided to go to school.

Actually, his decision to attend college was forced upon him. Ralph assisted his father in litigation in a court in Huntsville, Arkansas, over some money owed to his father. Acting as counsel, Ralph won the case. The judge, however, told Ralph that he didn't want to see him in court again as anything but a bonafide lawyer. Therefore, Ralph entered John Brown University in September of 1971. This is where I first met him. Ralph began talking about his experiences, and I began to learn about Arkansas politics — crooked and otherwise — land, national politics, cars, law, people, livestock, and crops. While he has a familiarity with all these topics, Ralph's real interest is politics and law. He is preparing for a career in both. He has been a notary public since he was nineteen, and in 1972 he was elected Justice of the Peace for White River Township, Madison County. He has also acquired a realtor's license. Having graduated from John Brown University with a B.S.E. in social studies, Ralph plans to enter law school at the University of Arkansas.

A first encounter with Ralph may be somewhat disconcerting. He introduces himself by saying, "My name is Ralph E. Hughey, H-U-G-H-E-Y, Hughey," making sure that his name would be neither mispronounced nor misspelled. Unless he wants something, his custom is to speak only when addressed. His manner is initially aloof and suspicious, yet sufficiently polite and friendly. When one ultimately becomes involved in conversation with him, the impression is almost that of a formal reading. Ralph's speech excludes slang and seems highly cultivated. He has developed his speech style with the intention of self-improvement both by impressing other people and by preparing for his law career.

THE STORIES

During Thanksgiving vacation of 1974, I visited Ralph in Siloam Springs in order to record some of the stories which he has told me many times. Assisted by a bottle of scotch, we recorded in a quiet motel room. Ralph sat opposite to me with one hand on the bottle and another on his glass. It should be pointed out that Ralph always speaks as if he is addressing a jury. Hence, while his language may seem overly formal, it is presented here naturally and without embellishment from a transcriber. The following stories are all based on actual events. These events, though, are filtered through Ralph's storytelling abilities and shaped by his prejudices. In some cases in the stories, names of people and places have been altered or omitted.

The New Year's Dance at Elkins

The first story was told to Ralph by a local resident of Elkins, Arkansas, who witnessed the event. Ralph especially enjoys telling this story and performs it whenever asked about it or reminded of it. The small community of Elkins is located in Washington County, about ten miles east of Fayetteville. It is perhaps typical of many of the towns in the northwest section of the state; events like those described in Ralph's story are frequent yet memorable occurrences.

It was on a New Year's night — of 1966 — at the Elkins Skating Rink and Dance Hall, which upon Saturday nights was used for the purpose of having a public dance, near the town of Elkins in Washington County, Arkansas. OK, now, the Elkins dance was a place that people of good will and those who liked to have a good time would go for an enjoyable Saturday night. Now, not everyone who went there was always a person who'd leave off drinking intoxicating beverages, and on this particular New Year's night, there was a deputy sheriff who was a guard at the dance named D.M. P_____ . He was about six foot, eight inches tall and weighed over three hundred pounds. And he also liked to smoke cheap cigars.

Along about eleven-thirty, not too far before midnight, and everybody was feeling pretty good, the music was playing; some guys decided they would even an old score with D.M. P_____ . He was leaning up against the doorway, watching the dance, ready to apprehend any drunks or anyone who might be causing any disturbance at the dance, when one of the partners to the crime went stealthily towards the fuse box. At the same time, the other one sneaked out behind Sheriff P_____ with a sixteen-ounce Coke bottle that just had come out new about that time. And he had it in a

90

raised position about the back of Sheriff P_____ 's head. About that time, the fuse box lever was hit, and the lights went off. And you hear a lot of cussing and groaning and profane language rending the air. But all you could see was the big ring of fire which was the fire of D.M. P_____ 's big cigar.

Just after that, there was the awful thump and a terrible groan as the sixteen-ounce pop bottle shattered over Sheriff P_____ 's head. At this time, other people began to bump into each other and Coke bottles began throwing and flying through the air and they were striking people with considerable force and the pop bottles were rolling across the floor. There was all kinds of cussing and people falling down, and the band kept trying to play "San Antonio Rose" right along. But somehow they still sounded kind of out of tune. Well, somebody in the midst of all the turmoil finally got back and got to the fuse box and turned the lights back on. And when they turned it on, it was the scene of almost complete disaster. Every person in the dance was either coldcocked and fighting, wallowing down on the floor, or some other bad shape. All except some old man and woman back in the back, and they were still up dancing.

Willard and the Mayor's Dog

Ralph lived in the small Madison County town where this story is set. He knows the people well and is familiar with most of the community's significant historical events. The incident described here was big news; the trial actually took place in Huntsville, the seat of Madison County.

Ralph: In the town of S.P., Arkansas, population 148, there lived a man named Willard S_____ , who was at that time around eighty-seven years old, and in all those years had never been convicted of any type of crime or any infraction against the law. Now the mayor of the town was one J.J. T_____ , a retired army man, who had come to the illustrious city of S.P. to live. Now, Mayor T_____ had a dog which he was rather proud of, but which was known to be a public nuisance to a lot of the citizens of S.P. This dog and others often caroused the streets at night causing considerable problems and keeping people from sleeping at night.

Now, Willard was tired of being kept up late at night by hollering, fighting dogs, and them gnashing their teeth, and huge packs of them roaming the streets, and so he vowed that he would put an end to this. The very next night, a pack of mangy curs happened to pass by the S_____ residence, and lo and behold, Willard had had enough. And the — it turned out the group of dogs had traveled right down the street and stopped right in front of his house. He lifted a twenty-two automatic rifle up from off the mantel, which happened to be loaded. He poked it out the window, and he opened fire at close range on the dogs. He said later when he testified in court, that he didn't intend to do any dogs any damage, or especially, he didn't have

91

any grudge against any dogs in particular.

But when the fracas was all over and the rest of the dogs cleared away, one lone dog lay dead at the side of the road. It turned out to be the carcass of none other than Mayor J. T_____ 's dog. Well, so it turned out, that the mayor should drive by the next day, and there laid his favorite dog. He came in and questioned Willard, and first Willard admitted nothing. But under closer examination he did admit that some shots had been fired on the previous evening, and was possible that shots fired from his house could have been the ones that were — ah, proved fatal to the mayor's dog. But it — death could have been due to some other source, however, according to what Willard said.

Mayor T_____ turned out to be enraged over the incident and went to the county seat at Huntsville and swore out a warrant for Willard. So the deputy served the warrant in a few days, and Willard was promptly hauled into the courthouse where he had to post bond. And trial, a few days later, was held. When that great seat of justice at the courthouse handed down his decision, the ruling was in favor of Mayor T_____ and against Willard. So finally at age eighty-seven Willard had committed his first infraction against the law and ended up having to pay the fine. To add insult to injury, Mayor T_____ sued Willard, who was known to be unusually stingy anyway, for a rather large sum of money for damages incurred due to the loss of this valuable animal. And there again the court ruled in favor of Mayor T_____ against Willard, and Willard had to cough up.

JMG: What was the charge against Willard that he had to pay the fine on?

Ralph: Oh, I believe that the actual charge against Willard in the warrant — let me see, how was the wording? I believe Willard was alleged to have unlawfully disturbed the peace, dignity, and tranquility of the State of Arkansas.

Bank Robberies

Ralph first told me these stories about bank robberies in 1972. We were waiting to get a haircut, and just across the street from the barber shop stood the fire station that used to be the bank referred to here. Ralph's mother told him of the first robbery; the second robbery was general knowledge in the community where it occurred.

Ralph: Well, on or about 1937, whenever the town of X_____ in Washington County, Arkansas, was far less from prosperous — and this is the story of a great bank robbery, as recounted to me by my mother who started high school there in 1938, only a year after that. Things were not going well at all around X_____ at that time. The depression was on, and the broth was getting pretty thin, so to speak. But there was one bank that always seemed to totter on the edge of insolvency. It was the major financial institute of that area. It probably had assets of not more than twenty-five or thirty thousand dollars at that time at the very most.

So some enterprising young men who decided they would like to make a few nickels on the side decided they would pull a bank job on the X_____ bank. The bandits waited — an opportune moment until the bank president, who was also about everything else in the bank, had gone home in the evening. And they got ready to begin their work. They had an old model truck — I'm not sure of the brand — that was mounted up with an old-time wench on the back. So they, under the cover of darkness — they drove up to the bank, and one member managed to get inside, evidently through jimmying the door or some other means. And once inside, he loosened a window, and they backed the truck up to the window, took the cable through the window, attached it to the vault, and then the man running the wench truck pushed the lever forward, winding the cable up on the wench, and pulled the vault right on out the window and right out onto the street, at which time his partner got back into the truck, and they drove off with the bank vault and about all the proceeds. The only witness to the crime was one old lady who lived across the street, who was afraid to report the crime for the time being. But the next morning when questioned by the local authorities, she told all.

JMG: What about the other bank robbery? There was another one, wasn't there?

Ralph: Well, let's see; could you refresh my memory? What city was that?

JMG: That was X_____ . They had two of them.

Ralph: Oh yes, the other one was in 1958. I remember that one. It turned out that in 1958, there again, things were not too prosperous. Fifty-eight was sort of a bad year. There was a recession on, and again the X_____ bank seemed on the verge of insolvency. At this time bank president — let's see, J_____ S_____, had got up to where he had two tellers working full-time along with him at the bank.

So they looked out the door one day and a car stopped, and in came three gentlemen with stocking masks pulled up over their faces. Once coming inside, one of the poor old tellers who worked in there thought it was all a joke, and when the men demanded money, he made some joking remark in return, thinking that these were friends of his who had come to play some type of prank on him. He was paid back by a rather large bump on top of his head which was left by the butt of a forty-five automatic. Once he had been clubbed to the floor, the bandits managed to secure the proceeds of the bank from the president and the other teller. In which time, they jumped in their car and drove off at a high rate of speed.

Unfortunately, the bank president and other tellers including the unconscious one had been left locked up in the vault, which was new and a better one than the one that had been driven off with at the 1937 robbery attempt. And it was a number of hours before that anyone came into the bank and heard anyone pounding on the door from inside of the vault.

JMG: Was the money ever recovered from these robberies?

Ralph: No, that was the strange thing about it. Although the civil authorities put up a giant dragnet around the area, the money was never recovered. An unusual thing about that — no leads were ever found to who that the gangsters might be that had done this evil deed. As a matter of fact, no one could ever seem to imagine. But one thing about it, the bank president's financial status seemed to improve after that.

The Farmers and the Wolf

This is a story told to Ralph by his grandfather early in the 1960s; his grandfather heard it on the radio news. Ralph enjoys this story and tells it regularly. It seems to fit the style of his sense of humor; the irony, the misunderstanding, and the protagonists' false sense of security.

It turned out, along back in the late fifties, somewhere up here across the Missouri line — I believe it might have been around Pineville or somewhere up in there on towards kind of up towards Joplin — that there was a bounty being paid for wolves and coyotes, bobcats, and other predators that were harassing farmers' livestock. So a number of people in the area, hoping to get rid of these varmints and at the same time hoping to collect a little bit of money of their own, decided they'd trap and shoot a few of these predators. So there was some people out hunting one day, and they saw a wolf jump up and they blasted away at him with a high-powered rifle and shot the thing stone dead. OK, it was — they hauled it in, thinking they done the community a considerable service — and probably had. But at least when they went to collect the bounty, they had somewhat of a problem collecting. Because that the wolf that they'd killed turned out to be the sheriff's German police dog.

D.C. Bruster and the Hershey Bars

When in a talkative mood, Ralph can build this story into a lengthy narrative. He wants the listener to see the surroundings and setting; he wants him to feel the peacefulness and calm so that the shocking intrusion at the story's conclusion will carry the necessary impact. He learned this story first-hand, and judging from the intense enjoyment Ralph expressed in retelling it, the protagonist must have been quite distraught and humorously so.

Whenever I was still living at S.P., Arkansas, there was some people that lived in a little place just above the place I owned. Now that if you've ever been to S.P., Arkansas, it's in the mountainous countries and part of the Ozark Mountains. S.P. was sort of a pretty town — most of it down in the valley by the White River, but part of it located on the mountainous slope down toward the town. Up on the mountain that overlooked the fair town of S.P., Arkansas, there was a large rock under a shade tree where the local people would gather especially in the summertime to visit and sit and watch the traffic go by on the highway and see who was going in the various businesses and post office and this and that down in the town of S.P. It was sort of a meeting place of the people that didn't have much of anything else to do. Now D.C. and Alice Bruster that lived up the from me — they frequently sat down there. And sometimes whenever I didn't have anything else to do, I'd go down there and join them.

One day I went down and D.C. and Alice seemed to be dis-wrought. And in the course of the conversation, D.C. said, "You know, Hughey, I just don't know what things are coming to around here. It seems like it's getting so you just can't trust anybody anymore. You know, the other day Alice went down to the store and bought — bought a box of Hershey bars. And we thought that it would be nice to sit up here and eat them now and then, but we'd be able to have just, if we wanted, oh, a couple one day. We'd eat them and just stick this box of Hershey bars back under the rock here. And we just figured it'd be all right. And say, you know those X_____ boys who live here, the ones that are always so mean? Well, you know, last night after we left, they came up here and when they was sitting on this rock, they evidently looked under it and found my box of Hershey bars. And do you know, they ate every one of them? And I'll tell you, Hughey, whenever Alice and me came down here this morning, Alice reached back under there and got the box of Hershey bars and took the lid off of it and started to reach in and get a Hershey bar, and, I'll tell you, Hughey, there wasn't any Hershey bars in it. There wasn't anything but a box of shit!"

The Klansmen and the Pope

This story is one of Ralph's favorites and obviously contains many of the elements characterizing his style of humor: gullibility, runaway rumor, and misunderstanding. Ralph gives the listener a good background and in doing so displays a considerable knowledge of historical, geographical, and political affairs. He heard the story from a political science professor at the University of Arkansas.

Back in 1923 the Ku Klux Klan was really going big at that time. I believe that it had around four million members in the United States in '23. There was two headquarters; originally there had been only one headquarters, which had been Atlanta, Georgia, but in '21 there had been a great schism within the Klan and the midwestern Klan broke off from the rest of the Klan. Most states stayed loyal except the midwestern states of Ohio, Indiana, Illinois, and I believe Wisconsin and Minnesota maybe. At least those who split off formed a new headquarters at the city of Kokomo, Indiana, which if for no other important reason that would give the town any fame was the hometown of a particular automobile works at that time. Kokomo was always sort of the center of Klan activity, and at one time in the summer of '23 over a hundred thousand Klansmen attended a meeting in Kokomo.

Now at that time the KKK had one all-consuming fear. They had the belief that the Pope in Rome was about to subvert America. It was just almost a sure thing that Catholicism was about to take over here in the United States — that almost any Italian or Irishman who was an immigrant was almost surely a agent for the Pope and was either a spy or saboteur sent here directly from Rome to do acts of sabotage and stir up the people. At the opportune moment the Pope would arrive from Italy with his army and what little resistance remained would almost surely be crushed. So the Klan decided they were going to deal with this menace and nip it in the bud before it got any worse than what it already was. Now in this kind of atmosphere people are likely to get their wires crossed and sometimes stories can begin to sound more menacing than what they originally were intended to be, and things could be added to stories.

Someone in Kokomo one day said, "You know, I reckon that the Pope has just about got America, that we're just about on the verge of being subverted and soon Catholicism is going to take over here." Evidently someone else repeated what had been said and added a little bit to it because they said, "Well, I already heard he was in the U. S. right now." This story was passed along with some concern evidently, and whoever passed it along evidently let the story grow — they saying, "Well, I hear he's already got Chicago, and Chicago's not very many miles away." The rumor began to grow by leaps and bounds. And the next thing was that someone said, "Well, not only has he already got to Chicago, but I hear he's coming on the southbound at two o'clock this afternoon and he's going to take Kokomo!"

Well, the news spread like wildfire. The loyal Klansmen, ready to fight to the last man against this insidious menace that had reared its ugly head and come across the great ocean from Italy to subvert the free and independent nation that we were — they went home. They got pistols, squirrel guns and shotguns. Some came armed with brickbats and anything else they could get. And they converged on the Rock Island Railroad station at two o'clock that afternoon. Right on schedule the Rock Island pulled into Kokomo. The conductor got off, ready to let the passengers dismount, and at that time an angry mob of Klansmen charged. It turned out that there was only one man on board the southbound that day. And he was a flour salesman for Pillsbury's Best Flour. And that day he had a rather difficult time explaining to the Klansmen that he really wasn't the Pope after all, especially considering that none of them really knew much about what the Pope looked like.

Fire at the Gobson Ranch

This story, as is apparent in the text, was told to Ralph by a friend in the mountains of Madison County. Ralph is related in some way to most of the people in these mountains, and Theobald Gobson is no exception. But kinship is not as important as a good laugh even at a cousin's expense, and Ralph enjoys telling a good story. He particularly likes painting the picture of flames blazing from an outhouse and recounting Ida Jane's refusing to answer her neighbors' call "on account of she was mad at them."

> *JMG*: Why don't you tell me something about the great fire they had on the mountain that time?
>
> *Ralph*: Let me see — great fire?
>
> *JMG*: D_____ C_____ was telling ...
>
> *Ralph*: Oh yes, down at the Gobson ranch. Yes, that was unusual. As a matter of fact, the election — during the election whenever I went over to vote and shake a few hands on account I was running for J. P., I saw D_____ C_____ and Theobald Gobson both, and the fire was discussed although I didn't bring the subject up. Well, it seems to have happened like this:
>
> Theobald Gobson, who is a second cousin of mine, and who owns a cattle and chicken farm in Madison County, had seemed to have been doing some improving in the last few years. The old outhouse out in back had been discarded for a new model of the indoor plumbing variety. It was installed in the back of his house and the old outdoor variety fell into disuse. OK, now this turned out that he — about the only thing he could use the outhouse for anymore was just to store some of the stuff that he traded in. So that might shed a little light on what the quality of his merchandise was. So at any rate he was gone on business for some reason one day, and his wife was there. His wife was named Ida Jane. And his two adopted twin boys were outside and Ida Jane didn't seem to be keeping a very close eye on them. They were supposed to have been big enough to take care of themselves. They were about fourteen years old, somewhere along like that. But soon the smell of smoke rent the air. And now, there had already been some warning. Some of the neighbors had tried to call and warn of the impending blaze that seemed to be occurring at the back of the house, but Ida Jane wouldn't answer the telephone on account she was afraid it was some of her neighbors that she didn't want to speak to on account she was mad at them at the time.
>
> Anyhow, the boys had evidently been in the toilet, and they had been playing with some matches and evidently got some papers or something on fire, and without noticing what had happened, they had gone off doing something else. When Ida Jane finally did look out the back door, the toilet was nearly in shambles. Flames were shooting twenty feet in the air. By the time that she could get the garden hose unwound and the hydrant turned on, it was too late. The

outhouse had burned to ashes.

JMG: Didn't some of the neighbors come from all around to...?

Ralph: It turned out that the neighbors, sure enough, the ones she was mad at, had spotted the blaze, and they ventured close enough to drive by about three or four times, but they didn't dare stop. So if the boys hadn't owned up to it, Ida Jane and Theobald might have even believed that sabotage had been the cause of the blaze. There again, that was, I guess one of the most serious blazes we've had in the area lately, whenever Theobald Gobson's toilet burned down. And that's really strange too because usually there's not very much in one of those that'll burn.

Labon Jacob and George Kess

This story is not one of Ralph's favorites, but to relieve himself of some of the bitterness associated with it, he tells it often. Indeed, the bitterness sometimes seems to outweigh the humor. The story tends to fluctuate in length at each telling depending on Ralph's time, interest, and mood. Sometimes when he digresses into the personalities of the protagonists and the foolhardiness of the people who believed Labon Jacob's hard-luck story, the story can become quite long.

Ralph: In 1969 I'd just been discharged from the Marine Corps. As I came back from California, I came back to S.P., Arkansas, and got a school-bus driving job and found out some new people had moved into the area while I was gone. It turned out to be the family of Labon Jacob and his, I believe, twelve kids. Now Labon Jacob had a wife that weighed about 220, sort of a fat, sloppy looking kind. About the only thing that I noticed at first meeting was that it didn't seem that these people seemed to wash or clean up too often. But that wasn't anything unusual because a lot of other people didn't either.

Well, now, Labon Jacob got to claim that he was in a bad shape. Whenever I got to talking to him in W_____ H_____ 's cafe one time, he told me that he had leukemia, that the doctors had given him only six months at the very longest to live. And that was about the most convincing story that I'd ever heard. For a person who's usually a skeptic, I swallowed this one hook, line, and sinker. So did nearly everyone else around S.P. who were usually pretty skeptical about people's hard-luck stories.

Well, it turns out that he did such a good job of selling his ailments to the people that he'd went to the grocery store run by O_____ R_____, and he told him that he was — his family was in desperate shape, that he needed three hundred dollars' worth of groceries on short notice. And he'd pay him the *first*. Evidently, it must have been the *first* chance he got because to this day the three hundred dollar grocery bill stands. Oh, now before that the effects of that had even been realized, they decided to have a pie supper for the Jacob family. They made up a pretty nice pie supper, around eight hundred dollars. And the proceeds of which was supposed to go to the Jacobs to build their new house with. Now at this time when I again was talking to Jacob, he mentioned that he had to go to the Veterans' hospital pretty frequently for treatment for his ailment and that he had won among other things both the Congressional Medal of Honor and a Navy Cross for valor beyond the call of duty while he served in the Second World War somewhere in the Far East.

Evidently no one was particularly more skeptical. The house began to be built on a piece of land over on the Ball Creek area. And they asked donations for — labor to help put up this house since Jacob just wasn't able to do any work. There was one man in the area that seemed especially anxious to help. This was George Kess. Now George Kess was a lumberman who was — had broke up with his wife not very long before that. And George Kess seemed to be there day after day. And so the old shack was finally put together without any cost to Jacob, of course. And the — George Kess became a rather permanent fixture around there. I believe George was somewhere around fifty years old. At this time there seemed — that Labon Jacob was going to go into the cattle business. And he put up a rather large sign right by the road where everyone could see it that said, "The Jacob and Kess Hickory Hill Stock Farm."

Although that they seemed to have gotten a lot of work out of George, not everything was going Jacob's way. They got something that they hadn't bargained for out of the deal, and that was two illegitimate grandchildren. Later on whenever more about Jacob became better known and George Kess became more or less a laughingstock in the area — when he was quizzed about the sign that said, "George — Jacob and Kess Hickory Hills Stock Farm," that was placed probably by the side of the road for all the world to see, he said, "I wish that they'd take that down."

JMG: What about his leukemia?

Ralph: Oh well, it seemed to be a rather mild case or a miraculous cure, one or the other, because that was 1969 and he only had six months to live. Something must have happened. I don't know whether it was faith healing or just what because Labon Jacob seems to be going about as strong as ever today.

JMG: Didn't they give him a big pie supper and thing ...?

Ralph: Oh yes, when they thought he was about dead. Not only that, to add insult to injury after he made almost complete fools out of everybody, then he got on a kick of trying to make everyone think he was really quite well off. This was about two years after his initial coming to the area. And one time he tried to tell me that he had — he owned a bunch of large lead mines around Joplin, Missouri, a three hundred and some acre farm worth a million dollars around Baxter Springs, Kansas — and I doubt if he'd ever been to Baxter Springs, Kansas — plus some more real estate down around Hot Springs,

Arkansas, and places like that that are very valuable.

Now all these tracts of land that seemed to be so good had one thing in common; none of them seemed to be around close enough that anybody around here had ever seen them. And for a person who now claimed that his real estate was so valuable, I couldn't resist asking him why that he didn't sell some of this considering — and I didn't say this — that it looked like he was living in sort of a dump. But he said that he just didn't want to sell them right now because the price wasn't right and he didn't want to have to sell these too low. I thought about asking him if I really looked ignorant enough to believe a story like that especially considering the family had been seen at the relief office in Huntsville only a few days before.

Most of Ralph's stories seem to hinge on humor of discomfiture. Local character types like the miser ("Willard and the Mayor's Dog"), the gullible bigot ("The Klansmen and the Pope"), and the freeloader ("Labon Jacob and George Kess") meet their matches in Ralph's stories. Although the surprise ending does not seem to characterize Ralph's storytelling style, he consciously presents contrasts between the idyllic settings in the Ozarks and the mundane buffoonery of his characters. Most of these stories are allegedly accounts of recent incidents. Hence, as of yet they have failed to adopt distinct elements from oral tradition. However, as stories of local characters, they represent an established tradition in American storytelling. Like the stories collected by Richard M. Dorson along the Maine coast,[1] Ralph's narratives are examples of a kind of folklore too frequently ignored by American folklorists.

NOTE

[1]For examples of local character stories collected by Dorson see *Buying the Wind, Regional Folklore in the United States* (Chicago: University of Chicago Press, 1964), pp. 65-77.

This article originally appeared in Mid-South Folklore *3:1 (Spring, 1975), pp. 3-11 and is reprinted here with the permission of the Ozark States Folklore Society.*

Some Folk-Ballads and the Background of History

John Gould Fletcher

I.

Arkansas's most famous literary son is John Gould Fletcher (1886-1950), the imagist poet. Born in Little Rock and educated at Harvard, Fletcher spent much of his life abroad but returned to Arkansas for his final years. His prolific publishing career began in 1913 with the book Fire and Wine, *and for the next thirty-seven years he produced essays, biographical pieces, poetry, art criticism, and translations of a number of French and German classics. In addition he wrote* Arkansas *(1947), a one-volume history of his native state. This latter work was presaged by* The Epic of Arkansas, *a long poem covering the entire history of the state, which first appeared in the Centennial Edition of the* Arkansas Gazette *(June 15, 1936).*

Less well known is Fletcher's interest in folklore, specifically that of Arkansas. Few references to the subject appear in his published poems, although he did include considerable dialect and references to frontier customs in an unpublished work, Bugles Blow Love Down. *Many folklore references are scattered throughout* Arkansas, *and he did publish at least two articles on ballads and folksongs.* Among the latter is "A Songbag from the Ozarks Hollows and Ridgy Mountains,"* Missouri Historical Review *45 (April, 1951), pp. 252-255, which is basically an expansion of a review from the* New York Times Book Review *of* Ozark Folksongs. *The second article on folksongs is the paper reprinted here in which Fletcher takes several texts from Randolph's* Ozark Folksongs *and comments on their relationship to Arkansas history. But the greatest evidence of Fletcher's interest in folklore is his role in founding the now defunct Arkansas Folklore Society, which he served as first president. He*

---

*Folklorists define ballads as songs that tell a connected narrative, whereas folksongs do not. They are, instead, merely lyrics that somehow seem to fit together. *(Ed.)*

collected a number of songs from the famous ballad singer, Emma Dusenbury of Mena, Arkansas, an experience that made him enthusiastic about other similar projects. Fletcher came to believe that the best way to stimulate other collecting was by having an organization devoted to such matters. Therefore, one Sunday afternoon in 1949, he brought together in Vance Randolph's study in Fayetteville a group including Randolph, Albert H. Carter, Wesley Davis, Merlin Mitchell, and Robert L. Morris, who started the Ozarks Folklore Society (the name was soon changed to the Arkansas Folklore Society), which lasted until 1960. Fletcher's hopes for this group are briefly discussed in his "The Ozarks Folklore Society," Arkansas Historical Quarterly 9 *(Summer, 1950), p. 115.*

The best source of information about Fletcher is his autobiography Life Is My Song *(1937). An obituary by Albert H. Carter appears in* Ozark Folklore 1:1 *(July 6, 1950), pp. 2-9.*

In looking through the four volumes of Mr. Vance Randolph's monumental work on Ozark Folksongs,[1] the most extensive collection of similar material so far published in the United States,* and by far the largest ever gathered from any single region, one is struck by the fact that a certain number of these ballads, accumulated by Mr. Randolph during the years 1922-1942, relates to actual historical events. The entire work is arranged as follows; in the first volume, there is a section devoted to ballads of traditional British origin (following the scheme set up by Professor Child)** which were brought, no doubt, by the ancestors of the present Ozark population, from Tennessee and North Carolina, Kentucky and other southern border regions, to their present home. As Mr. Randolph has pointed out, more than three-fourths of the ballads from the United States so far collected, have come from the South, mostly from Virginia; and are essentially akin in their general outlook on life and destiny, to the attitudes taken up for centuries by the British people, especially those who have lived on both sides of the Scottish border. Of the one hundred and seven traditional Child ballads so far collected in the United States, Randolph has found forty-one in Missouri and Arkansas and Eastern Oklahoma; following them by seventy-nine listed as later importations. With almost no exceptions, all these are from that part of Europe previously covered by Bishop Percy, in his

---

*This statement was true in 1950 when this article was originally published, but it is no longer true. The largest collection by a single collector is contained in *The Frank C. Brown Collection of North Carolina Folklore*, a multivolume work published between 1952 and 1964. Only Volumes 2 and 3 of the seven total volumes are devoted to ballads and folksongs. Still, Randolph's is the second largest collection yet published. His four volumes contain 891 songs with an additional 744 variants, while the Brown compilation has 972 songs with 1,231 variants. Brown, however, was a professor of English at Duke University who frequently relied on his students for help in turning up songs and singers, whereas Randolph was an amateur with no such advantages. *(Ed.)*

**This refers to the classic work, *The English and Scottish Popular Ballads*, produced by Harvard professor Francis James Child (1825-1896) and published between 1882 and 1898. These are the oldest ballads in the Anglo-American tradition and the ones Child considered the best examples of the genre. *(Ed.)*

"Reliques of Ancient British Poetry" in 1765, and by Sir Walter Scott in his "Minstrelsy of the Scottish Border" in 1802. That they have persisted, with some modifications of text, to be sung by hardy mountaineers all the way from the Atlantic seaboard to the Oklahoma prairies, says more than many volumes of text concerning the nature of American customs and usages, or the supposedly purely economic origin of the American Constitution.

The ballads of specific American origin, on the other hand, are of chief interest as displaying the new attitudes toward life developed by the Ozark people at the conclusion of their Western migration. These ballads are in Mr. Randolph's second volume, under the titles, "Songs about Murderers and Outlaws," "Western Songs and Ballads," "Songs of the Civil War," and "Negro and Pseudo-Negro Songs." This list, in itself, reveals a good deal concerning the attitude of the Ozark people to the new environment in which they found themselves. Having crossed the Mississippi, and by sheer self-dependence and pioneer spirit, having made homes for themselves in what had been a wilderness, they found the prairies open before them to the westward, and a new type of pioneering called for by necessity. Of the thirty-two western songs printed in Mr. Randolph's second volume, all were presumably known to that great Texan, John A. Lomax — though Mr. Randolph prints one or two which never appeared in any of Lomax's collections. This interest in the West, stimulated no doubt by the vast rise of the range-cattle industry and the heyday of the Cowboy, during the period 1840-1860, was also immensely stimulated by the sensational news about California gold, in the early months of 1849. Josiah Gregg, the most famous of Santa Fe traders, had already investigated and followed the Canadian River Route, starting at Fort Smith, which he recommended as being generally superior to the usual one followed from Independence, Missouri, along the course of the Upper Arkansas, before he wrote his classic "Commerce of the Prairies." What Gregg had explored, other expeditions, hurrying to get to California, and stake out good claims, were ready to follow. During the early months of 1849, hundreds of wagons lined the meadows between Van Buren and Fort Smith — and dozens of adventurous youths framed themselves into Arkansas' "California Army."

All this is reflected by "Sweet Betsey from Pike," which Randolph prints; no doubt the Pike County mentioned in this rollicking ballad is the one by that name in Missouri. It is also reflected in "Oh Susannah," which Stephen Foster wrote without thought of California — and found, no doubt to his surprise, becoming a folksong, with the word "California" substituted for the original "Indiana." After this episode, the main body of the Ozark people, no doubt, still tended to cling to their mountain fastnesses; the conservative elders among them going on with "Barbery Allen," "The House-Carpenter," and "False Lamkin"; the youngsters, especially if they had taken part in the Mexican War or the California Gold Rush, coming back (with pockets full or empty) to sing "The Texas Rangers," or "The Dying Cowboy," or "Little Joe, the Wrangler." These last, found by Mr. Randolph in the Ozarks, could not be picked up so readily by any ballad-collector in either Tennessee or North Carolina.

But it is the songs about murderers and outlaws, as well as those about the Civil War (Mr. Randolph prints forty-six of the former, and forty-three of the latter, so that the interest is fairly divided) that should most engage any reader's interest. For the purposes of this essay, I propose to discuss the songs about murderers and outlaws last, in the second section of this essay. The Civil War ballads, on the other hand, have been the most difficult to obtain — and they reflect more, I think, on the actual objective sequence of events, than on the peculiar psychology of the Ozark people. Many of them, as Randolph has pointed out, exist in both Northern and Southern versions, thus revealing how the "borderland of the South" represented by Southern and Central Missouri, North Arkansas, and the "Indian Nation," found itself fixed in its first great historic dilemma, by being divided in its loyalties during the struggle that still separates, psychologically, a great part of the nation.

As early as the 'fifties, German settlers began to make their appearance in some number in Northwestern Arkansas, as some had settled in Little Rock — or along the Southwest Trail that led to Texas even earlier. These settlers were, for the most part, refugees from the convulsions that had torn Central Europe apart and had finally destroyed the shadowy ghost of the old Germanic Empire, in the wake of Napoleon's conquests, by 1806. In most of the German States, especially in those, which being Protestant, were but little allied in spirit to conservative, Catholic Austria or Bavaria, there had grown up, since the days of Frederick the Great (parallelling in time the American Revolution) — an intense desire for unity. Slavery was non-existent among these States, and serfdom had been abolished, I think, by Prussia as early as 1802. For the rest, Hanover tended in its policy to lean towards England; Saxony followed Prussia; Bavaria remained loyal to Austria. But as early as 1785, a league was formed among the German princes, comprehending Saxony, Hanover, and six other smaller dukedoms and principalities; and in 1806 on the eve of the dissolution of the Holy Roman Empire, Napoleon himself formed the Confederation of the Rhine, which ultimately included all German-speaking people except the Austrians, the Prussians, the inhabitants of Brunswick, and those who lived in the dukedom of Hesse.

Union was the great dream of all the German exiles, who now began to come out of their ravaged countries and to move down from New York and Pennsylvania along the Ohio and down the Mississippi, in the wake of the Napoleonic wars. Cincinnati as well as St. Louis came early under their influence. Freedom from religious persecution was important, but union was still more important. Unlike their compatriots left at home, they were not easily stirred, either, to make wars on each other. The second great wave of German settlers, who came over after the Revolution of 1848 had been crushed, felt even more disposed towards Union, and to a republican form of government. They brought with them special technical skills, a love for books and music, a higher degree of education, than the Ozarks could boast, as they moved into the Ozark country.

As early as 1853, as Professor Clarence Evans has shown in a valuable paper (Memoirs, Letters and Diary Entries of German Settlers in Northwest Arkansas, 1853-1863; *Arkansas Historical Quarterly*, Vol. VI, number 3, Autumn 1947) two brothers, both born in Germany, with their wives, founded the Hermannsburg settlement, now known as Dutch Mills, where they became millers, farmers, and doctors. No doubt they were regarded by their neighbors with suspicion as the Civil War came on. That they did not favor secession, owned few negroes, spoke a peculiar jabber (soon corrupted from "Deutsch" to "Dutch"), were thrifty and neat, kept to themselves, made all the difference. They were subject, during the period that elapsed between the secession of Arkansas and the Battle of Prairie Grove, to immeasurable annoyances, acts of vandalism — and finally escaped to join a brother-in-law in Missouri, in December 1863. This brother-in-law was serving with the Union Army.

No doubt these people, who later compiled a rare book on their attitude, and their sufferings, at first enjoyed being in Arkansas. They were made to suffer, and finally to lose one of their number (the wife of the older brother, Johann Heinrich Hermann, died soon after their exodus) because the very same Ozark people who had at first been tolerant had turned against them. These hillmen were the people who in the first Arkansas Convention held to consider Secession, had refused to go out of the Union. They owned few, if any slaves. But they accepted the idea of Secession after Sumter had been fired upon, out of a poetical and highly impractical desire for independence and self-government.

The German population of St. Louis, and of the hill country southward, had also been skillfully organized under General Nathanael Lyon (a West Pointer from Connecticut) and Franz Sigel (a refugee from the Revolution of 1848) to oppose the Missouri State Government, in its attempt to get out of the Union. On August 10, 1861, Lyon and Sigel, with only about five thousand volunteers, opposed Sterling Price, who had recruited twice as many from his Missouri slave-holding neighbors, and who was aided by a few Arkansas troops, at Wilson's Creek, about ten miles Southwest of Springfield — and Sigel's men had broken, and had run away. Lyon held his ground, but was killed on the field, and his men retreated, leaving Springfield to be captured the next day. Price's Confederates, actually not recognized as an official legal army, by the Richmond government, but acting at a time when Missouri had not yet gone out of the Union, pressed on to the Missouri River Valley, and took Lexington, not far from Kansas City. But Fremont, sent to the spot by Lincoln, reorganized the Union forces sufficiently to drive them back to Springfield, and out of the State, by the winter of 1861-2.

Mr. Randolph prints in his second volume, no less than five ballads: "The Battle of Pea Ridge," "Manassa Junction," "I Fight Mit Sigel," "The Yankee Dutchman," "Joe Stiner," which with the "Dick German, The Cobbler" song in the first volume, are all markedly satirical toward the German in the Civil War. The attitude is perhaps best summed up in "The Yankee Dutchman": —

> *My heart is broken in von little bit,*
> *I'll tell you all what for;*
> *My sweetheart was a very patriotic girl,*
> *She drove me off mit de war.*

> *I fight for her de battle of de flag,*
> *Just as brave as ever I can;*
> *But a long time ago she nix remember me,*
> *And ran off mit anudder man.*

> CHORUS: *Oh, Florrie, what makes you so unkind,*
> *As to go mit Hans in Germany to dwell,*
> *And to leave poor Schnapps behind.*

We travelled all day when the rain came down,
So fast like Moses flood;
I slept all night mit my head upon a stump,
And I sunk down in de mud.

De nightmare came, and I catch him mighty bad,
I dreamt I slept with a ghost;
I woke in the morning frozen in the mud
Just stiff like one stone post.

At length we took one city in de South
We held it one whole year;
I got plenty of sauerkraut
And lots of lager beer.

I met one rebel lady in the street,
Just pretty as ever can be;
I made me gallant bow to her
And ach, she spit on me!

One should compare this reference, along with the references to "Feds and flop-eared Dutch" in "The Pea Ridge Battle" and to "Tories and dirty Dutch, Hessians and Yankees bloody" in "Manassa Junction," and also with "I Fight Mit Sigel" in order to see that — for a considerable time in the Civil War, — the Ozark people despised and ridiculed the Germans. Certainly, the Ozark attitude of suspicion of all "furriners" — an attitude which covers up a certain shyness, natural enough to a people rather remote and independent by nature — was intensified by the struggle incidental to the Civil War. The way in which the German was seen, as rather a figure of fun, in these ballads, may have come from the initial success of the Confederates at Pea Ridge. Having myself examined a considerable collection of Confederate Civil War ballads in the Huntington Library, I can testify that it was only the early fights of that contest that were riotously celebrated. Before the war came to an end, most of the Confederate troops were singing dirges of the most doleful description. Many of these, too, appear in Mr. Randolph's collection. They were certainly later in date than the ones I mention.

II.

The Ozarkers' independence of spirit, their desire not to be "messed around with" by outsiders, their determination to be let alone and to govern themselves, rather than be governed, is even more manifest in the section which Mr. Randolph devotes to "Songs about Outlaws and Murderers."

He ascribes the popularity of these songs, much more easily obtainable than the Civil War ones (after all, the Ozarks people suffered about as much from the depredations of lawless bands of bushwhackers and jayhawkers as did Professor Evans' Germans, and were left with little enough to boast about) to the natural belligerency of spirit frequently manifested in the region. But this is not

106

the only reason. Pride of place is justly given to the "Cole Younger" and the "Jesse James" ballad, with its contempt for the betrayer, Robert Ford: —

> *It was Robert Ford, the dirty little coward,*
> *I wonder how he does feel;*
> *For he ate of Jesse's bread, and he slept in Jesse's bed,*
> *Then he laid poor Jesse in his grave.*

What was the reason why the Ozark people should glorify such a cold-blooded killer as was Jesse James, and his bandit accomplice, Cole Younger, so that the former, at least, appeared to them like a veritable Robin Hood — "he robbed the rich and gave to the poor"? No doubt, the reason was highly complex. The James boys did not begin their career of banditry till after the Civil War. Unquestionably, they often hid out in the Ozarks wilderness, between their exploits. They were generous with their stolen money, to many a poor Ozark family. They, quite possibly, magnified their own early service under Quantrill's guerillas, on the Kansas border into a life-long devotion to the lost cause of the Confederacy which may have been, in heart at least, sincere — for no historian can say to this day just what side Charles Quantrill really was on! Moreover, the James boys — and their like — especially appealed to the Ozark people precisely because the mountain folk, after espousing the cause of the Confederacy out of a poetic desire to attain independence than for any better reason, had gone back to the Union, only to find themselves again let down by the Carpetbaggers. Let us remember that the year 1871, when Pulaski County, out of sheer hatred for Powell Clayton and his regime, refused to grant lands for the establishment of a State University, but Washington County gave the land required, was also the year when Pope County (also in the Ozarks) flared up in open warfare against Clayton's militia and one of his sheriffs.

To be an outlaw, even a murderer, was in those days of Reconstruction, not so bad a thing. There could be heroism in it, when to most of the hillmen, any form of government, except self-government, had become despicable. Moreover, the James boys were respectable in other ways. Jesse James, I have read, always went to church on Sundays, and his older brother, Frank, was, in his later years, a Baptist elder. If they swore or used dirty talk, they presumably did not do so before ladies.

Mr. Randolph is perhaps right in saying that the Ozark toleration for outlawry and killing, did not extend to horse-thieves and other petty villains. His main evidence on this point seems to me to be the very remarkable "Horse-Traders' Song" which is so good and so unique in many respects that I give it without comment:

> *It's do you know those horse-traders?*
> *It's do you know their plan?*
> *It's do you know those horse-traders?*
> *It's do you know their plan?*
> *Their plan is for to snide you,*
> *And get whatever they can:*
> *I've been around the world.*

107

They'll send their women from house to house
To git whatever they can;
They'll send their women from house to house
To git whatever they can;
Oh yonder she comes a runnin', boys,
With a hog-jaw in each hand;
I've been around the world.

It's look in front of our horses, boys,
Oh yonder comes a man;
It's look in front of our horses, boys,
Oh yonder comes a man;
If I don't git to snide him,
I won't get nary a dram,
I've been around the world.

Oh, now we stop for supper, boys,
We've found a creek at last;
Oh, now we stop for supper, boys,
We've found a creek at last;
Oh, now we stop for supper, boys,
To turn out on the grass,
I've been around the world.

Go saddle up your snides, boys,
And tie 'em to the rack;
Go saddle up your snides, boys,
And tie 'em to the rack;
The first man that gets 'em
Will pay us to take them back;
I've been around the world.

Come on now, boys,
Let's go get a drink of gin;
Come on now, boys,
Let's go get a drink of gin;
For yonder comes the women, boys,
To bring us to camp again,
I've been around the world.

III.

To summarize this argument, the Randolph collection is one that should be read by future Arkansas historians, as a vivid and rewarding experience, often more indicative of the actual temper of the people under stress and strain, than pages of impersonally phrased war reports, or reams of official correspondence, or legislative acts can ever be. Without a sense of the human element involved in making history, all history — however well documented — is worthless. Voltaire, himself an excellent historian, said that history was a pack of tricks played by the dead upon the living. Emerson said that it was the lengthened shadow of a man; Carlyle, and others, seem to have held that what mattered after all was the deeds of great men, rather than what the people lived through — but Mr. Randolph's anonymous authors give us the true point of view of the people. To them history is grim tragedy or sentimental pathos: —

> 'Twas just before the last fierce fight,
> Two soldiers drew a rein;
> With a parting word and a touch of a hand,
> They might never meet again.
>
> One had blue eyes and curly hair
> Eighteen scarce a month ago;
> The other was tall, dark, stern, and proud
> With haggard eyes to show.
>
> They rode along to the crest of the hill,
> While the cannon shot and shell,
> While volley after volley came,
> To cheer them as they fell.
>
> Among the dead and dying lay
> A boy with curly hair;
> And close by his side lay a tall dark man
> Who was dead beside him there.

I have slightly modified, for the sake of shortening, this particular text. It can only be matched by the following:

> In eighteen hundred and sixty-one,
> Hurrah, hurrah,
> In eighteen hundred and sixty-one,
> Hurrah, hurrah,
> In eighteen hundred and sixty-one,
> The great Rebellion is just begun;
> We'll all drink stone-blind;
> Johnny, come fill up the bowl!
>
> In eighteen hundred and sixty-five,
> Hurrah, hurrah,
> In eighteen hundred and sixty-five,
> Hurrah, hurrah,
> In eighteen hundred and sixty-five,
> We'll git Abe Lincoln dead or alive,
> We'll all drink stone-blind;
> Johnny, come fill up the bowl!

"Brief is the choice, yet endless" between history considered as a fate that may befall us all, and which must be met with resolution befitting such dignity as we may muster, and history becomes relentless madness and vengeance. Both sides are fairly presented by Mr. Randolph. The historians, this collection of folk-balladry tells us, should write not only from the documents themselves, but from the heart.[2]

NOTES

[1]*Ozark Folksongs*, collected and edited by Vance Randolph, edited for the State Historical Society of Missouri by Floyd C. Shoemaker, Secretary, and Frances G. Emberson, research associate, in four volumes, published by the State Historical Society of Missouri, Columbia, Missouri, 1946, 1948, 1949.

[2]All quotations in this essay are taken from Randolph's *Ozark Folksongs*.

This article originally appeared in the Arkansas Historical Quarterly *9 (Summer, 1950), pp. 87-98 and is reprinted here with the permission of the Arkansas Historical Association and the editor of the* Arkansas Historical Quarterly.

Earl Ott: Fishing on the Arkansas

Diane Tebbetts

To many readers it may seem that the following essay does not deal with folklore, and — in the sense of treating folk narratives, songs, ballads, proverbs and the like — it doesn't. Instead, this paper is an example of a study in material culture, by which is meant those traditions that result in a tangible material item. These might be such things as chairs, fences, cabins, houses and barns or, as in the present example, traditional methods of fishing and constructing fishing equipment. Most such studies have been concerned with the survival and variation of traditional patterns or with their geographic, historical or cultural distribution. Tebbetts, however, is not so concerned with these matters as she is with placing them within the context of an individual tradition bearer's life — that is, she also treats such traditional items of folklore as stories and anecdotes, beliefs and proverbial comparisons. Thus, she demonstrates that collecting from one's own family can be a highly informative and worthwhile project. For those totally inexperienced in fieldwork, collecting from immediate family members may be the best approach for reasons already outlined in the introduction to this book.

Earl Ott was born 10 July 1921 on a farm near Searcy, Arkansas, a small town about fifty miles northeast of Little Rock.[1] He was the oldest of four children born to Bill and Ina Blackshire Ott, both natives of Dexter, Missouri, in the southeastern corner of that state. When he was four or five, he caught his first fish and brought it home for his mother to cook. After the family moved to North Little Rock in October of 1928, he soon became familiar with the Arkansas River. By the time he was eleven, he had associated with the local "river rats" enough to advance from using the casual fisherman's line and pole to fishing with nets from a flat-bottomed boat. He began building his own boats and selling a few fish to supplement the family's small income when he was thirteen. By age

111

fourteen he was building his own nets as well so that he could catch more fish.

His teachers in boat-building, net-building, and riverlore were Charlie Gill and L. C. Bumgardner, two of the "river rats." Gill, born about 1900 and raised around North Little Rock, was a World War I veteran who moved onto the river during the Depression. A man who could do almost anything he set his mind to, he was a successful fisherman and by 1936 owned a new car, numerous nets, twenty rowboats, a motor boat (gas boat), and a houseboat. Unfortunately for him, he also drank heavily and within a year lost everything, never managing to get ahead again. Every Fall he would build a boat from used lumber, make a few nets, pack up a large tarpaulin to use as a tent, and head downriver to trap, hunt, fish, and drink until Summer, when he returned to Little Rock. Gill, who was the best line fisherman Ott ever knew, died about 1955. L. C. Bumgardner, who was about twenty years older than Gill, was born in North Carolina, but he lived near the North Little Rock dump for years, where he scavenged metal and sold it. Eventually he built a houseboat from scrap obtained there, but after this home sank in 1941, he too lived up and down the riverbank under a piece of canvas. Bumgardner was better organized than Gill — a hard worker who never drank. One of his industrious habits, however, was extremely dangerous and wonderfully showy. He retrieved dud shells from a World War I artillery range and hoarded them until he had enough to make a good-sized batch. Then he built a bonfire and burned the shells, thus obtaining lead to melt down for his sinkers and steel to sell as scrap. This recycling effort produced a fireworks show so spectacular that the "audience" rapidly retreated behind trees and boulders to escape being shot.

In addition to these two men, Ott observed many other individuals and families on both the Arkansas and White Rivers and absorbed their knowledge and values. In the 1930s several hundred families were a part of this Arkansas fishing culture. Born on the river, they knew no other life and rarely left their houseboats. One old man reportedly did not go to town for over thirty years, sending for the few supplies such as coffee, flour, or sugar that he could not produce himself. These people lived off the land, raising a few chickens, ducks, and pigs. Those who drank, especially on the lower White and the lower Arkansas near the Mississippi, made their own liquor. Some of these moonshiners sold their product for ten dollars per five-gallon keg. They rarely got caught, for they would run their goods downriver using only one of their boat's two cylinders. For the return trip they hooked up both so that the boat could not be identified by sound. They were, Ott said, "slick as a mink." Moonshining was not, however, prevalent in the relatively heavily populated Little Rock area.

For most river people the year's work consisted of fishing in Fall and Spring, trapping in the Winter, and digging mussels in the Summer. They also would pick up pecans to sell, scooping them out of the water during the regular Fall flooding. It was a rough life, but the people were independent and made their own living.

Their social code was simple: don't fish another man's territory, keep away from another man's woman, and mind your own business. The people who lived on White River and the lower Arkansas were an especially closed group. They solved their own problems and did not tolerate intrusion by the law. Murder was a common end to arguments, and feuding was not unknown, as one of Ott's stories shows:

DT: Could you tell me the one about P_____ ?

Ott: Who?

DT: P_____ wanting to buy the — the shells. That's — that's a good one.

Ott: It was over on — I was over on White River there hunting one morning. It was during the war. You couldn't buy — couldn't buy any shells, guns, or anything. He was asking if I knew where he could buy some forty-four shells. I asked him what he wanted with a forty-four. Said he had to kill a guy. He just pulled his jumper back and had the forty-four. Next time I saw him he wanted to know if I knew anybody wanted to buy a forty-four. He said he didn't need that one anymore. His wife was sitting over there: "Yew talk too much" (said very slowly with pronounced drawl). That's the way she talked all the time.

DT: She sounds like a — a woman of few words.

Ott: She was.

DT: Did they live on the river or ... ?

Ott:: Well, they lived in a houseboat when I first met him, but this guy he was going to kill burnt his boat. I guess that was the thing that really made him get rid of him. He may have left the country, of course. He never did ever say what happened to him. He wasn't going to tell off on hisself. He said he wasn't around anymore.

Lawmen were usually smart enough to leave these people alone, but two different sorts of game wardens illustrate what could happen:

DT: Tell me about the game wardens.

Ott: Well ...

DT: That sounds like a wild bunch of people down there.

Ott: Well, they wasn't wild; they just had their own law. They were the only law that was there. When you left DeWitt, there wasn't nobody — there wasn't no sheriff going to go out of DeWitt looking for anybody. Of course, this game warden — his job was to check the people for licenses. He didn't go just out throwing his weight around, he'd get in his boat and take off up the river. When he'd come to a houseboat, he'd pull in, knew all of them, talk with them an hour or two and eventually get around to asking if they had their license. They'd tell him if they did have it. They say, "Yeah, we've got them." If they didn't, they tell him, "Hadn't been able to get them yet." Lots of times the people'd be waiting for him to come. He'd just sell them the license then. If they didn't have them, he'd just write them — write them up and give them their license — tell them to send the money, give it to somebody. He'd be back later — something. The guy that came in there and took the job over after he left picked up one — one or two guys and carried them to DeWitt. Next time he went back down there they found him — they just — they found him a day or two before I went into the Navy.

DT: What had they done to him?

Ott: They just killed him. Shot him.

DT: Shot him.

Ott: Ah, there was no way — wasn't nobody going to go in there and investigate.

As late as 1955 the Pine Bluff sheriff would not go after an AWOL serviceman for whom there was a $25 reward. "I wouldn't go after him for $25,000," he said.

Fishing involved the whole family. Everyone knitted webbing, but the women were usually acknowledged as the more skilled at this task. While the women knitted nets, the men fished. A family of accomplished knitters would produce the webbing for a hoop net in half a day. Extra webbing was sold to fishermen outside the family. In Ott's family, however, only he fished or made nets.

The flourishing river society has been gone for about twenty years now. "Progress," as is too frequently the case, destroyed as much as it helped. The building of dams on White River, with a resultant drop in water temperature, changed the ecology of the stream so that catfish, the choice catch, no longer thrived. Paper mills built on the Arkansas at Pine Bluff discharged toxic wastes into the river. Fish could no longer effectively migrate upstream, and minnows and shrimp almost completely died out. Few fish lived long enough to become big old-timers. Although most of the older people never left the river, the younger ones moved out — joining the armed forces, going north to Michigan to pick fruit, or entering the unskilled labor pool.

But when Earl Ott was a boy, river life was still alive and well, though difficult.[2] Because, as he said, he had no "connections," he was unable to find a job which paid anything. And the family was — like most — desperate for money in the 1930s. Ott delivered circulars, scrounged metal out of alleys and the dump, and worked at a small dairy. Fishing, however, paid better. Having gone to the river like most teenagers go now to the local hangout, he just "grew into" fishing. Anytime he wasn't in school or working at odd jobs, he was on the river, often staying out all night. A younger brother fished with him some, but no one else from the family was really interested. But the fishing got into Earl Ott's blood. "A drunk can't stop drinking," he says, "and I guess I just can't quit fishing."

In 1940 Ott joined the Navy, where he received eighteen months' training as a metalsmith. During World War II he served in Alaska and the Solomon Islands, where in addition to metalsmithing he was a rear seat gunner on a dive bomber. Throughout the next several years he enjoyed using his metalworking abilities in his free time to make jewelry, boxes, and other items from scraps of steel and aluminum, as will be further discussed later. In 1945, back in the States at Ottumwa, Iowa, Ott married a WAVE at the same Naval station. He remained in the Navy until 1960, serving several years as a recruiter at Pine Bluff and Little Rock, finally retiring to a 400-acre farm on the Arkansas River at Conway, thirty miles north of Little Rock. During the time he was stationed in Little Rock, he fished, leaving home before daylight, going on to the office, and then returning to fish until after dark (Fig. 1). He continues to fish part-time now to supplement his Navy retirement pay, dreaming of someday escaping the headaches of living on the land by moving aboard a large, modern houseboat and going wherever he wishes on it.

Yet things will never be as he remembers them in the thirties. Ott complains about the pollution of the river, saying that fish are now three times harder to catch and expenses are three times higher while the selling price of fish has remained at 1950s levels. Because he can barely catch enough fish to pay his expenses, he has taken all of his nets out of the river and says he will probably never fish again. He compares himself to the American Indian shown on a television public service ad deploring litter and other forms of human destructiveness: "I guess I could cry too," he says. He is bitter and yet resigned about the way the river is being killed by industries dumping wastes, the Corps of Engineers building dams, and some "sport" fishermen "telephoning" (electrocuting) vast numbers of fish and — whether intentionally or not — destroying expensive (up to $500 for some individual nets) handmade nets and tackle. He sees little chance of improvement. But he continued to fish long after it was truly profitable because he had always done so and because he could not find other work that paid anything while allowing him to be his own boss.

As is proper for the practitioner of a traditional occupation, Ott is a craftsman, producing nearly all the equipment he needs for fishing. His first boat, built in 1934 when he was 13, was a fourteen-foot flat-bottomed river boat. It was not, however, long enough to be very safe, and so the next Fall he built a sixteen-footer that could easily cross shoals. In the 1930s nearly all boats on the river were inboard "gas boats." (Ott remembered only one outboard on the river at that time.) The motor was used only for such special tasks as taking fish to market. Otherwise fishermen rowed to conserve gas, often six miles each way to run nets or lines. Building a boat was itself an economical undertaking. Ott scrounged wood for ribs, ends, and seats from the dump and then nagged lumber dealers for bargains until he got five twelve-inch boards for the body of the boat.

Occasionally the inboard motors could be dangerous. That first fourteen-foot boat Ott built he swapped to a Howard Morgan in 1937. Morgan was crazy for machinery — anything that moved. If he couldn't trade for an item, he would steal it. Any delicate engine parts, like magnetos, he kept under his bed. One day his mechanical expertise failed him:

> *Ott:* Howard Morgan was coming back up the river one afternoon after he'd been down at Little Rock selling a load of fish. This motorboat had a set screw on the propeller shaft held the thrust

(Fig. 1) Ott and daughter with 42½-pound catfish caught in May of 1952 in North Little Rock

bearing, stuck out about an inch away from the shaft which is real dangerous. He went back — he went up in the front of the boat and went back. As he went by it, his overall leg drug past over the head of the set screw, and it wound his overalls up — tore them off of him. That's all he had on. There was people lying along side the — living on the riverbank there. (laughter) You got me bugged worse than ever. Only thing he had in the boat to cover up with was that old piece of canvas that he had the fish covered up with. He come putting (pronounced as in *putt-putt*) in that afternoon wrapped up looking like a — an Indian, Indian blanket — wrapped up in that old stinking piece of tarpaulin.

DT: You said when you told me about it before that people gave him a hard time for a long time after that about his striptease act.

Ott: Yeah, Bumgardner was the one gave him a bad time. He accused him of putting on a show right in the middle of Little Rock for everybody. In fact, I don't think he went to Little Rock for two or three months after that. They was wanting to see another performance.

Another of Ott's favorite boat stories illustrates the well-worn theme of duping an outsider:

Ott: Now this motorboat that talking about on White River that run on water was a one cylinder; I think it was four and a half horsepower, model U Gray single cylinder engine. On the gas tank they had put a piece of pipe that stuck up about an inch inside the tank. This old boy came down and wanted to buy the boat. Going down the river and run out of gas, he just took the scoop, reached over, poured a couple of scoops of water in, cranked the boat, cranked the engine, and took off back up the river. That old guy thought that it would run on water. He bought it, filled the gas tank up, and couldn't get it to go.

DT: Where — where was he from, do you know?

Ott: He'd came down from up north; I don't know just ...

Although Ott has used only outboards for the last fifteen years, he continues to prefer the inboard and speaks enthusiastically about their pleasing sound, as exemplified in the name of his last inboard: *Putt-Putt*. He has *Putt-Putt's* engine stored away in a barn and speaks hopefully of building a replacement someday. He still uses solid wood for ribbing, seats, and ends, but has substituted marine plywood for the curving, flat bottom. He has also begun putting chunks of styrofoam under the seats to ensure the boat's floating in case of an accident. The main problem with the wooden boats is that splintering along the sides snags the nets as he is putting them out. But he wouldn't own any other kind and scoffs at commercially produced metal boats.

His tackle consists mainly of several types of nets. The first step in making any net is knitting the webbing (Fig. 2). This requires three pieces of equipment: a yarn holder, a needle, and a block. Ott owns two types of yarn holders, both of which he made. The older one (c. 1946), similar to devices used to wind skeins of knitting worsted, was made to hold the skeins of cotton or linen yarn used when he began making nets. When he began using nylon twine, which came wound on cardboard spools, he made a different device on which the spool could be mounted and the yarn then reeled off as it is loaded on the needle. Traditionally the needles were hand-carved from oak or another hard wood so that they would not break easily. The sizes of needles vary depending on the size of mesh being made. The needle loaded with thread has to go through the mesh. In 1940 Ott began making aluminum needles for his own use. As far as he knows, he is the only person who has ever made metal ones. At one time he made a needle of 1/16-inch welding rod to go through the mesh of a minnow net. Metal needles are, of course, much more durable than the traditional ones which break rather easily unless carefully handled. Ott also keeps a few commercially produced plastic needles around because they are lightweight and durable. These he keeps on the boat to patch holes made by "musrats and beavers." He keeps the aluminum needles at home to prevent their theft. The blocks, traditionally made of wood in a rectangular shape and thicker at the bottom than at the top, determine the size of the mesh. They are a little oversize to allow for shrinkage of the thread. Ott has blocks for mesh from one inch up to four inches. Block size increases in quarter-inch increments. They must be made of wood that "polishes up slick" so that the twine will slide off easily. Ott's first ones were red cedar, but he switched to walnut because he had cut and cured a log. He also made a few flat aluminum blocks, including the large one used for the outer walls of trammel nets. Unlike the aluminum needles, the blocks did not please him because they were too heavy.

Knitting the mesh is always done in the same way, using the same knot, regardless of mesh size or net type. According to Hiram F. Gregory, "The knot is at least as old as that in the Neolithic netting found in the bogs of western Europe."[3] The aboriginal nets of some eastern American Indians also used the same knot.[4] For gill nets, trammel nets, wings, hoods, and seines the mesh forms a flat rectangle. For hoop nets and dip nets it is cylindrical. Mesh size varies from one inch for some seines, to 2¼ inches for hoop nets, 3¼ inches for the inner wall of trammel nets, and as much as sixteen inches for the outer walls of trammel nets.

The hoops used to give hoop nets their shape come in a variety of sizes and materials. In the 1930s most were made of second growth white oak. The best ones were made of wood cut in August when the sap was right and then bent over a Model A tire rim. The lathes were cut with a draw knife. Some hoopmakers steamed the wood to help it bend into the circular shape, a weakening process which "killed the wood" and was necessary only for wood harvested at the wrong time. When Ott tried to make a set of oak hoops once, he decided that was the hardest part of net building. He had more success making hoops from quarter-inch galvanized spring steel wire. He still uses these as the second and last hoops on each net to help sink it. He now uses commercially produced fiberglass hoops in place of the old wooden ones, which eventually would weaken.

(Fig. 2) Knitting a net

Gregory describes how a hoop net is put together: "Hoop nets are constructed in sections. The outer 'walls' are hung over the hoops and the 'flues' or throat section which traps the fish is 'hung' inside. Tapering the 'flues' is an extremely exacting task for the knitters and while almost all fishermen can knit passably, the 'taper,' if one can afford it, is done by an expert, often a woman."[5] Ott, who says "throat" instead of "flue," does all his own knitting.

After it is all put together, the net must be tarred. When nets were still made of cotton or linen, they were tarred with refined coal tar or, better yet, pine tar, which was reputed to attract catfish. Pine tar was always hard to find. The tarring process was hot, messy, and potentially dangerous. The round tar vat, large enough to submerge a whole net, was raised off the ground on legs so that a wood fire could be built underneath. A fifty-five gallon barrel of coal tar was dumped in and heated to just under a boil. It had to be hot enough to melt old tar off the already-used nets, but not hot enough to boil over or burn up the nets. Each net was individually attached to a rope and pulley, dipped into the tar for two or three minutes, and pulled out to hang, frequently in a tree, for at least twenty-four hours. Each hoop was struck with a broom handle as it came out of the tar to remove any excess. Tarring sets the knots, sets the throats in the correct position, protects the fiber from rotting, and helps the net shed trash. Nets are re-tarred when the white of the cord begins to show through — that is, after about ten days in fast water. The net is then pulled out, allowed to dry thoroughly, cleaned, and re-tarred. Fishermen, therefore, must own twice as many nets as they are fishing at any one time. The last time Ott tarred nets was in the Summer of 1951 on a very hot day, a day when everything went wrong. First, the tar boiled over and caught fire. After that was extinguished, fourteen nets were dipped, one by one. As he knocked the tar off the last hoop of the last net, it flipped, slapping him in the face. Burned by the creosote in the tar, Ott went to a local movie theater for the rest of the day, staying until it closed, trying to get cool. Nylon nets are not tarred because the high temperature would melt them. Instead they are treated with Texaco Net-Set to set the knots and help the net shed trash and a coral-like animal resident in the river.

After tarring, a new net was ready to get an anchor, which was attached to the closed end of the net by means of a tail rope about twenty-five feet long. This held the net in place. Ott's anchors are made by Bill Johnson, an eighty-six-year-old blacksmith at Des Arc, Arkansas, on the White River. A less sophisticated anchor can be made by tying a rope to a heavy rock, as Ott did in the 1930s.

Ott's hoop nets consist of the cylinder of mesh stretched over seven hoops, each one three inches smaller than the preceding one (Fig. 3). Hoops are "tied in" every 5½ meshes. Throats are constructed on the second and fourth hoops, stretching toward the tail of the net. The first throat serves as a guide while the second throat forms the actual trap. The first hoop can be eight to ten feet in diameter, but five feet is the largest Ott has seen used in Arkansas. He has used four-foot hoops, but currently favors hoops measuring three and a half feet. The net is anchored off with the tail rope and is held straight downstream by the current, with a bleach bottle or other jug floating at the end of the thirty-five-foot head line to show where the net is. The fisherman pulls the net into the boat, hoop by hoop, removes any fish or trash, and drops the net, again hoop by hoop,

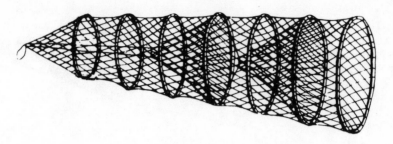

(Fig. 3) Hoop net

back into the water. In Summer and Fall these nets can be baited with cotton-seed meal cake to attract catfish. Ott owns forty hoop nets and fished them in the Summer and Fall.

Sub-types of the hoop net are numerous:

1. *D nets.* The first hoop is shaped like the capital D with the straight side six feet long. This flat side lies on the river bottom to give a wide catching area. It is fished off sand bars in Spring, Winter, and Fall. Ott always had one or two of these in the 1930s.

2. *Wing nets.* This type usually has nine hoops with three throats located on the second, fourth, and sixth hoops. Because of the net's length, fish are removed through the rear of the net by means of a lace string which closes the tail. Two wings, flat rectangular pieces of webbing like seines, have corks on the top and sinkers on the bottom. They are attached to the front hoop and flare out from it to guide fish into the net. These are fished off sand bars in the Winter.

3. *Hood nets.* Much like the wing net, this type "hoods" over the net with wings ten feet deep and twenty-five feet long. The corks on the wings cause them to pull the wings downstream, thus forming an "umbrella" over the net. Ott has used trace chains for weights on these pieces. This net is used against the bank in fast water during Spring, Fall, and Winter.

4. *Heart and lead net.* This is the most complex of all the nets (Fig. 4). It is fished in backwater and requires two people to set it out. Preferably, before a rise an area is cleaned out to assure a smooth bottom, and willow poles are stobbed into the ground to provide a framework for part of the net to be laced to. The lead is a piece of rectangular webbing twelve feet deep and fifty yards long. It is tied off to the bank, stretched out taut at a ninety-degree angle to the bank, and laced to a pole. Fish swimming either upstream or downstream strike it and are guided into the heart, which is composed of two square pieces of webbing twenty-two feet on a side. These are attached to a net in the same way as with the wing net. Each piece is

121

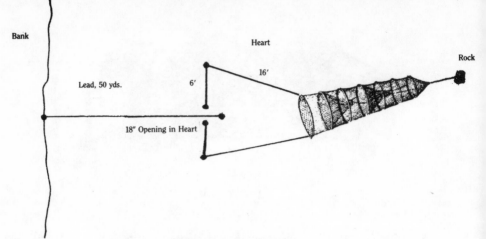

(Fig. 4) Heart and lead net

then stretched toward the bank, one slightly upstream, the other slightly downstream. Sixteen feet from the net they are lashed to poles. Then the ends are pulled in toward each other and again lashed to other poles, leaving an opening about eighteen inches wide. Protruding about ten inches into this opening is the lead. Fish who enter the triangular trap seldom escape. The hoop net is weighted with a rock anchor to keep it straight, more or less in line with the lead, and is then tied off to a tree. The fisherman pulls up the rock and opens the net with a lace string to remove his catch. This net is fished in backwater in the Spring.

5. *Live nets.* These are small nets with two hoops and a drawstring, used to store live fish.

Two flat nets — the trammel net and the gill net — are also widely used. The trammel net consists of three layers of mesh (Fig. 5). The inside wall is a 3½-inch mesh of light-weight twine, while the two outer walls are sixteen-inch mesh of heavy twine. The fish swims through the first large mesh, pushes the light mesh through the third layer to form a bag, and thus "trammels himself." This net, a type of tangle net, is fished at sea off Kent and Lancashire in England.[6] In Arkansas, it can function in two ways. As a "whip net" it is set out around a

(Fig. 5) Trammel net

122

(Fig. 6) Gill net

submerged tree top. The water is then whipped or beaten to scare the fish out of the brush and into the net. The net is then taken back up and moved. As a set net, the more common use, it is set out from the bank in running water so that fish accidentally swim into it. The gill net is made of light-weight 3½-inch mesh. Most are leaded on the bottom with corks on the top (Fig. 6). Fish attempting to swim through hang up at the gills. This kind of net, with stone sinkers and wooden floats, was used by some American Indians.[7] Ott uses two sub-types. The "shirt-tail gill" is unleaded. Because it is fished in still water, its own weight causes it to hang straight, but the fish roll up in it when they hit it. The second sub-type, the "tie-down gill net," has a heavy cord running vertically every eight feet which is shorter than the depth of the net, thus causing the net to bag (Fig. 7). Again, fish roll up in it.

Seines are also made of flat rectangular webbing and like the nets discussed above are corked and leaded. For all three cases, corks were formerly made of white cedar from old telephone poles. The lead sinkers were made by sticking a wire through a piece of cane to open it up, pouring in lead, and then cutting the cane into short pieces. Ott now uses a mold for the sinkers and commercially produced floats.

Two types of line complete Ott's equipment. Back when they were made of cotton, they were preserved with a liquid made by boiling one part coal tar with six parts kerosene. The snag line is a hundred yards long and consists of a heavy cord with limber drops six inches apart. Each supports a 0000 English steel limerick hook. These are fished in lakes, with about a thousand yards used per lake. The fish are driven to the end of the lake where, panicked, they turn and

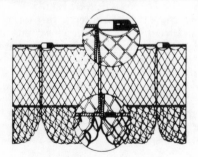

(Fig. 7) Tied-down gill net

123

swim back through the lines. This type of line is seldom used anymore, and Ott feels it should be outlawed because it can clean out a lake. Many times more fish are wounded and subsequently die than are caught. The snag line is also dangerous to the fisherman because it is easy to get hooked, especially when handling a big fish. "It's as dangerous a thing as they are to fish with," Ott says. The trotline is 150 feet long with hooks spaced three feet apart. When live bait was still readily available, Ott would use worms in Winter, shrimp beginning around 1 March, then crawfish, and finally minnows beginning around 1 June. By using this bait and setting the line across the river, Ott could catch catfish and drum. Or in Summer and Fall when the water was low and clear, he baited the trotlines with doughballs and fished them up and down the river to catch buffalo. Doughballs provided the only area where Mrs. Ott became involved, even though unhappily. She would boil water and stir in white or yellow cornmeal until the mush became too thick to stir. After cooking it as long as she dared, she turned it out onto meal-covered paper and patted or rolled it to a half-inch thickness. (She stated that she always rolled it because it was "too damn hot to pat." Mrs. Ott is not a swearing woman.) The flattened dough was then cut into half-inch cubes, which were sprinkled with more meal so they wouldn't stick together.

Except for an occasional fish fry, Ott sells all his catch because, unlike most river rats, he doesn't like fish, having gotten "burned out" on it during a childhood fishing and hunting trip. What he can't sell live, he has to throw out because Health Department regulations forbid his dressing it out. If he has a big order to fill for a fish fry, however, he skins the fish, removes the fins, head, and guts, and stores it in his freezer.

As is the case with occupational crafts nationwide, traditional fishing is dying out on the Arkansas. Most of its practitioners are older than Ott. A living exemplar of the work ethic, Earl Ott seems to connect his continued fishing in the face of rising costs, approaching old age, and lack of familial support with a Golden Age where money was scarce, but people worked hard, minded their own business, and retained their independence. Fishing, although hard work under sometimes unpleasant and even dangerous conditions, was his way of making a little money, a way strongly connected to his memories of a better past and hopefully connected to a happier future.

NOTES

[1]An earlier version of this paper was delivered at the 1975 American Folklore Society meeting in New Orleans. While the basic interviewing was done in Earl Ott's home in 1975, he was reinterviewed in October of 1977 on some points and was recorded telling the stories quoted in this paper. Ott was completely open and at ease with me at all times because I am his daughter.

[2]For information on a similar culture on the Ohio River, see Ernest Theodore Hiller, "Houseboat and River-Bottoms People," *University of Illinois Studies in the Social Sciences* 24 (1939).

[3]Hiram F. Montgomery, "The Black River Commercial Fisheries: A Study in Cultural Geography," *Louisiana Studies* 5 (1966), p. 20.

[4]Charles F. Waterman, *Fishing in America* (New York: Holt, Rinehart and Winston, 1975), p. 23.

[5]Gregory, p. 20.

[6]Willy Elmer, *The Terminology of Fishing*, Cooper Monographs on English and American Language and Literature, No. 19. English Dialect Series (Bern: Francke Verlag, 1973), p. 74.

[7]Waterman, p. 23.

This article originally appeared in Mid-South Folklore *5 (Winter, 1977) pp. 101-112 and is reprinted here with the permission of the author and the Ozark States Folklore Society.*

The Jonesboro Tornado: A Case Study in Folklore, Popular Religion, and Grass Roots History

William M. Clements

One area of American folklore that has been little treated is that of folk religion. Most of those who have broached the topic have not been trained folklorists and have generally taken the tack that there are "folk religions," by which they usually mean Southern fundamentalist and highly emotional churches. It is true, of course, that such groups do have elements of folk tradition in their worship practices and beliefs, but then so do all other churches. Even the members of a highly structured and formal denomination such as the Roman Catholic or Episcopal Church have a great deal of folk belief mixed in with their official dogma. Those who doubt the truth of the last sentence need only read a book like Carla Bianco's The Two Rosetos *(Bloomington, Indiana: Indiana University Press, 1974), particularly the chapter titled "Traditional Life in Roseto, Pennsylvania," pp. 70-121, which illustrates how the official religious tradition and the folk religious tradition are intertwined in one community. An important study of the folklore of another religious denomination, the Church of Jesus Christ of Latter Day Saints, commonly known as Mormons, is Austin and Alta Fife's* Saints of Sage and Saddle *(Salt Lake City: University of Utah Press, 1980; reprint of a work originally issued in 1956). A discussion of aspects of folk religion found throughout several American regional cultures is contained in Richard M. Dorson,* American Folklore *(Chicago: University of Chicago Press, 1959), pp. 74-134. An important regional study is Bruce A. Rosenberg's* The Art of the American Folk Preacher *(New York: Oxford University Press, 1970) which, despite its title, is only concerned with black preaching.*

In the following essay Dr. Clements, one of the foremost American students of folk religion, focuses on a natural disaster that happened in Jonesboro, Arkansas, in 1973 and reveals how religious beliefs helped shape popular attitudes toward the event. He has also published two other papers that will be of interest to anyone concerned either with folk religion or Arkansas folklore. In "The Rhetoric of the Radio Profession," Journal of American Folklore 87 (October-December, 1974), pp. 318-327, he studies the radio sermons delivered by Pentecostal members of two Arkansas counties. His "Conversion and Communitas," Western Folklore 35 (1976), pp. 35-45 is a consideration of conversion rituals and social structure of Baptist and Pentecostal sects of northeastern Arkansas.

Over a quarter of a century ago, Theodore Blegen wrote, "The pivot of history is not the uncommon, but the usual, and the true makers of history are 'the people, yes.'"[1] In order to get at this grass roots history, Blegen recommended the utilization of such documents as immigrant letters, diaries, advertisements, and even material possessions recovered from attics and storehouses. This material provides a perspective about events, movements, or periods of history different from that afforded by the writings of celebrities or by official reports. Grass roots documents reveal the attitude of unreflective folk instead of the more or less contrived, formalized expressions of writers aware of a public, contemporary or future, who will read what they write. Any sort of writings, though — and to a lesser degree the accumulation and storage of material possessions — reveals a certain lack of spontaneity. A letter writer, for instance, has time to ponder what he will write and to weigh its effects upon his reader. Even a diarist who may not expect that his writing will ever be read by anyone must organize and codify his thoughts before setting them to paper. His attitudes may become stylized by the very act of writing. In order, then, to delve as perceptively as possible into grass roots history, it would be nice if documents existed which reflected popular notions untainted by the formalization inherent in the secondary skill of writing. From these the historian could extract popular reactions to historical matters without the possible adulterations of sources like those cited by Blegen.

To suggest a relationship between history and folklore may, on the surface, seem paradoxical. After all, one idea about the term "folklore" is that it is synonymous with "misconception," the antithesis of historical, scientific, or theological fact.[2] However, it is the contention here that folklore is precisely where the historian may find the purest materials of grass roots history. Two arguments support this contention. First, it must be emphasized that the notion that "folklore" can be equated with "misconception" is completely a popular idea. Professional folklorists are normally not concerned with the factual validity of the material they study and never incorporate the question of "fact" or "fiction" into their characterizations of "folklore." Although no consensus of definition could ever be attained, perhaps a fairly comprehensive definition of "folklore" would be the "unofficial culture" of a complex society;[3] the beliefs, behavior, and artifacts which occur or have been produced outside the auspices of the society's power structure. Many folklorists might restrict this definition to include only oral manifestations of that unofficial culture. At any rate, "misconception," or a related term, is not part of the definition. Second, because the grass roots historian is more interested in attitudes than in facts which can be retrieved from conventional sources, ultimately it does not matter whether or not folklore is true. It reveals attitudinal truth even when factual data is imprecise. For example, it must be granted that an item of folklore, which may owe its vitality primarily to oral dissemination, is subject to forces like faulty memory and mishearing. These forces cause variation and hence the possible transmutation of the factual material which spawned the item of folklore. An excellent illustration is afforded by a native American ballad entitled "The Mountain Meadows Massacre" (Laws B 19).[4] This narrative folksong recounts an incident which occurred in southern Utah in 1857. A band of armed Mormons, accompanied by Indians, promised safe passage to an emigrant wagon train, only to butcher mercilessly all of the adults and many children. One text of the ballad places the blame for the massacre squarely on Brigham Young, president of the Mormon Church. However, other versions of the song shift the responsibility to the Indians or John D. Lee, the local Mormon leader.[5] At least two of the versions are factually inaccurate; however, any text of the ballad graphically reflects grass roots attitudes toward the incident, toward Mormondom in general, and perhaps toward Brigham Young. These attitudes are much more unconscious and spontaneous — and hence more representative of grass roots opinion — than those in written documents treating the same event. Any folklore item with a historical focus has the same potential as "The Mountain Meadows Massacre": despite the transmutation of facts concomitant with oral transmission, the grass roots attitudes are accessible to the historian.[6]

Because the grass roots historian who works with folklore may often be involved with orally transmitted materials, his activity appears to parallel two other branches of historical research. One of these is ethnohistory, the study of the pasts of groups like American Indian and African tribal societies. When these groups are nonliterate, it is necessary to rely on their oral traditions for historical data. In a succinct technical discussion Africanist Jan Vansina has shown that oral traditions as historical sources "can provide reliable information about the past if they are used with all the circumspection demanded by the application of historical methodology of any kind of source whatsoever."[7] By subjecting oral accounts of historical matters to a number of different texts, Vansina argues, it is possible to discover the degree of factual authenticity inherent in a particular account. It should be obvious that the similarity between ethnohistory and folklore as grass roots history extends only to the fact that both employ oral materials. While the ethnohistorian seeks to extract facts from oral traditions and separate them from the subjective attitudes which characterize the traditions, the grass roots historian using folklore is particularly interested in those attitudes and concerns himself with fact in folklore only to illuminate his study of beliefs, biases, prejudices, and the like.

When the grass roots historian uses folklore, his methodology also suggests that of the oral historian, who often interviews participants in significant historical events. In this time of electronic communication and easy mobility, many decisions affecting the course of history are never recorder on paper. Hence, the oral historian may seek out a key figure in decision-making, interview him using a tape recorded, transcribe the tape, and submit the transcript to the informant for editing and correction. There is slight similarity, though, between this methodology and that of the grass roots historian using folklore. First, the emphasis of oral history is usually on the celebrity instead of "the people, yes." Second, the submission of transcripts to informants for correction destroys whatever spontaneity might have been achieved in the orally recorded interview situation. The celebrity informant has plenty of opportunity to evaluate what he has said and its possible effects on users of the interview transcript. Occasionally, a grass roots attitude may creep into an interview by an oral historian, but the collector is usually interested primarily in the factual information and unique views of his informant.[8]

For several decades, Richard M. Dorson, Director of the Folklore Institute at Indiana University, has been urging the use of folklore in historical research.* A number of his essays on the subject have been collected in *American Folklore and the Historian*. Dorson has suggested that folklorists can appreciate the significance of American folklore only if they are aware of its historical context; likewise he has proposed a number of ways in which the historian can use folklore. Most of the published studies treating the relationship between folklore and history have been undertaken by Dorson's students, who have demonstrated that historians can use folklore to reveal grass roots attitudes, to bolster the concept of "myth" as it is used in intellectual and cultural history, to supplement the factual material found in conventional historical documents, and to provide data on minority groups whose history may not be available elsewhere.[9] For example, W. K. McNeil has shown that the use of folklore data collected from mountaineers in eastern Kentucky results in an image of the people much different from the shiftless, feuding hillbilly whose stereotype is perpetuated in officially-oriented historical works by figures like Arnold Toynbee and native Kentuckian Harry Caudill.[10]

When they have dealt with historical matters, folklorists generally have concentrated on one genre of orally transmitted folklore. Historical legends are oral prose narratives set in the historical past which usually are believed to be true by the people among whom they circulate. A series of historical legends which deal with the same person, event, or period comprise a folk history of the relevant matter. This folk history may serve as a source for facts which are not available elsewhere, but the grass roots historian is primarily interested in the spontaneous attitudes apparent in the narratives of the folk history. Perhaps these grass roots attitudes can be equated with what folklorist Alan Dundes has called "folk ideas," traditional notions that a group has about the nature of man, about the relationship between man and his environment, and about specific features in its history.[11] These folk ideas occur not only in historical legends, but in all kinds of folklore. They may even occur in other types of expressive culture, such as literature, but are corrupted there by the stylization inherent in writing. One folk idea that has been part of the culture of many groups which believe in a transcendent supernatural being is a belief in that supernatural being's direct interference in human affairs. In Christian groups this belief is called "provi-

---

*Richard Mercer Dorson (1916-1981) was one of the most prolific and influential folklorists of the twentieth century with twenty-five books and hundreds of articles to his credit. As Clements notes, most of the scholars who have studied extensively the relationship between folklore and history have been Dorson's students. *(Ed.)*

dence" and is particularly associated with the Calvinists of Tudor and Stuart England and colonial New England.

In order to illustrate the use of folklore by the historian interested in grass roots attitudes, a natural disaster which struck Jonesboro, Arkansas, will be utilized here. The focus of the discussion will be on anecdotes and commentaries collected orally and comprising a folk history of the disaster. The basic folk idea pervading this folk history is the notion that the disaster was in some way providential. While the belief in providence is an article of most Christian doctrines,[12] its relevance in regard to the Jonesboro disaster is accessible to the grass roots historian only if he looks to folklore materials.

The belief that the hand of God can be discerned in even the most trivial events affecting humanity has been accepted to a greater or lesser degree throughout Christian history. At least since St. Basil, Christian commentators have attempted to substitute providence for the pagan ideas of destiny and fortune. All post-Reformation theologians seemed to agree that every earthly event represented a warning, a reward, or punishment for appropriate human conduct, a testing of a believer's conviction, or occasionally just a reminder of supernatural power and human weakness. God controlled everything from the forces of the weather to economic fluctuations. However, He did not act according to whim, for everything that befell man had a divine purpose which a believer could discover. Hence, a plague or economic crisis could be a punishment for the sins of those affected. When a whole community suffered affliction, the cause might be the collective wickedness of the population or the presence of an especially sinful person in their midst. In the latter case, the sinner had to be discovered and delivered to justice before the community's afflictions could be alleviated. But if God punished for sinfulness, it followed that He rewarded for virtue. Thus, the notion that material wealth and physical well-being reflected godly behavior was illustrated by examples of rich and pious merchants and farmers. Yet theologians recognized that affairs did not always work so neatly; the apparently virtuous were known to suffer while the wicked prospered and flourished. The explanation for this circumstance was that God might bring suffering to test a believer's mettle. Physical well-being, then, could be a sign of God's lack of interest in an individual just as easily as it could reflect that individual's virtue. Given these theories, Christians strove mightily to explain human fortunes and misfortunes in terms of God's beneficence or wrath. Any incident with extraordinary qualities of any sort was especially suitable for providential interpretation. The result was a number of devotional literary works containing anecdotes about remarkable occurrences which obviously revealed God's providential interference in worldly matters.[13]

Jonesboro, Arkansas, is the seat of Craighead County in the northeastern section of the state. This city of 25,000 people rests on Crowley's Ridge, a gentle, forested uplift which overlooks the fertile delta of the Mississippi River on the east and the flood plains of the Cache and White Rivers on the west. The city's wealth, which is apparently quite great for a community of its size and location, comes from agriculture (soybeans, cotton, rice), industry (printing, electronics), and education (the state's second largest university). At about 12:45 on the morning of Sunday, 27 May 1973, Jonesboro suffered what the local newspaper described as "probably the greatest destruction in the history of Arkansas storms."[14] Two or three tornadoes swept across the city, taking a northeasterly path through an upper-middle-class subdivision and then a commercial district of several shopping centers and single businesses. Estimates of property damage suggested a loss of over sixty million dollars. However, the casualty figure was quite low: three people died in a rural community south of Jonesboro; one man died in the city itself, but his death was attributed to heart failure. The local medical facility treated 257 people for storm-related injuries, but hospitalized only twenty-one of them. This was Jonesboro's second tornado in five years; in 1968 a smaller storm hit a lower-middle-class residential area, killing thirty-four persons.[15]

Providence was the basic folk idea running through the folk history of the disaster. For at least three months after the event, the Jonesboro tornado provided a major topic for conversation, and those who had lost their homes in the storm or who had just been in the city when the winds struck developed a repertoire of anecdotes about their personal experiences or the effects of the disaster upon their acquaintances. Auditors who had not experienced the tornado firsthand were expected to marvel at two features which appeared to stand out in the anecdotes: the vast amount of property destruction and the low casualty figure. Of special interest was the folk idea of providence which was encouched in commentaries often accompanying the recitation of a tornado anecdote. This body of oral data, anecdotes and commentaries, came to my attention forcefully during field research which I understook during the summer of 1973 among the folk churches in the general Jonesboro area.[16] This research included observation of worship events, where the tornado was occasionally a referent, and tape-recorded, nondirective interviews with folk Christians. From responses by informants during these interviews, I was able to formulate some notions about providential interpretations of the tornado.

Supernatural involvement in the storm was cited in regard to both the vast destruction of property and the preservation of human life. It is possible to subsume folk ideas about the providential character of the tornado experience under five categories: divine punishment for sin, reminder of the transitory nature of material goods, demonstration of divine power, demonstration of diabolical power, and manifestation of God's protective care.

Divine punishment for sin. The most obvious providential interpretation of a community disaster like the Jonesboro tornado is that it represents divine retribution for the community's wickedness. For example, Lewis Bayly in *The Practice of Piety* (1613) suggested that two fires which destroyed the English village of Tiverton could be attributed to the inhabitants' allowing their preparations for market day to profane the Sabbath.[17] An illustration of direct relevance to the Jonesboro disaster is afforded by a narrative folksong from the repertoire of Almeda Riddle, a traditional singer from Heber Springs, a town about a hundred miles west of Jonesboro. Entitled "The Storm of Heber Springs," the song tells of the destructive force of a cyclone which struck the town and concludes with the following stanzas:

Some people in that city
Declared it was God's wrath,
To course the great tornado
To take them on its path.

They pointed to the churches
Where they'd refused to go
To pay to their Redeemer
The debt of love they owed.[18]

Despite these precedents, the idea that God used the tornado to punish the sins of Jonesboro was rare in the anecdotes and commentary comprising the folk history of the storm.

Relatively speaking, Jonesboro does not seem to be a wicked community according to conventional usage. Churches are numerous and well attended, the sale of alcoholic beverages is prohibited by law, and the crime rate is one of the lowest for American cities of its size. Hence, the tornado was seldom seen as divine punishment. An exception to this idea was provided by an Assembly of God pastor from nearby Harrisburg. He insisted, "I honestly believe the reason we're having all these tornadoes and all these things is the result of our backslidden condition with God."[19] While this comment was meant to have an applicability more general than the Jonesboro storm, a local Baptist preacher said that the high wind "looked like it almost made a Sodom,"[20] thus comparing Jonesboro to one of those Old Testament cities whose name has become synonymous with sin. However, the most direct association between the tornado and sin came not from an oral source, but from a letter to the editor of *The Jonesboro Sun*. In a document which reflects grass root attitudes, but not as purely as folk history might, the correspondent reacted to "streaking" incidents which had occurred on the campus of the local university during the spring of 1974. He wrote:

About a year ago a preacher stopped at the service station on the corner of Church and Huntington [Streets] and forgot to zip his pants up before proceeding on to Fred's Dollar Store. Someone called the police on him, and he was charged with indecent exposure and fined. This preacher doesn't even believe in wearing short sleeve shirts.

Nowadays, respectable people cannot go about Jonesboro without seeing nude people on the streets. Gen. 19: God destroyed Sodom and Gomorrah with over 300,000 people. If He doesn't do something to Jonesboro, he should call those people back and repent to them. In the 5th chapter of Mark, there was a man that was possessed with unclean spirit [sic] who stayed in the tombs naked and the Lord cast the spirits out into a herd of swine, and the next thing you read about this man, it says he was clothed and in his right mind. The Lord is great in power and will not acquit [sic] the wicked, and He has His way in the storm. Watch the next tornado that comes across Jonesboro. The Lord's children don't go naked in the public. Whose child are you?[21]

132

The fact that the tornado was seen as a mirror of divine wrath only in two folk history sources and in a stylized commentary suggests that this element of the folk idea of providence was less relevant to the Jonesboro storm than might have been anticipated.

Reminder of the transitory nature of material goods. The Jonesboro tornado was seen as providential education more frequently than as punishment. The vast amount of property damage could easily be interpreted as an explicit reminder by God that material goods are always subject to destruction and that men should turn their full attention to spiritual matters. This idea was proposed by another writer of letters who stated, "I am thankful to Almighty God for His sparing our whole city from more destruction of lives, and from the Double Tornado that hit us, reminding us that we still owe our allegiance to God and His Church FIRST — and if we do not pay a large part of our income to His Church and its work, He will surely take it from us ... SOMETIMES NOT IN A VERY GENTLE WAY."[22] However, this view of providence was not restricted to written expressions, for a number of oral commentaries also stressed it. For instance, a Holiness pastor noted, "And thinking God can take away the property and all, but I feel that He's trying to do something to get people to stop and think. These were just temporal things. There's more — something more valuable than just temporal things."[23] A Pentecostal teenager discovered the tornado's message in the fact that its effects were felt primarily by the economically advantaged. She said, "And these people — most of the people that were hit were rich people. And I don't know how they feel or anything else, but ... if it was me, I think I'd think that He was trying to show me that I wasn't so high and mighty that I couldn't be knocked down off my big old rock house or anything else. So I really think that He was trying to show people that He could do anything He wanted to and that they — no matter how much they had down here, they didn't have anything unless they had Him."[24] Particularly for those who were not as wealthy as persons who lost property as a result of the storm, the tornado operated as reinforcement for the idea that wealth and property were valueless anyway.

Several commentators, however, had scant hope that the lesson of the tornado would actually have much effect on the behavior of the citizens of Jonesboro. A young woman's pessimism was validated by an experience shortly after the storm. She recalled, "I don't know if you're acquainted with it or not, but there's a club on the way to Trumann [south of Jonesboro] they call the Cotton Club. And, you know, it was completely demolished — I mean, completely blown away. And they — there were so many people in it that night, you know, and just had left and people that were still there. And none of them there were really hurt. And yet the very next time we were by there.... They were right down the road — there were twice as many people as could've possibly been there at a different beer place.... It makes you wonder how that people can come that close to death and then still yet they don't seem to be concerned."[25] A Baptist preacher lamented, "And I notice some of our preachers have said that the attendance in church is less *since* the storm than before."[26] The belief that God sent the tornado as a reminder of the transitory nature of material goods is an obvious

133

folk idea in oral accounts of storm incidents. It is interesting to note that the idea is strengthened rather than debilitated by the apparent lack of heed that was paid to this powerful reminder.

Demonstration of divine power. An occasional providential interpretation of the tornado was that it represented merely a show of force on the part of God, a less than subtle illustration of the vast power at His disposal. Complacent man might forget the tenuousness of his condition if God did not compel him to recall it. A young Pentecostal woman suggested that the tornado was God's attempt "to show people that there — that He is — *does* hold the highest power and that He is the almighty power."[27] One of her coreligionists said, "And I think He done it to show us that He really could just come at anytime and He could destroy anybody at anytime."[28] However, this folk idea of providence as divine saber-rattling — yet with man's ultimate good in mind — was not as popular as other views of the tornado. Perhaps such a notion does not jibe with the characterization of God as essentially benevolent which colors many notions about His nature.[29] Its occurrence in only two folk history sources implies that it is relatively insignificant as a grass roots attitude concerning Jonesboro's disaster.

Demonstration of diabolical power. On the other hand, a number of informants suggested that the winds represented the power of Satan, whom God allowed to destroy the city so that men might be reminded of the forces which the devil can command. This providential view of the Jonesboro tornado, essentially Manichaean in perspective, appeared in oral accounts from informants who subscribed to scriptural literalism as part of their belief system. For them Satan was second in power only to God and thus a personage to be treated warily. As a Missionary Baptist preacher put it, "God releases the devil for a few minutes just to show people how destructive he could be if he were turned loose." He continued, "But He lets him go so far, and that's enough — just like He did Job, you know." He based his interpretation of the tornado's destructive power on comments by one of his own pastors:

> I had a pastor one time — we's visiting. I don't know — some way or the other the subject came up. It come up something about the storms and tornadoes and so forth. And somebody made mention of one town where they lived. A tornado hit and tore down everything but the saloon. And somebody spoke up and asked the question why was that. The church was destroyed, people's homes, and quite a few people killed.
> The pastor says, "Well," he says, "I've studied quite a bit about tornadoes," and he says, "I've come to the conclusion that God turns the devil loose for a few minutes to let people know how — see how much destruction he can cause. The devil's got a lot of power. And if he had — but God limits his power to a certain extent. He lets him go so far." And I thought that was about as good an explanation as I ever heard for tornadoes.[30]

The analogy between the Jonesboro tornado and the tribulations of Job, whose sufferings resulted from Satan's actions, but were limited by God, was suggested by other informants. Two recounted the same story concerning a supernatural compromise on the tornado. A Presbyterian layman presented one account: "We agreed in our Sunday school class — and I think it's a fairly predominant feeling around town — that God protected the people, and He let the devil have everything else. And someone put it — the way they phrased it — said, 'God told Satan — said, "You can have the houses, but don't touch my people."'"[31] The analogous text, this one from another Missionary Baptist preacher, showed little variation: "And someone said to me — and I'll give you this little story which meant quite a bit to me. A lady said to me — said, 'Brother Jewell, I heard a little joke about this tornado the other day.' Said, 'Somebody said that the devil and the Lord had a meeting. And the devil said, "I'm going down there to Jonesboro and destroy the city." And the Lord said, "You go down there and destroy it, but you don't bother my people."' I said, 'Now wait just a minute. You may have more than you think you have.' I said, 'This could be the case. This could easily be the case, but I'm not saying it is the case.'"[32] It must be noted that even when Satan was held to be directly responsible for the Jonesboro disaster, God was envisioned as still holding the highest authority and exercising His permissive will.

Manifestation of God's protective care. While the destruction caused by the tornado was afforded a number of interpretations according to the general folk idea of providence, the low casualty rate appeared to be viewed always as a definite illustration of God's concerned care for His people. Most tornado anecdotes, in fact, tended to focus on this aspect of providence while explanations for the destruction were relegated to a secondary place. For example, one anecdote related a child's coming into his parents' bedroom at midnight, forty-five minutes before the storm, and expressing his fear of having to sleep in his own room that night. He entered the parents' bed, and a telephone pole crashed into his room during the tornado, crushing his bed. Another narrative focussed on how a man, who was not harmed by the tornado, asked God to guide him to where his assistance was needed. He was told of a woman, alone with two children, whose house had sustained severe damage. He found her and addressed her by name although they had not known each other previously.[33] An elder in the local Presbyterian church told the following: "Now I'll tell you one story — one I heard afterwards. That a woman in Bono [northwest of Jonesboro] had said that on Saturday afternoon she saw a band of angels all over Jonesboro. And she just decided that — that these were angels looking over God's people."[34] A Baptist clergyman suggested that the prayers of the populace caused God to show mercy. He said, "I was just wondering if God was just deciding whether to — to really show us His wrath. But then people began — there was a lot of people began to pray and seek God that night. And it seemed like the Lord just lifted it."[35] God, essentially good and merciful, was thus an agent of protection who prevented the just from being harmed. This theme, one of the most popular in oral religious narratives crossculturally, has appeared in American folklore especially among the Mormons of Utah, who have a rich corpus of stories concerning

135

the Three Nephites, guardian angels who help the Latter Day Saints whenever needed.[36] Obviously, the notion of providence as God's protective care can emerge in response to events even when a religious group as closely knit as the Mormons is not present.

This point of this discussion of the various providential interpretations of the Jonesboro tornado is that such a discussion could not occur if the historian relied only on official documents. From them he could learn the amount of property damage, the casualty count, and the kind of programs for community recovery that were set in motion. However, he would have available nothing to suggest that providence was a relevant factor in reactions to the storm. The grass roots historian who used sources like those recommended by Blegen, on the other hand, would recognize providence as the predominant grass roots attitude regarding the tornado. The letters quoted above would provide the relevant data. However, using only these documents as source material, the grass roots historian would misinterpret the nature of providence in this particular case. For instance, the correspondent who saw the tornado as punishment for Jonesboro's sins might be taken as representative since such an interpretation is perhaps expected. However, the grass roots historian using folklore knows that this interpretation is not typical. It is one of at least five — and a minor one at that — ways in which the tornado was viewed providentially in anecdotes and oral commentaries regarding the storm. The folk history of the tornado is pervaded by providential interpretations. In order to appreciate the nature of those interpretations, the grass roots historian must be cognizant of that folk history.

It might be argued that the case for the grass roots historian's using folklore as a source for grass roots attitudes, or folk ideas, is not fairly illustrated by the folk history of the Jonesboro tornado. The material used here, after all, is virtually all firsthand accounts collected shortly after the event. If the grass roots historian were not fortunate enough to be on the scene, he would have difficulty gathering such data. However, I strongly suspect such an argument is invalid, for those who were affected by the tornado or who believed the stories that portrayed the tornado as providential will probably preserve the basic features of the folk history. A decade from now, the grass roots historian will be able to gather material on the Jonesboro tornado from oral sources. The factual information may not be as clearly presented as in some of the immediate accounts, but the folk idea of providence will still be the operative force in characterizing recollections of a major event in a community's history.

APPENDIX: INFORMANT LIST

A. Male, Assembly of God minister, about thirty years old, interviewed on tape in Harrisburg, Arkansas, on 20 July 1973.
B. Male, Missionary Baptist minister, thirty-seven years old, interviewed on tape in Jonesboro on 21 June 1973.
C. Male, Church of God (Holiness) minister, about sixty years old, interviewed on tape in Jonesboro on 14 August 1973.
D. Daughter of assistant pastor at an independent Pentecostal church, eighteen years old, interviewed on tape in Jonesboro on 17 July 1973.

E. Female, member of a gospel trio that performs during worship services at various Pentecostal churches, about twenty-five years old, interviewed on tape in Jonesboro on 16 July 1973.
F. Male, Missionary Baptist minister, about seventy years old, interviewed on tape in Jonesboro on 31 July 1973.
G. Male, Presbyterian elder, about fifty years old, interviewed on tape in Jonesboro on 31 July 1973.
H. Female, Presbyterian, twenty-eight years old, interviewed using notebook in Jonesboro on 20 September 1974.
I. Male, independent Pentecostal minister, about fifty years old, interviewed on tape in Jonesboro on 14 June 1973.
J. Male, Missionary Baptist minister, about sixty years old, interviewed on tape in Jonesboro on 6 September 1973.

NOTES

[1]Theodore Blegen, *Grass Roots History* (Port Washington, New York, 1969; originally 1947), vii.

[2]Consider, for example, the following quotation from Prince Philip on the reliability of newspaper reporting. It appeared in the *London Daily Telegraph:* "I think what happens is that you get these stories which circulate in which the dialogue assumes a certain folklore." Reprinted in Richard M. Dorson, "Use of *Folklore* in English Newspapers," *Journal of the Folklore Institute,* 2 (1965), 364-66.

[3]Richard M. Dorson, "What Is Folklore?," *Folklore Forum,* 1 (1968), 37.

[4]When referring to narrative folksongs indigenous to America, folklorists often employ the letter and number designation assigned to them in G. Malcolm Laws, *Native American Balladry, A Descriptive Study and a Bibliographic Syllabus,* revised edition (Philadelphia, 1964).

[5]Austin E. Fife, "A Ballad of the Mountain Meadows Massacre," *Western Folklore,* 12 (1953), 229-41. Historical matters concerning the event are treated in Austin and Alta Fife, *Saints of Sage and Saddle, Folklore Among the Mormons* (Gloucester, Massachusetts, 1966; originally 1956), pp. 70-73. [It has since been reprinted by the University of Utah Press. Their edition appeared in 1980 with a new preface by the Fifes. *(Ed.)*]

[6]The matter of folklore as a source for grass roots attitudes is discussed by Richard M. Dorson, *American Folklore and the Historian* (Chicago, 1971), pp. 132-34.

[7]Jan Vansina, *Oral Tradition, A Study in Historical Methodology*, trans. H. M. Wright (Chicago, 1965), p. 183.

[8]The distinction between goals in folklore and oral history has been summarized in Robert C. Cosbey, "Proposal for a Saskatchewan Oral History Project," in *Conceptual Problems in Contemporary Folklore Study,* ed. Gerald Cashion (Bloomington, Indiana, 1974), pp. 37-38.

[9]Dorson, *American Folklore and the Historian,* pp. 129-144. For a collection of studies relating history and folklore, see Richard M. Dorson, ed., *Folklore and Traditional History* (The Hague, 1973). A major piece of relevant scholarship by one of Dorson's students is William Lynwood Montell, *The Saga of Coe Ridge, A Study in Oral History* (Knoxville, Tennessee, 1970).

[10]W. K. McNeil, "The Eastern Kentucky Mountaineer: An External and Internal View of History," *Mid-South Folklore,* 1 (1973), 35-53.

[11]Alan Dundes, "Folk Ideas as Units of World View," *Journal of American Folklore,* 84 (1971), 93-103.

[12]For example, consider the following from *A Brief Statement of Belief Adopted May, 1962, by the General Assembly of the Presbyterian Church in the United States* (n.

p. 1962), 8: "We believe that our destiny and that of the world are not subject to chance or fate, but to the just and loving sovereignty of God." Compare this with a statement from Informant I: "There's no such thing as luck in the Christian life."

[13]A thorough discussion of providence in Tudor and Stuart England appears in Keith Thomas, *Religion and the Decline of Magic* (New York, 1971), pp. 78-112.

[14]*The Jonesboro Sun*, 28 May 1973, 1A.

[15]Facts and anecdotes concerning the Jonesboro tornado have been assembled in *The Jonesboro Tornado, May 27, 1973* (Lubbock, Texas, 1973).

[16]The results of this research constitute "The American Folk Church, A Characterization of American Folk Religion Based on Field Research Among White Protestants in the South Central United States" (unpublished doctoral dissertation, Indiana University, 1974). The complete transcripts of interviews cited here comprise the appendices for the dissertation.

[17]Thomas, *Religion and the Decline of Magic,* pp. 84-85.

[18]Roger D. Abrahams, ed., *A Singer and Her Songs, Almeda Riddle's Book of Ballads* (Baton Rouge, 1970), p. 22.

[19]Informant A.

[20]Informant B.

[21]*The Jonesboro Sun*, 10 March 1974, 3B.

[22]*The Jonesboro Tornado,* 9. The ellipsis is in the original.

[23]Informant C.

[24]Informant D.

[25]Informant E.

[26]Informant B.

[27]Informant E.

[28]Informant D.

[29]For example, the Presbyterian *Brief Statement of Belief,* 3, states, "God is holy and perfect, abundant in goodness, and the source of all truth and freedom."

[30]Informant F.

[31]Informant G.

[32]Informant J.

[33]Informant H.

[34]Informant G.

[35]Informant B.

[36]Fife and Fife, 233-249.

This article originally appeared in the Red River Valley Historical Review 2:2 *(Summer, 1975), pp. 273-286 and is reprinted with permission of the author and the Red River Valley Historical Association, Inc.*

Social Customs and Usages in Missouri During the Last Century

Mary Alicia Owen

*One of the most important names in the history of Missouri folklore studies
is Mary Alicia Owen (1850-1935). A member of an influential St. Joseph family,
Owen had two sisters who gained international reputations in their chosen
fields: Luella (1855-1932) became a well-known geologist and Juliette (1863-
1943) an ornithologist and botanist. Mary Alicia was a pioneer both in the study
of Afro-American lore and Native American traditions. Her* Old Rabbit the
Voodoo and Other Sorcerers *(1893) was a major collection of Negro folk narrative that was gathered mainly from blacks around St. Joseph. Her* Folk-Lore of
the Musquakie Indians of North America *(1904) was an important addition to
the literature on the North American Indian. She was one of the founders of the
Missouri Folklore Society in 1906 and served as president of the organization
from 1908 to 1935. Because she was the main contributor to the society's
publication fund, Henry M. Belden's* Ballads and Songs Collected by the Missouri Folk-Lore Society *(1940) was dedicated to her memory.*

*Despite Owen's fame during her lifetime, she has been largely forgotten
today. Much of the blame for this situation is due to her association with
Charles Godfrey Leland (1824-1903), the folklore authority who most influ-
enced her work. Although an American by birth, he was peripatetic and spent
as much time in Europe as in his homeland. Being so closely associated with a
scholar who, for all practical purposes, was European-oriented, Owen's influence was less extensive in the United States than it otherwise might have been.
But her fall from favor is also because her work now seems dated. For more
about Owen see Elizabeth Robins Pennel,* Charles Godfrey Leland, a Biography,
*2 volumes (Boston: Houghton, Mifflin and Company, 1906); Bartlett Boder,
"The Three Owen Sisters ... Famous Scientists,"* Museum Graphic *8:2 (Spring,
1956), pp. 2, 9; and W. K. McNeil, "Mary Alicia Owen, Collector of Afro-
American and Indian Lore in Missouri,"* Missouri Folklore Society Journal *2
(1980), pp. 1-14.*

In the following essay, one of her last publications on folklore, Owen departed from Afro-American and Native American folklore to concentrate on the folk traditions of the European immigrants and other white settlers of the frontier. In a clearly written essay she provides considerable information about such topics as food, house raisings, sap collecting, sugaring off, corn shucking, plowing contests, bonnet day, infares and various holidays. This paper is must reading for anyone interested in the history and folkways of the Missouri frontier.

Ever since the pioneers set their blaze on the trees along the river courses and built cabins whose sites were prophecies of cities, hospitality has been the dominant impulse of Missouri's social customs and usages. "Light and tie, Mister, the latch-string's out," was never an empty form of words as the weary traveler found, be he priest, peddler, circuit-rider, agent for ague pills, pelt-hunter, or explorer merely. For him, whoever he was, the ask-cake was baked on the hearth, the prairie-hen roasted in the Dutch oven, pork, if the wolves had spared the razor-back pigs, fried in a long-handled skillet over clear, red, hickory coals. For him was fresh coffee made, of the real berry if his hostess had it, of rye if she had not, while choice was given of "short sweetening" from the maple-sugar crock, or "long sweetening" from the honey jar.

Parenthetically, I must state that for every purpose "long sweetening" was the favorite. It is said that the famous Honey war, the dispute as to the ownership of the strip of land claimed by both Missouri and Iowa because of its bee trees, determined the stand of certain families during the Civil War. "Don't you take the side of Robert E. Lee, son," was the advice of parents along the Missouri border. "He's the man that gave our bee trees to Iowa," a mistake still prevalent. Major Albert Miller Lea was the government engineer sent to settle the boundary.

It was only after the guest had declared he "couldn't eat another bite" that it was proper to fill up the corncob pipes, reverse the little brown jug and ask eager questions concerning the outside world. Occasionally, but not as a rule, the hostess joined in the conversation and, if she made excuse that her hollow tooth needed the soothing effects of nicotine, in the smoking. The children, according to the old time admonition, were seen and not heard — except in giggles. Certainly, girls of that day, unlike their modern prototypes, had no practical knowledge of cigarettes.

When the whippoorwills ceased marking the time and the owls began, it was the host who suggested that "we men folks better step out of doors a minute and let the women get to bed." On the return of the men, they found the tallow-dip extinguished, but by the glow from the fireplace they could discern the pallets of the family spread on the floor and the one bed reserved because of its tick of feathers, hay or shucks — "husks" is not a frontier word — for the weary traveler.

It must not be omitted that if the traveler happened to be a preacher, he read, or declaimed from memory, a chapter of the Bible ere preparations for bed were made, and followed it by a long prayer in which, to everyone's edification, he roundly abused himself and his entertainers to the Almighty.

When the refreshed visitor resumed his journey, he was pressingly invited to return when he could stay longer, unless he had offered remuneration for his visit, in which case he was coldly informed that he had not stopped at a tavern.

As the cultivated areas increased with the influx of Virginians, Tennesseeans and Kentuckians, who emphasized their common name, "American," in contrast to the French and Spanish who had fought no war of independence, but were reft from their mother countries by treaty and purchase, frolics and dances added to the zest of pioneer life. These frolics were of as many varieties as strong, bold, gay young people of exuberant health could invent from the peculiarities of their new environment, copy from the annals of their ancestors, or take over from foreign born or foreign bred acquaintances. They included: house-raising, house-warming, sap-collecting, sugaring-off, corn-shucking, all forms of helpfulness combined with fun and laughter and hospitality. Even plowing contests, races of mowers, cradlers and hacklers were followed by simple feasts prepared by the women and girls, and games where the forfeits were kisses. Of all the amusements, however, dancing was the most popular. To the jigs and reels of the "Americans" were soon added the quadrilles, gavottes and boleros of the French and Spanish of St. Louis, Ste. Genevieve and Cape Girardeau and the waltzes and polkas of the Germans and Bohemians, who were pouring into the state as the new land of freedom and opportunity.

It seems almost incredible that, after the strenuous labors of the day, such as spinning, dyeing, weaving, making garments for both sexes, besides the ordinary labors of the household, for women, and clearing, tilling, tanning, shoemaking and all the other drudgery necessary where man has not yet conquered nature, for the sterner sex, whole families would ride twenty miles or more to a dance, even with babies on the saddle in front of them. Once there, only the young people danced, both sexes being arrayed in new suits of homespun — linsey-woolsey in cold weather, pure linen in warm. Only occasionally did some dandy make himself conspicuous by the addition of a calfskin vest with the red and white hair still on. Symbolical dancing such as the present day is accustomed to had not been heard of, but now and then an enthusiastic dancer with blistered toes took off her heavy calfskin shoes and continued her exertions in comfort. The matrons sat on benches ranged against the wall, and as the wails of their indignant offspring permitted, criticised the dancers, exchanged gossip and recipes, or tendered invitations to the quilting-bee to be held as soon as a few more patches were "pieced." The older men and the bashful boys stood near the door and discussed their labors, crops and sports. Golf clubs were not in fashion, but hoes were, and skill with the flail received as respectful consideration as their grandsons would accord a tennis championship. The whole state was, without gainsay, the most magnificent country club in the world.

Sometimes instead of a dance, there was a fiddlers' contest. There might be only two, but, more frequently, there were four or five, some of whom had come a long way to put their claims of superiority to the test. Quite often a zest was added by some local troubadour, who sang, to the tune of a familiar hymn, a ballad of his own composition, treating of some absurd or tragic happening near by. In vain the indignant revivalist thundered his denunciation at these gatherings. He was met with a stubborn response of this sort:

"Now, see here, Brother Smith, you just render unto Caesar them things that are Caesar's and we'll render unto the Lord the things that are the Lord's. We don't aim to worship the Lord by machinery. Have your camp meetings and we'll raise the tunes without even the help of a tuning-fork, and sing all the hymns you give out, but, you please let this outside business alone. If Thomas Jefferson cleared his mind of care by playing the fiddle, it is good enough for us."

It was the school teacher in the new schoolhouse who took the place of the fiddler, with his singing school and spelling bee, and he in his turn was remanded to oblivion by what Judge Henry M. Vories of the Missouri Supreme Court characterised as the "piano epidemic of the late '50's." Every girl had to have a piano, which she played if she could and thumped if she couldn't — to the intolerable anguish of sensitive ears and the anathemas of mothers who sought vainly to put the children to sleep. It is not definitely known what benefactor shut those old square pianos and littered their covers with china-painting and decorated rolling-pins and other ordinarily undecorated kitchen utensils.

Men's games, such as wrestling, leaping, jumping, running, lifting weights, pitching quoits, or "shoes," as the old game with the discus was called, where no women were present, were not always peaceful. Disputes sometimes ended in bloodshed.

The "Americans" saw to it that the Fourth of July was celebrated properly, and their enthusiasm drew in the French and Germans. The French loved to hear Lafayette eulogized and the British abused, and, after all, this was their country whether they liked the newcomers or not. The Germans of that first immigration were enraptured with the new freedom, and sang "My Country, 'Tis of Thee" with as much fervor as any man whose great-grandfather had belonged to the Jamestown Colony. Very early the people began to assemble in front of the cross roads' store, at the schoolhouse, or the courthouse, if the county seat boasted of one. Some came on foot, some on horseback, in wagons, buggies, carriages. A minister opened the services with a prayer of thanksgiving, somebody read the Declaration of Independence, a flustered little girl in a white dress presented a bouquet of common or garden flowers embowered in sprays of asparagus to the orator of the day, and the orator of the day, who was, generally, a patriot who had held, was holding, or wished to hold office, after kissing the little girl and tickling his nose with the asparagus, plunged into that style of oratory technically described as "spreadeagle," and soared until a hungry audience drowned his voice in applause, or the singing of the national anthem. After the "exercises" came the barbecue, oxen, sheep and swine roasted over a pit of coals. For those who did not care for roast meat, there was burgoo, a highly seasoned stew of rabbits, fowls, venison and a great variety of vegetables. To the feast the women brought pickles, bread and cake — they never attempted a barbecue, and seldom, a burgoo.

In the afternoon were horse racing, sack and potato races, climbing greased poles and catching greased pigs. Sometimes the young men insisted on having a tournament, which little resembled the jousts of the Knights of the Round Table. With a wooden spear, the modern knight caught rings from a bar, and if he had more rings to his credit than his rivals, he received a wreath, with which he crowned the lady of his choice "queen of love and beauty."

In the evening, then as now, Missouri blazed with fireworks, and the day ended as it had begun with the noise caused by ignited powder. Every boy had been expected to wake his family with a fusilade, and did it — some thought, overdid it.

In the last hundred years Hallowe'en pranks and customs have not perceptibly varied, nor have those of Thanksgiving Day — the customs of the day, that is, but Christmas observances, are not quite the same. The open hearth is gone, and with it the yule log, especially dear to the slaves of ante-bellum days because as long as it burned they need do no work. They were the ones who chose it, selecting carefully the largest and greenest log, not from the wood pile, but from the wood lot, so as to be sure that it was green as well as of large size. When it was burned down to the last charred brand, this was intrusted to a careful old mammy to be kept to light next year's log. Any work done while the Christmas back-log was burning must be paid for. If anyone chose to absent himself, he must have a "pass" written by his master, and return to his home by the morning of New Year's Day.

Until after the advent of the Germans, the "American" children hung up their stockings at the fireplace, in the happy confidence that St. Nicholas, the ascetic saint of Asia Minor, metamorphosed into a jolly Father Christmas, would come through the air in a sleigh drawn by reindeers, and fill them with toys and candy. Very early, Christmas morning, the children and slaves were awake and shouting "Christmas gift" at everyone. Later the stockings were examined, and breakfast was attended in disorderly fashion, but eaten only by the adults. With the Germans came the evergreen tree, supposed by some to typify Ygdrasil, Tree of Life, of Teutonic mythology, and renamed by the early Christian Church, while others maintained that Martin Luther, after watching the stars over a grove of firs one Christmas Eve, went home and prepared a little tree to put his children in mind of the Star of Bethlehem. Whatever its origin, we Missourians speedily made it ours, and have since dramatized St. Nicholas, or Santa Claus, to stand beside it. Also, commerce has captured both tree and saint, perhaps to the pleasure of the children who see them in shop windows.

The little French or Spanish children had no tree, but they placed their shoes on the hearth for the Christ-Child to fill with presents. To put them in mind of what the celebration meant, there was what the French called a "creche," the Spanish a "posada," a box or alcove prepared to look like a little cavern, and tenanted with little figures of the Holy Family, the Magi and their camels, the donkey on which the Madonna rode and the oxen in their stalls. Our new citizens, the Mexicans, have the same observances, and, in addition, a great earthenware jar dressed in tissue paper, to look like a sort of Santa Claus. This is filled with sweets and toys and hung from a bracket. Every child is invited to break this "pinata" by striking it with a wooden wand. When it withstands youthful taps it is shattered by the father, who is not expected to join in the scramble for the presents.

Sir Henry Cole invented Christmas cards in 1846 and had John Horsley, the artist, make the design for him, but it took a score or more of years for us to incorporate them into our observances, along with holly and mistletoe decorations, Christmas trees, interchange of presents, banquets of turkey, cranberry sauce, mince pie and the national-pie a rich custard flavored with pumpkin and called by its name.

New Year's Day, which some of our foreign visitors referred to in their letters as "Gentlemen's Day," because it was the general custom for men to call on their friends on that day and partake of their hospitality, has been spoken of as a day whose observance was introduced by the French. Truly, it is a day beloved by that people in all climes and under all skies since the day of the Druids, who on that date cut the sacred mistletoe from the oak tree and, later, exchanged gifts in commemoration of their freedom from the hated Roman taxes, but the Scotch Covenanters who desired a "silent" or "silenced" Christmas as ardently as did Cromwell and the Puritans who substituted Thanksgiving in November for Christmas in December because the Cavaliers kept it, with noise and wassail, had Watch Night and saw the Old Year out and the New Year in, and brought the custom, as well as that of visiting, overseas.

The second of February, "Candlemas Day," so called because Jesus, "The Light to Lighten the Gentiles and the Glory of Israel," was presented in the temple on that day, has lost prestige with many. The general public call it "Ground Hog's Day," because of a folk tale almost forgotten. It related how a marmot, alias ground hog, alias woodchuck, stepped out of his burrow to warm himself at the bonfire of withered Christmas decorations, which are burned on Candlemas Day, because every leaf of them left over means a trouble in the house. The sunlight was so brilliant that the "beastie" cast a very black shadow, which he concluded was a trouble for him. He ran into his burrow without warming himself, and shivered and shook till he heard the birds, six weeks later. Boys still hunt the woodchuck, making pretense that they wish to improve the climate, but we do not hear of their going to the Candlemass, or blessing of the candles that are to be used in the churches.

St. Valentine's Day, February the fourteenth, has always been observed with little feasts made gay with darts and hearts, and the supposedly anonymous missives composed of rhymes, roses, paper lace, cupids and other accessories of what some one has styled "tentative love-making," as well as that pictorial attack on the sensitive, the alleged "comic" valentine, but its interest is transient, owing to its proximity to Washington's birthday.

The Father of his Country, who was as great a dandy in his time and as fond of dancing as his enemy, George the Fourth of Great Britain and Ireland, who ceased to be regent and became king the year Missouri became a state, would feel honored if he knew how many hundreds of balls this state has given in his honor, and how many thousands of young Missourians have, for such revels, arrayed themselves in the costumes which were copies of his and his Martha.

There is nothing archaic about the bonnet show, excepting the name, seeing that even grandmothers wear hats at the present time, but it was once a title that fitted the recurring pageant. What it was and is, I quote from Mr. John Barber White, who quotes Col. D. C. Allen, who quotes Mr. W. S. Embree, who was ninety-six years old in 1918:

"Merchants of Liberty began to purchase for local trade fine goods, bonnets and the like in Philadelphia. *** Their purchases began to arrive in Liberty during the latter part of March or the forepart of April. *** It was a race with all the girls for the first pick of the new bonnets. *** The origin, then, of the bonnet show was near 1826. Then, and for many years later, there was no church in Clay county which attracted so many persons to its religious service, particularly on the second Sunday in May, the annual exhibition of the spring bonnet show, as did the Big Shoal Meeting House, the church of the Primitive Baptists. *** Nothing could be more natural than that the bells and beaux of all the surrounding country should instinctively flock to the Big Shoal Meeting House at the great annual meeting on the second Sunday in May to see and chat with each other. By that time the ladies, young and old, would have secured their new bonnets and dresses. The girls could display their charms to the very best advantage. The side of the church allotted to the ladies would be a mass of colors, topped by a gorgeous array of spring bonnets."

Bonnet day is still kept — one might almost say, practiced — in all the churches, but it is a day of hats and suits, and is a movable display, having been transferred to Easter Sunday, which is the better date. A sweet girl is at her sweetest hour when she looks from under the brim of her flower-crowned hat to the flowers that deck the altar of our risen Lord.

Of course, a girl's supreme moment is when she stands before the altar as a bride, but it is not always her prettiest. Her face may be pudgy from crying, or yellow from having partaken of many prenuptial entertainments. Her grandmother's fashion was better for the looks and nerves on the wedding day, but it must have been equally trying in the days that followed. She lived in complete seclusion for several weeks previous to the wedding, and even the bridegroom could not see her on the wedding day until she was ready for the ceremony, arrayed in

*"Something old and something new,
Something borrowed and something blue."*

to insure good fortune. Part of it, perhaps, was the omission of the rice and shoe-throwing. She stayed at home that night and was ceremoniously escorted to her room by her bridesmaids, the one who had found the thimble in her slice of bride-cake taking off her shoes, and the maid who found the ring, and was therefore, to be the next bride, removing her veil.

Next morning, after a breakfast almost as elaborate as the supper of the evening, she and the bridegroom went to his people for the "infare," at which his mother did her best to outshine the entertainment of the night before. There was an elaborate dinner, a still more elaborate supper, and dancing. The bride's dress for the infare was a heavy silk of bright color, made low in the neck, with a little cape to fit over the decolletage like a yoke, and long sleeves set within short sleeves called caps. For dancing, the long sleeves and cape were removed. This dress made its second appearance at church. One Catholic bride, Miss Barada, told of, came to grief because of the fashion. The day was very warm, she was plump, she laid aside her cape. An indignant young priest, asperging the congregation, flung a whole vessel of holy water on the unguarded frontage. Such was the potency of the sacred liquid, that the beautiful green silk was turned an ugly yellow wherever the water ran.

The bridal festivities continued as long as either of the high contracting parties had a relative well enough off to give an entertainment, and wherever the bride went, the bridegroom, like Mary's little lamb, was sure to go. No doubt, a bridegroom invented afternoon teas, ladies' luncheons and other strictly feminine functions.

When mother was married, she had palms, flowers, bridesmaids, ushers, and, incidentally, father and a best man, at church. When supper at home was over, she donned a "going-away gown" and hat, and went off, of course, with father, on a "tour," starting amid a shower of old shoes and rice, for a railroad train.

When Sister Jane went into matrimonial partnership with William Smith, last fall, she entered the family drawing-room, through a lane bounded by white ribbons, and holding father firmly by the elbow to keep him from straying into anything. When the best man handed William out of a corner into her keeping, they were married before an "improvised" altar, under a bell of white flowers. When the happy couple were ready to set out in a limousine, destination unknown, Sister Jane threw her bouquet of orchids and lilies among her bridesmaids, told her mother to be sure to get a man to pack the presents not later than the day-after-tomorrow, and, with the admonition, "Hurry, Bill, you know you're always late," set out on her adventures as a married woman.

Weddings, long ago, were expensive, but the expense was not comparable to that of funerals. Oftentimes, families were impoverished by the cost of funeral feasts and processions. Friends and acquaintances came from near and far. They must be entertained with lavish hospitality. The watchers who sat with the corpse during the night must have a midnight banquet. There must be an expensive coffin, an expensive shroud, an expensive hearse, flowers and very many hired carriages. When settlements were scattered and churches few and not provided with a settled minister, frequently, the funeral sermon was not preached for months, or even a year or more. One old lady enjoyed telling her grandmother's experience:

> I loved Mr. A., but my children were small and I could not afford to hire all the help I needed, so I married Mr. B., in a year and a day after Mr. A. died. In a year and five months, Brother C. came to preach Mr. A.'s funeral sermon. I had to go and take the children, but I just could not put on my crape again. I studied and studied as to what would be respectful to both gentlemen, and made up my mind to wear my new black silk Mr. B. gave me for a wedding-present and my purple bonnet. I took off the buttercups and purple strings from the bonnet and sewed on the black strings from my crape bonnet, and felt that all was genteel and suitable.

Those old churches were the scene of many curious life dramas, and what labor and self-sacrifice — mostly of women — they represented. Their foundations were laid in egg-money, their shingles were ice-cream saucers, the "main edifice" was the result of festivals, socials, oyster-suppers, chicken-pie dinners, concerts and those humble forerunners of the movies, tableaux, not to forget Rebecca at the lemonade well, the post-office and gypsy-fortune-teller. The debt — there was always a debt, it is fair to say — was substantially reduced at times by some brother, who was unwilling to have all his religion in his wife's name.

The sewing societies of the various churches, then as now, were missionary institutions, but the supper that followed the sewing must have been worth more than the heathen received. A letter written by a Mrs. Sykes, in 1854, says, "It is my turn to have the sewing society next week. How I dread it. I wish I had the courage to do as Mrs. Sarah Josefa Hale advises in the last *Godey's Lady's Book*, and have only four kinds of cake and preserves."

What could they have had to eat at those old donation parties the preachers hated so cordially? Nobody seems to remember. Missionary boxes are on the same order. Perhaps, the recipients hate them in the same degree.

After roads were made, the older members of the family went to church in a wagon or carriage, but the youths and maidens preferred to ride horseback, the maidens protecting their Sunday finery from horse hairs and lather by slipping on a long skirt of black "glazed muslin," which was dropped off at the horse-block. This skirt was very long. It had need to be, for there was a sort of chickencoop arrangement of tapes and steel called crinoline, underneath it and some other skirts. One old lady, after the lapse of half a century, was still indignant at one of our ex-Governors. "He was so clumsy," was her plaint, "that when he tried to help me off my horse he jerked me forward so that my hoop-skirt caught on the horn of my saddle and tore apart, so that it all flattened out. I had to go straight home." If the lady who could not appear unless she had a skirt-circumference of six yards or more, could see her grand-daughter in a street skirt, or riding-breeches!

It is said that more horses were swapped on Sunday mornings than during all the rest of the week.

More popular than even the Christmas tree, or the Easter egg-rolling, has always been the Sunday-school picnics, which is not to be wondered at, considering how popular all sorts of picnics are with Missourians. "As the twig is bent, so is the tree inclined," the youngster who starts with the Sunday-school picnic, progresses, as the years go by, through a series of entertainments in God's out-of-doors: the gathering of wild fruits, berries and nuts furnishing one set of excuses for eating chickens and pickles under a tree and boiling coffee in a pot balanced precariously over a fire of twigs; the county fair, another set for spreading a tablecloth where ants do least abound, and assembling thereon the choice from a well stocked larder, to which are added peanuts, popcorn balls and pink lemonade from the various "concessions" which really make part of the fair; while all sorts of associations, secret societies, and orders, political, financial and philanthropic, have their outings, at which the skill of housewives and the genius of orators are taxed to their utmost.

There was another sort of picnic, or near-picnic, which, of late years, has been taken over by the kindergarten, the May festival. Formerly, the prettiest and most popular girl from one of the upper classes of the school was crowned Queen of the May, in some pleasant glade, and sat on a little dais, with a chunky scepter of flowers in her hand, to watch her subjects tangle the ribbons of a May-pole. After the "exercises," it was the privilege of the parents and certain favored young gallants, to serve what was termed "a cold collation." It is in the chronicles of St. Joseph, that the May-queen of Mr. J. T. Robinson's Select

147

School for Young Ladies, in 1856, was Vinnie Reame (Mrs. Hoxie), the sculptor.

It is said that the pioneers did not play cards, esteeming it beneath the dignity of a man who had a horse to bet on, but play was very high among those who came on the steamboats. We are told that the "dead man's hand" — according to gamblers' superstition, two black jacks, two red sevens and any fifth card — was drawn by some one on almost every trip, and the inevitable tragedy occurred before it could be played. In strong contrast was the card or trictrac game of the French inhabitants. The farmer came to town early Sunday morning, attended mass, had a noon dinner of chicken — with rice, tartines, *pain d'epice* — a sort of glorified gingerbread — a compote of fruit and a cup of coffee "cleared" with a dash of ratafia, with his relations. Then he played a few games of cards, drank a glass of light wine, ate a cookie, which he called a *petite four*, and jogged, cheerfully homeward, behind his oxen or heavy-footed work-horses. Neither he nor his next-of-kin lived to see auction-bridge come into fashion.

Some of our guests — visiting statesmen, Chautauqua lecturers, club speakers, reformers, faddists, etc., have said, doubtless when feeling overly-cheerful from repletion, that Missouri could not begin, or end anything without a banquet. Why not? Brillat-Savarin said, "Tell me what you eat, I will tell you what you are" *(Dis-moi ce que tu manges, je te dirai ce que tu es)*. Providence has given us an unusual variety of the kindly fruits of the earth and in due time we enjoy them and share with the less favored, knowing that we are rendered cosmopolitan, and hoping to expand any narrow-minded Cassius who comes among us. However, it is not always necessary to refresh the body as well as the soul of the properly nourished. In the many clubs, scientific, civic, literary, musical, artistic, patriotic and athletic, the luncheons and dinners are occasional and an adjunct to toasts and speeches. When we attend the circus, "to take the children," the refreshments are very light, consisting mainly of peanuts, popcorn and pink lemonade. When we "dilate our emotions," to quote Rufus Choate, with the theater or opera, supper follows the performance.

Wholesome, hearty, cheerful people, with vigor to spare after the tasks of life are done, Missourians give banquets, but they do not enjoy them in supine contentment, their exuberant vitality finds outlet for itself in balls and processions, as well as in less elaborate forms of amusements. It is a matter of history that when Lafayette came to this country, in 1824, by special invitation of the American people, Missourians fired national salutes and had torchlight processions in his honor as if he had been present. In 1825, April 29, to be exact, Lafayette hurried away from a ball given in his honor at Natchez, Mississippi, and hurried up the river to what was then an outpost of civilization, St. Louis, where almost the entire population of the new state had assembled to greet him. An impromptu procession fell in behind the carriage in which he was seated, reaching almost from the levee to Pierre Choteau's house, where a reception was held. In the evening, was a ball, as brilliant as any St. Louis has given in the subsequent years, and, at midnight, the great Frenchman parted from his entertainers with tears. Since then, what pageants of wealth, of strength, of beauty, have been exhibited in the streets and ball rooms of Missouri's towns and cities: Veiled Prophets parades, Priests of Pallas parades, flower parades, Shriners, Labor Day, all sorts and conditions of parades and processions of secret societies, bodies civic and military, and the balls that followed, besides deb-utantes' balls and balls for other epochs, or none. In a way, both marching and dancing have been a preparation. The feet that stepped so lightly carried heroes through the Civil War, the Spanish and the battlefields of France.

This article originally appeared in the Missouri Historical Review *15 (October, 1920), pp. 176-190 and is reprinted here with the permission of the State Historical Society of Missouri.*

La Guillonnée: A French Holiday Custom in the Mississippi Valley

Rosemary Hyde Thomas

It cannot be said of the Missouri French that they have not attracted scholarly attention, for they have been studied more than most ethnic groups in the Show-Me State. In 1935 Ward Allison Dorrance published The Survival of French in the Old District of Sainte Genevieve, *which was based on fieldwork conducted in that river town. Two years later Joseph Medard Carriere produced* Tales From the French Folklore of Missouri, *a collection gathered in the community of Old Mines. Subsequent academics have shown an interest in the Missouri French. In the late 1960s, Clyde Thogmartin did a linguistic study of Old Mines which he used as the basis for a Ph.D. dissertation. During 1978 and 1979 a St. Louis-based group, the Missouri Friends of the Folk Arts, did a broad-ranging survey of various aspects of the French tradition then existing in Old Mines.*

Most of the linguistic and folklore work on the Missouri French has been survivalistic in nature. In other words, the researchers were seeking French items that survived over many decades. The following paper by Professor Thomas, a member of the Missouri Friends of the Folk Arts team, is in the same tradition. Here she traces how a French holiday custom changed during the past century, focusing primarily on La Guillonnée as found in Ste. Genevieve and Old Mines in Missouri and Prairie du Rocher in Illinois. For further information about Missouri French folklore see Rosemary Hyde Thomas, It's Good to Tell You: French Folktales from Missouri *(Columbia, Missouri: University of Missouri Press, 1981). For an example of the La Guillonnée song see the double album* I'm Old But I'm Awfully Tough: Traditional Music of the Ozark Region, *which was produced by the Missouri Friends of the Folk Arts and contains the song as performed by Rose Pratt of Old Mines, Missouri.*

150

La Guillonnée! La Guignolée! La Gaie-Année! Throughout communities of French origin in the Mississippi Valley and in Vincennes, Indiana, these words excite a deep feeling of pride and reverence for the old traditions. All three terms refer, in different communities, to a rollicking New Year's Eve celebration. Usually this involves a band of ten to twenty singers who disguise themselves and go from house to house performing an ancient French song and dance, receiving some reward of food, drink, and perhaps money at each house. This ceremony has been documented in a fairly large number of publications throughout the twentieth century, and with good reason, for it stands as a cohesive symbol of the old French culture that once flourished everywhere in the French settlements of Mid-America. At least until after World War I, Guillonnée groups were still active in Ste. Genevieve, French Village, Bloomsdale, and Old Mines in Missouri; in Prairie du Rocher and Cahokia in Illinois; and Vincennes in Indiana. By 1977 the only Guillonnée group which had enjoyed an uninterrupted existence was that of Prairie du Rocher. Groups in Ste. Genevieve, Cahokia, and Old Mines have lapsed and been revived with enough continuity of transmission to preserve the variants peculiar to each community. The custom is said to be fairly widespread in French Canada and has been documented at Perche and St.-Onge in France.[1]

In Old Mines, Prairie du Rocher, Ste. Genevieve, and St. Louis (where the Guillonnée survived until the mid-nineteenth century), we have anecdotal information and observations on the conduct of the custom. In all four communities, the original procedure was for a group to assemble at about seven in the evening of New Year's Eve and to visit twenty to thirty homes on a preselected and probably traditional itinerary continuing into the early morning. At each home the singers would sing a portion of the Guillonnée song as they stood outside on the front gallery. In Prairie du Rocher, the first two verses of the song would be sung. In Old Mines, it was the first eight verses. At the end of this predetermined outdoor performance, the householder had the option to admit the Guillonneurs to his house or not. If they were admitted, the singers would start singing at the beginning of the song and sing it through. If they were not admitted, they would go on to the next house. It was rare for the singers not to be admitted, since their performance was generally anticipated with great eagerness by both adults and children. Even if the Guillonneurs did not arrive at a house before the early hours of morning, the children would be aroused to watch. A fantastic sight it must have been for a small child in the middle of the night, this band of masked and costumed revelers with their fiddler, their singing, their dancing, and their pranks. There was a chance, of course, if the Guillonneurs were not admitted, that the householder might find he had made a contribution to them anyway from henhouse or field.

One resident of the Old Mines area told how the Guillonneurs had come to her family's house when she was a child. A relative in another place was ill, and both parents were attending the sick person. The children had been told to allow no one into the house. The Guillonnée had never come that way before, but that night they did come and sang the first verses on the porch. The informant remembers watching the glowing ends of the performers' cigarettes from the window as they sang and went on their way as well as her vivid regret that for that one time in her life she did not get to have them perform in her house.

151

In earlier days each community had as many as three or four Guillonnée groups, each with its own traditional territory, its own slightly different version of the song, and its own rules on who might participate. Groups went from house to house on foot, and each house on the chosen route was solicited for admittance. Sometimes it would be raining or snowing, and the fiddler would have to try to protect his instrument between houses by hiding it under his coat as best he could. Traditionally the groups were composed of men only. However, there is evidence that even in the early days occasional women accompanied the groups and even brought along their children. After World War I women's Guillonnée groups came into existence in both Prairie du Rocher and Old Mines. And since World War II Guillonnée groups in these two communities as well as Cahokia have included both men and women on a regular basis. Only one group has existed in each community since that time, and the singers have gone from house to house by bus or car since they have had to cover greater and greater territories. The Guillonnée group in Ste. Genevieve has remained all male.

Another innovation that occurred when multiple groups of singers disappeared from communities was a change from visiting private homes to performing in public places and at New Year's Eve parties in such locations as church halls, restaurants, Knights of Columbus halls, or American Legion halls.

After their performance at each location, the singers have traditionally been offered refreshments: wine or whiskey to drink; sandwiches, cookies, or cakes to eat. In Ste. Genevieve and Prairie du Rocher there is a Sergent d'Armes whose job it is to maintain order and regulate the drinking. Along with the posts of leader and fiddler, this is a traditional office in the Guillonnée group. All three of these positions tend to be hereditary, passed on where possible from father to son. In Old Mines each group had one fiddler. In Prairie du Rocher there might be two musicians, one of whom sometimes played guitar.

Ideas on costumes varied from community to community. Most of the communities now prefer that Guillonneurs dress as Indian chiefs, pierrots, French voyageurs, or colonial gentlemen; these are the costumes one sees today in Ste. Genevieve, Cahokia, and Prairie du Rocher. Formerly in these communities and today in Old Mines, people generally turned their coats inside out, wore red neckerchiefs, and blacked their faces or wore stockings over their faces. Stories circulate about men after the Guillonnée who could not get black shoe polish off their faces without a week or more painful scrubbing. A kind of make-up more easily removed was soot from the top of a woodburning stove. Women wore old dresses or dressed as men. If there were no women in the group, at least one man dressed as a woman and was called "La Fille Aînée." In Old Mines a hat was also a necessary part of the costume; it was doffed when the group came to the apology part of the song. In Old Mines, also, the leader and fiddler would not dress up, but this does not seem to have been the custom in other communities. In the Prairie du Rocher group today, leader Percy Clerc is resplendent from head to toe in a costume of corn shucks which he made some twenty-five years ago, instructed by his grandmother.

The actions which accompany the song vary from community to community. The Prairie du Rocher singers and the Cahokia singers stand still, although formerly some kind of dance step was done. In the Prairie du Rocher group, however, the leader beats time while he sings the solo parts. The Ste. Genevieve singers dance a shuffling step counterclockwise around the fiddler and leader throughout the song. In Old Mines the Guillonnée group jumps up and down, shuffling their feet and occasionally turning around, during the responses they sing. They stand still during the solo verses.

Ida Schaaf states that in St. Louis and Ste. Genevieve there was a pause in the middle of the Guillonnée performance for the dance of the Fille Aînée to be done.[2] If there were enough daughters in the house being visited, this would be a quadrille. Also, a jig or "Rag Dance," called "danse de la Guénille," would be done at the end. The only remnant of the Fille Aînée dance today is in Old Mines, where it is a brief twirl of any likely and available member of the audience. Traditionally, when the Guillonnée group was still mostly male, a member of the group would dance with the eldest daughter of the house. If there were no eldest daughter present, this same member would dance with the man who had dressed for this purpose as the Fille Aînée. The Guénille seems to have disappeared entirely. I have not been able to find anyone who remembers more than its name. People do jig at dances, but no one recalls any connection of this step with the Guillonnée. The Old Mines Guillonneurs, however, do bow and doff their hats to the audience at the end of the carol when mention is made of dancing La Guénille in certain versions of the song.

The collection made at the end of the Guillonnée has had different aspects and purposes over the years. The author of the "Coleman Family History" even speculates that the collection was in early times the main purpose of the performance and that its goal was to fill the church poor box.[3] It is certain that the collection has been an integral part of the Guillonnée. However, throughout the French-speaking portions of Mid-America, what was usually collected by the Guillonneurs was either provisions or pledges of provisions for the King's Night Ball to be held on 6 January. Typical provisions sought included coffee, sugar, chickens, pies, cakes, and similar foodstuffs, which were to be brought to the ball or collected prior to the ball by members of the Guillonnée group. This was true in Old Mines as in the other communities. However, the Old Mines Guillonnée lapsed from about 1930 to about 1950. When it was revived for a few years in the early 1950s by the Reverend Edward Bruemmer and Dr. George Creswell, the collection was indeed taken up to fill the coffers of St. Joachim's Church.

The King's Ball or King and Queen's Ball or Guillonnée Ball, as it has variously been called, seems to have been less longlived in most French communities than in St. Louis, where it survives as the Veiled Prophet Ball. A custom similar to that which still characterizes the Veiled Prophet Ball, one of St. Louis' major debutante parties, is described from earlier times by the author of "The Coleman Family History":

> The King's Ball is held on the "Jour des Rois" or the evening preceding Epiphany. ... They danced until Midnight when the patriarch would take a bouquet and give it to the girl that he considered most beautiful. Then the guests all cried "Vive la Reine." She in turn would take the bouquet and pin it on the man she chose, and he became her king, and the crowd shouted "Vive le roi," and they

would take hands and dance around them singing.

The queen then cut an immense cake known as the queen's cake and which contained a bean. The girl who got the bean became the next queen, and she chose her king, and they were in turn the king and queen of the ball to be held two weeks later. This went on during the season and culminated in the grand ball of "Mardi Gras" which was held the Tuesday preceding Ash Wednesday, when all social activities ceased.[4]

In Cahokia the ball was revived in the 1960s after a lapse of about a century. In Prairie du Rocher the ball was revived in 1976, having ceased to take place on the eve of World War II. In Old Mines the Guillonnée ball continued up to the time when the Guillonnée itself lapsed in about 1930, but only in a vestigial form. It continued to be a combination of banquet and dance, but the choosing of monarchs and the cake had disappeared. The Guillonneurs were admitted free, but other people who came had to pay at the door. In Old Mines the custom of having balls and dances every week or two between New Year's Day and Mardi Gras continued until the 1940s, but the choice of hosts was very informal, people making their own decisions as to whether and when to host a party in their homes. There was generally, also until World War II, a dance on Mardi Gras in this community.

People in Cahokia and Prairie du Rocher seem to have remembered more faithfully the procedures for the King's Night Ball than did those in Old Mines. In Prairie du Rocher the cake was eaten by the men, and four beans were to be found, commemorating four wise men who visited Bethlehem. Being king in Prairie du Rocher, however, was not tied to hosting other dances. Pledges for dances between the King's Ball and Mardi Gras were collected along with provisions for that first ball during the Gaie-Année. In Cahokia traditionally one bean was baked into a cake which the men ate. The man who found the bean chose a queen and then hosted, or at least presided over, all the balls till Mardi Gras. In St. Louis and Ste. Genevieve, according to Ida Schaaf, the men searched for three beans in the cake.[5] The first one to find one was king. The other two, with their ladies were his courtiers. Before World War I in Old Mines, a ring and three beans were baked into the cake. Only the men took pieces until all four objects had been recovered. The one who found the ring reigned over all the balls of the season with his chosen queen. The men who found the three beans were his courtiers with their chosen consorts.

When asked what the term "Guillonnée" or "Gaie-année" or "Guignolée" means, people do not generally have a clear answer. A number of etymologies have appeared over the years. Schaaf believes that the word "Guignolée" comes from "Guignol," meaning a "clown," and that the Guignoleurs are a "band of puppets, clowns, or revelers."[6] In "The Coleman Family History" McCormack states that "Gui-année" comes from "Le Gui de l'an neuf," meaning mistletoe of the New Year and therefore that the custom evolved from a Druidic ceremony having to do with gathering mistletoe as a part of religious ritual.[7] This belief has been encountered in Cahokia recently, but from someone of fairly recent Canadian origin. A popular explanation for "Gaie-année" is that it means "Happy

154

New Year" and that it is the spirit of the custom. McDermott cites other forms less common in the Mississippi Valley: "ignolée," "aguilanieu," "guil'an-neu," "avilonneau," "guil'an-neou."[8] The custom dates back at least as far as the court of Louis XI,[9] and whatever the word means now, it undoubtedly had other senses during the Middle Ages. A search of Grandsaigne d'Hauterive's *Dictionnaire d'ancien francais* reveals the following definitions:

1. *avilanir*: "injurier, dire des vilénies, déshonorer";
2. *aguillener*: "darder comme use aiguille";
3. *guignier*: "farder, masquer";
4. *guile*: "ruse, tromperie";
5. *guionage*: "sauf-conduite, escorte";
6. *guische*: "tromperie, mauvais tour, ruse."[10]

All of these words, with the exception of *guionage,* which comes from Latin *guidonem,* "to lead," are listed as being of uncertain etymology. Any one of them, with the possible exception of *aguillener,* can be considered as descriptive of some important aspect of the Guillonnée. It seems at least likely that the several modern forms of the word came from several different older words similar to those listed above and that over the years these words merged in their semantic fields. One hypothetical etymology, that of Harnett Kane, does seem to stem from an obsolete word which he says meant "the beam of a steelyard, or a balance."[11] From this meaning, he deduces that the Guiannée is of Christian origin and involved asking for help for the mass box so that poor people who had died would not be weighed in the balance and judged wanting for lack of a few masses. Unfortunately, Kane does not provide the French word he was thinking of.

Although, like many other ancient customs, it has been repeatedly adapted by the Catholic Church for its own purposes, the Guillonnée is most likely not of Christian origin. The words of the song, first of all, have no religious references, being a combination of broad irony and tender love song. Second, there is definitely a circle dance of some kind attached to the custom; this, too, was not a feature of Christian observances. And the spirit of revelry which accompanies the disguise and drinking is not typical of post-Renaissance Christian observances. Indeed, although it does not seem possible to pinpoint the origins of the Guillonnée from any information presently available, the resemblance of this ceremony to many other customs throughout northern and western Europe and transported to various regions of the United States is startling.

In England and Scotland there were sailing, mumming, and boxing, all of which customs involved bands of revelers, often in costume, making rounds of homes, performing, and asking for various kinds of rewards. Carolers do likewise, adding a circle dance to the ceremony. Guise dancers participate in a similar act led by a "Lord of Misrule." The songs performed in each of the customs are characterized by a spirit of nonsense and revelry, and sometimes of debauchery, at least involving eating and drinking. Coffin describes one of these kinds of groups in Scotland: "Men and women, boys and girls, dressed themselves in strange costumes and blackened their faces or otherwise disguised them, and went off to villages and farmhouses, sang songs, and danced, to the banter and amusement of onlookers."[12] All of the above activities occurred around the end of the year. In addition, in the British Isles sword dancing, morris dancing, and the maypole bear some resemblance to this same type of traditional merrymaking. Referring to this impressive list of apparently related festivities, Coffin states,

> There is little doubt that these and related festivities have an immemorial history which weaves back to winter rites designed to purify the houses and fields at the New Year, and to confound the spirits by disguise, mocking the sacred, switching sex roles, noise and unusual dress or behavior.[13]

In support of his assertions about the ancient origins of these customs, he cites Caesarius of Arles, writing in the sixth century, regarding the January Kalends: "On those days the heathen, reversing the order of all things, dress themselves up in indecent deformities ... put on counterfeit forms and monstrous faces."[14] The "heathens" referred to here, of course, were residents of what came to be known as France. This would seem to indicate that customs similar to those still rather widely known in the British Isles existed in early times in France as well.

There are likewise similar customs on the North American continent. In Newfoundland on Christmas Eve, men go out mumming and "scoffing." They go from house to house singing, playing music, and dancing. At each house they get something to eat and drink before going on. There were until recently Christmas mummers' plays in Kentucky. The mummers' celebration in Philadelphia which is now televised as a mammoth holiday parade used to be done on New Year's Eve, with disguised men going from house to house and performing in exchange for refreshments. There is a New Year's Carnival in Mobile with noisemakers, dancing, and masked men. There were "Fantastics" or "Christmas Riders" elsewhere in Alabama, who traditionally spent Christmas Day riding from house to house dressed as clowns or Spaniards. Similar riders, known as Calithumpians, went out on New Year's Day in Little Rock. There were New Year's shooters both in western North Carolina and in parts of Missouri. On New Year's Eve bands of men armed with old rifles and muskets, or with fireworks, would go from house to house singing an ancient chant of greetings to all in the house and of wishes for a happy love life, ending the song with a huge racket from the firearms. Kane theorizes that these shooters stem both from English mumming and from Germany and parts of eastern Europe.[15] In Germany and Bohemia, he notes, people for centuries have "shot in" the New Year, sometimes for the purpose of frightening witches. In addition to these year-end traditions there are other celebrations at other times of the year in America such as Mardi Gras and Halloween that may provide analogues for the Guillonnée.

All of these celebrations share most of the following features with the Guillonnée: disguise (ragged clothes and blacked or masked faces), suspension of ordinary rules of behavior, a traditional chant or song, some kind of circular dance performance, refreshments as a reward for the performance, a leader and a band of followers, visiting private homes, and at least a latent threat of pranks if treats are not proffered. There are three main times of the year when such festivities occur: Harvest, Winter Solstice, and Spring. Most, like the Guillon-

156

née, are Winter events, taking place in modern times most often on Christmas and New Year's Eve.

A final source of evidence for the relatedness of the Guillonnée and others of this group of holiday festivities at some time in the distant past is the song itself. Like the wassail song it contains a formulaic greeting to the whole household: "Bonsouere la Maître et la Maîtresse,/Et Tout le monde du logis." The wassail song has a rather unusual musical arrangement, the verse being in 6/8 time and the refrain in 4/4 time. In the Guillonnée the verses are in 4/4 time, but the solo part is in 6/8 time. The traditional chant of the New Year shooters in North Carolina also begins with the same type of greeting: "Good morning to you, Sir,/I wish you a happy New Year." One version of that chant, like the Guillonnée, goes on to address the lovelife of the lady of the house: "I wish you lovers of every kind,/To suit your heart and please your mind." An English translation of similar lines in the Guillonnée song reads,

> *As for the maid who has no lovers,*
> *How can she live?*
> *Slumber she knows not, day or night;*
> *Wakefulness is hers.*

While none of these similarities is astounding, they do make it possible to theorize that at least some of these songs and their accompanying rituals evolved from similar observances in the distant past.

Another feature of the song which seems to hark back to more ancient times is the solo and response sequence. In the Guillonnée each verse is first sung as a solo by a leader and then repeated in chorus by the whole band of singers. In Old Mines this pattern is carried out throughout the song. In Prairie du Rocher the "solo" part, in which an apology is offered for any foolishness that may have occurred and is followed by an enigmatic promise to "do better" next time, is sung by the leader along with no echoing chorus. In discussing the medieval Fete des Fous in France, Ehret describes the format of the carols which were sung to accompany the farcical, masked processions typical of this observance:

> They began with a "burden" or refrain, sung by the spectators as members of the procession danced. A verse sung by a solo voice followed, during which the dancers rested and caught their breath. The burden was repeated, followed by another solo verse, and so on. As might be expected, the carols had many verses, each sandwiched in between the danced burdens.[16]

This festival took place at New Year's and was typical of other "Misrule" activities, especially those of Great Britain, in their singing, dancing, farcical intent, and masked costumes. The Guillonnée as it is practiced in Old Mines seems to preserve something of both the burden-response format and the notion that only the choruses are danced while the performers catch their breath during the solo verses.

Another characteristic of "Misrule" carols is that they don't make much sense if approached logically. This is certainly true of La Guillonnée, where a four-foot pork backbone is supposed to make a fricassee ninety feet long and where we skip blithely from warming the feet of the Fille Aînée with our rowdy dancing to hearing the nightingales sing in the woods. Such lines as "When we were in the midst of the woods, we were in the shade" and "He who sleeps neither day nor night is always awake" are surely in the best tradition of Misrule tomfoolery. Singer Jean Ritchie says that a song she learned from her father in the Kentucky mountains turned out to be a mumming tune known in parts of England. In "Fair Nottamun Town" we find verses of a similar type, such as "They laughed and they smiled, not a soul did look gay,/They talked all the while, not a word they did say."[17]

Whatever its origins, it seems fairly certain that La Guillonnee goes back several centuries at least. People will probably never cease speculation on its origins and quite possibly will never discover any hard evidence to explain them fully. Although it is awe-inspiring to realize how old customs may be in spite of increasingly rapid changes in the material and philosophical environment, what is most important is that these customs continue to enrich people's lives with joy, fellowship, and merriment.

NOTES

[1]John F. McDermott, *A Glossary of Mississippi Valley French: 1673-1850*, Washington University Studies-New Series, Language and Literature No. 12 (St. Louis, Missouri, 1941), p. 84.

[2]Ida M. Schaaf, "The Passing of an Old Custom — La Guignolee," *Mid-America*, 20 (1933), 170.

[3]E. Curran McCormack, "The Coleman Family History," 1932, typescript in Washington County Public Library, Potosi, Missouri, p. 16.

[4]McCormack, p. 16.

[5]Schaaf, p. 167.

[6]Schaaf, p. 168.

[7]McCormack, p. 16.

[8]McDermott, p. 84.

[9]McCormack, p. 16.

[10]R. Gandsaigne d'Hauterive, *Dictionnaire d'Ancien francais, moyen âge et renaissance* (Paris: Librairie Larousse, 1947).

[11]Harnett T. Kane, *The Southern Christmas Book* (New York: David McKay, 1958), p. 176.

[12]Tristram P. Coffin, *The Book of Christmas Folklore* (New York: Sentry Press, 1973), p. 148.

[13]Coffin, p. 134.

[14]Coffin, p. 134.

[15]Kane, p. 103.

[16]W. Ehret, *International Book of Christmas Carols* (Englewood Cliffs, New Jersey: Prentice-Hall, 1963), p. 6.

[17]Jean Ritchie, *Dulcimer People* (New York: Oak, 1975), p. 96.

This article originally appeared in Mid-South Folklore 6:3 (Winter, 1978), pp. 77-84 and *is reprinted here with the permission of the author and the Ozark States Folklore Society.*

Survivals of Old Marriage Customs Among the Low Germans of West Missouri

William G. Bek

William G. Bek (1873-1948) was a historian primarily interested in the study of Missouri Germans and particularly concerned with the nineteenth-century writer of promotional literature, Gottfried Duden, and his influence.* In the present article he turns his attention to other matters: the traditional customs surrounding the marriage ritual that are practiced (or were when this article was written) by those western Missouri immigrants speaking the Low German dialect. This distinction between Hochdeutsch *(High German) and* Plattdeutsch *(Low German) is primarily a linguistic rather than a caste or economic division. Bek, like most Americans writing on folklore at the turn of the century, was primarily interested in survivals, in this case of European customs, and was concerned not so much with the commonplace as with the unusual. This explains his emphasis on "peculiar" marriage customs; contemporary scholars would also be interested not only in the peculiar but in the usual.*

As Bek's article points out, the marriage rite is very tradition bound; it remains so even today. Perhaps some of the practices described here are no longer followed, but many other customs are. It is safe to say that marriage is the most tradition-regulated personal ceremony in American life. Wedding customs begin with the "shower," in some cases several of them to emphasize different kinds of needed gifts. There is also often a "stag party" held for the

---

*Gottfried Duden (1785-1855) is now best remembered for the several editions of *Bericht über eine Reise nach den westlichen Staaten Nordamerikas* (Report on a Journey to the Western States of North America) issued between 1829 and 1840. He painted a very — some would say overly — optimistic picture of the possibilities for Germans in America and was by far the most important person influencing German emigration before 1860. His most famous book has been reissued in a very well-annotated edition (Columbia: The State Historical Society of Missouri and University of Missouri Press, 1980). *(Ed.)*

groom. Certain recreations are reserved exclusively for these events, such as the practice of writing down the words of the future bride as she opens gifts. These remarks are read aloud later as "what she will say to her husband on their wedding night." Other wedding customs include the dress of participants, the seating of guests, the choice of attendants, kissing the bride, throwing rice, playing pranks on the married couple, and decorating the car. Because such matters have been rarely studied by folklorists, a useful project for students would be to collect various folk traditions associated with marriage ceremonies in their community. This would also be one occasion where no one would be likely to object about a person taking photographs of the happenings.

The people whose peculiar marriage customs I shall describe inhabit a portion of western Saline County, northwestern Pettis County, northeastern Johnson County, and a large portion of Lafayette County in west Missouri. The nucleus of this settlement is Concordia in Lafayette County, a small prairie town of about nine hundred inhabitants. An irregular line, varying from eight to twenty-five miles in distance, roughly includes the region in question. Barring a few small centres where the English have retained their hold, this domain is singularly German. Survivals of European customs are met at every hand. The major portion of these people hail from Hanover or are descendants of Hanoverians. The broad dialect of this province, therefore, naturally prevails. However, the more pointed speech of the Westphalian and that of the inhabitant of Lippe Detmold is also sporadically heard. The High Germans and Swiss who have strayed among these Low Germans are very few in number. So strong is the influence of the Low German dialect that the descendants of the High Germans soon acquire the prevailing Low German dialect.

The first Hanoverian who ventured into the wilds of west Missouri was Heinrich Dierking, whom the older generations of that region still familiarly call "Troester" Dierking. He settled either in 1838 or 1839 near the present site of Concordia. It is rather singular that a lone German should venture so far inland. Usually the first settlers remained close to the larger rivers. Investigation reveals the fact that Heinrich Dierking had married an American woman soon after his arrival in America. When he arrived in Lafayette County he was accompanied by one Dick Mulkey. He therefore drifted so far west in company with English friends, and most probably with the kin of his wife's family. The fertile prairies of Lafayette County and the rich, well-wooded creek bottoms pleased this German pioneer exceedingly. His letters to his friends and kin in Hanover soon brought them to his neighborhood. And thus, through "the Consciousness of Kind," this region became settled by a people, bound together by like tradition, like speech, and in many instances by blood-relationship. All of them came to seek improvement of economic conditions. They came unprompted and unaided by settlement or immigration societies, not, like the settlers of Hermann, Missouri, to found a new German state in this country, nor, like the Keilites of Shelby County, Missouri, to carry out the whim of their leader, nor, like the religionists of Perry County, to transplant the Lutheran faith to this western soil, but simply as farmers who found the tillage of their small, worn-out acres in Germany too meagre a source of income. Once having gotten a foothold in that rich agricultural country of west Missouri, they, by the peaceful method of purchase, drove, as they still are driving, their English-speaking neighbors farther and farther out, until now one may journey for many miles without meeting an Englishman in this region. No price seems too high for them, provided the land is good and conveniently located. Many of their English neighbors, still clinging to a cheap aristocracy, find themselves compelled to sell to them to avoid the foreclosure of the mortgages which rest on their estates. In this peaceful manner this prosperous community, year by year, stretches farther and farther in all directions.

Of a foreign-born population of 2342 (cf. U.S. Census of 1900) in Lafayette County, 1589, or almost 68 per cent, are German. According to the same census, Saline County has 560 foreign-born Germans. Most of these are living in the western part of this county. We are, therefore, safe in assuming that 460 of them live in the region under discussion. Johnson County has 270 foreign-born Germans, at least 200 of whom belong to the Concordia country. Pettis County has 784 Germans of foreign birth, most of whom are living in or around Sedalia. It is entirely safe, however, to say that 150 of them inhabit the region here discussed. This gives us a total of 2399 foreign-born Germans in the Concordia country. It must at once be manifest that this number does not nearly represent the total number of Germans in this district. The settlement is an old one for this western country, and the families are very large. It is, therefore, entirely safe to reckon the German population at four times the number 2399, or 9596.

By reason of their occupation and of their great number, these Germans have become very seclusive and rather self-satisfied, mingling comparatively little with the outside world. Church and school have contributed their share to keep things German very much alive among them. The customs which their fathers brought from beyond the sea live and are being perpetuated by succeeding generations. And so it happens that customs have survived among them in this, a foreign land, for three quarters of a century, customs which had their inception many centuries ago in another land. The very customs which I shall speak of are discussed among other old customs by Hans Meyer in his "Das Deutsche Volkstum," pp. 276-279.

During a few years of residence in this settlement, I had ample opportunity to observe some of the customs of these people. They are a pleasure loving people. Their parties, shooting matches, picnics, and similar gatherings are very largely attended. All the means of amusement and social intercourse, however, dwindle into insignificance when compared with a typical Low German marriage feast. I shall describe one of these as I observed it, and I shall let it serve as a type.

The engagement of a very wealthy young couple had been rumored for some time. On a certain day, the brother of the groom-to-be made his appearance at our house, in the capacity of *Hochzeitsbitter* or *Brautbitter* (that is, the person who invites guests to the wedding). He was mounted on a thoroughbred. The bridle and saddle were gayly decorated with many ribbons. The hat of the *Hochzeitsbitter* was also adorned with a mass of bright-colored ribbons, varying in length from one half to two yards. So numerous were these streamers, that the hat itself was invisible. In the stiff March breeze, which was augmented by the speed at which the horse travelled, the horse and rider were one splendid confusion of colors. It was with the greatest difficulty that the rider retained possession of his head-covering. In addition to these ribbons, the hat-band was studded with coins and paper money. While approaching the house, the *Hochzeitsbitter* uttered short piercing cries and discharged a heavy pistol. After entering the house he delivered his invitation by reciting in an awkward manner, a short poem, which in a long drawn out way bade those present to attend the ceremony at a certain time and place. His mission ended, he sped on, uttering shouts and discharging his pistol, as at his approach. The wedding ceremony took place in a small country church. Crowds of invited guests, from far and near, attended. After the simple, brief ceremony every one hastened to his horse or conveyance. The bride and groom rode in a new spring wagon, drawn by two thoroughbreds. The *Hochzeitsbitter* officiated as driver of this wagon. After he had gotten a fair start, the whole crowd dashed after this wagon at a dead-run. The home of the groom's father, where the celebration was to be continued, was five miles away. Up and down the rolling prairie the mad chase took its course. Every one attempted to overtake and, if possible, to pass the bridal pair. Suddenly the whole racing procession came to an abrupt halt. It was discovered by us who were in the rear, that a strong chain had been stretched across the road. It was the work of the small boy. The groom cast a handful of small coins among the youngsters. The chain was lowered and the mad chase resumed, to be checked a second and a third time in like manner. Finally, with foam-bedecked horses, we reached the home of the groom's father. A sumptuous feast was awaiting us. After this had been thoroughly enjoyed, the dishes of the table at which the bride had eaten were quickly cleared away. The table-cloth was seized by the married women, and a lively scramble ensued in an attempt to ensnare one of the girls with the table-cloth. Finally one of the young women was caught. The blushing maid was led back in triumph, amid the congratulatory shouts of all those present, who hailed her as the next bride-to-be. Later in the afternoon the whole party adjourned to a nearby meadow. Here the bride and groom took their stand at one end of the spacious field, the groom holding a broom in his hand. The young men all retired to the opposite side of the meadow. A foot-race followed, the winner seizing the broom in triumph, which victory symbolically designated him as the next groom to be. In the evening there came a dance, which lasted until daybreak. The following night occurred the charivari in its most deafening form.

It may not be out of place to explain some of these peculiar practices. There is no doubt that many of them date back many, many years in the history of our race. That they should survive in the land where they originated is not so surprising. But that they should prevail in an entirely foreign environment, surrounded by strange customs, is indeed noteworthy. The voluntary isolation of these people in a measure explains their existence.

The ribbons which adorn the hat of the *Hochzeitsbitter* are the contributions of those persons whom he has invited. The coins and paper money on his hat-band come from the same source. The money becomes a part of the bride's dowry. The giving of the ribbons, I take it, is a survival of a custom of giving much more valuable gifts. At the bride's home, or wherever the ceremony is continued, the *Hochzeitsbitter* always wears his decorated hat, which in itself shows how many persons have been invited. The guests bring presents to the wedding, and it is the duty of the *Hochzeitsbitter* to receive and arrange them. Besides these duties, he has others, the chief of which is the entertainment of the guests. He is a very busy person and in his odd attire a most striking figure. Not only the *Hochzeitsbitter* is decorated with ribbons on the wedding-day, but also the guests adorn themselves. The buggy-whip always bears a long ribbon in order that every one may know the persons are going to the wedding as invited guests.

The chase which I described is no doubt a survival of a very old custom. In doubtless dates back to the time when men secured their wives by a chase; that is, they took them by force. This is, of course, not realized by those who participate in the race from the church. All that this chase means to them is that if any one succeeds in passing the bridal pair, the guests are given license to play all sorts of pranks at the place where the celebration is continued. The obstructions which the small boys placed in the way of the procession, and the accompanying ransom paid by the groom, most probably are a remnant of the time when women were secured by purchase.

I stated that the *Brautbitter* delivered his invitation in poetic form. I have been fortunate enough to collect a few of these poems. They are now getting rare and rather hard to obtain. The practice seems to be dying out, as the younger generations are succeeding the old. The poems are usually handed down by word of mouth. The persons who now possess them have, as a rule, served in the capacity of *Brautbitter* themselves. When a young man has to perform this duty, he seeks some old man who knows such a poem, and with much labor learns it from him. Like most things that come down to us by word of mouth, there are doubtless many things in these poems at the present time which may, with certainty, be regarded as interpolations. As will be seen, they are in High German. Although these people use only the Low German dialect in their daily intercourse, they always write in High German, and what poetry they may have is in High German. It is the language of the church and school, and whatever elements of culture may come to them in German come to them through the High German medium.

The following are some of the poems recited by the *Brautbitter*: —

Hier bin ich her gesandt,
Werde ein Brautbitter genannt.
In diesem Hause bin ich wohl bekannt.
Hier nehme ich meinen Hut und Stab
Und setze meinen Fuss darein
Dass ich möchte willkommen sein.
Sollt' ich nicht willkommen sein,
So bitte ich um eine Flasche Wein.
Eine Flasche Wein ist mir zu viel,
Ein Kleiner Schnaps macht auch Pläsier.
Ich bin noch jung an Jahren,
Habe noch nicht viel erfahren,
Was ich erfahren hab' und weiss
Das will ich Euch sagen mit Fleiss.

163

Ich soll ein Kompliment bestellen
Von Junggesellen_____ und Jungfrau_____
Sie haben sich vor einigen Wochen
Verlobt und versprochen,
Dass sie nächsten Sonntag Hochzeit halten.
Dazu lade ich Euch ein,
Herr und Frau, Söhne und Töchter, Gross und Klein,
Die im Hause zu finden sein.
Ich möchte, dass ihr sie besucht und ehrt
Und die Mahlzeiten verzehrt.
Zehn Kühe, zwanzig Ochsen, dreissig Gänsebraten,
Vierzig Schweinebraten, die werden schön geraten.
Und ein Fass Wein ist noch nicht über den Rhein.
Und wenn die Musikanten die Saiten lassen erklingen.
So kann ein jeder nach seinem Believen tanzen und springen.
Und gutes Kartenblatt,
Damit ein jeder sein Vergnügen hat.
Nun kränzelt mein schön Hütlein
Mit vielen schönen Bändlein.
Habe ich meine Rede nicht gut gemacht,
So habe ich sie doch zu Ende gebracht.

The following is a rather free prose translation of this poem: —

Hither I have been sent, I am called the Brautbitter. *In this house I am well known. Here I take off my hat and rest my staff and enter in. I trust I may be welcome. Should I not be welcome, then I ask for a flask of wine. A flask of wine is too much for me, a drink of brandy gives pleasure, too. I am still young in years, have not had much experience. What I know, however, I tell you with diligence. I am sent to deliver the compliments of Mr. _____ and Miss _____ . They became engaged a few weeks ago, and promised to get married next Sunday. To the wedding I invite you, lord and lady, sons and daughters, great and small, as they are in this house. I wish that you visit them and do them honor and consume the feast. Ten cows, twenty oxen, thirty roast geese, forty roast pigs, will be well prepared. And a barrel of wine is not yet over the Rhine. And when the musicians strike up the strings, then may each one after his liking dance. Also good card games will be prepared, that each one may have his pleasure. Now decorate my pretty hat with many a fine ribbon. Have I not said my speech well, I have at least brought it to a close.*

Another poem of this kind is the following: —

Guten Tag in diesem Haus!
Alle die in Küche und Keller sind kommt 'mal heraus

Und horet zu
Was ich Euch erzählen tu'.
Hier komm' ich her geritten
Und nicht geschritten.
Mein Pferd habe ich müssen bei der Pforte lassen stehn,
Und muss zu Fuss zum Hause eingehn.
Was ich will ist Euch wohl bekannt,
Hochzeitsbitter bin ich genannt
Und ausgesandt
Von Bräutigam und der Braut.
Der Bräutigam ist_____ und die Braut_____
Die Beiden lassen Euch freundlich grüssen und bitten,
Knecht und Magd, Jung und Alt, Gross und Klein,
So wie sie in Hause zu finden sein,
Die sollen von mir gegrüsset und gebeten sein.
Und wenn Ihr meine Bitte wollt recht verstehn,
So könnt Ihr nächsten Dienstag zum Hause des-zur Hochzeit gehn.
Und darnach könnt Ihr Euch laben,
Mit dem was wir haben_____
Mit kaltem Bier und Branntewein.
Denk' da wollen wir anfangen ein wenig lustig zu sein.
Da sollt Ihr dann sehen
Den Bräutigam bei seiner Geliebten stehen,
Und die Kopulation anhören,
Wie der Mann die Frau und die Frau den Mann soll ehren.
Und wenn dies alles ist geschehn,
So sollen die Tische mit vielem gerüstet stehn.
Und wenn es Euch nicht mehr lüst' und schmeckt,
So werden die Tische wieder abgedeckt.
Und darnach will ich Euch verschaffen Raum und Platz, Feu'r und
*   Licht,*
Damit ein jeder kann sehen was er verricht.
Doch von weiterem zu erzählen fällt mir zu schwer,
Gebt mir 'mal was zu trinken her.
Ein Glas Bier ist nicht zu viel,
Zwei ist mein rechtes Ziel.
Wollt Ihr mich 'mal traktieren?
Sonst will ich lieber ein Haus weiter marschieren.
Und wer nun eine schöne Jungfrau will sein,
Die schmücke mein' Hut mit ein' schön Bändlein.
Was ich nicht bin, das kann ich noch werden,
Und was ich nicht weiss, das kann ich noch lernen.
Habe ich meine Rede nicht gut gemacht,
So habe ich sie doch kurz zu Ende gebracht.

A free translation of this poem is the following: —

165

Good day to all in this house! All who are in the kitchen and cellar, let them come out and listen to what I shall tell you. Hither I have come riding and not walking. My horse I had to leave standing at the gate and come a-foot to the house. What I wish is well known to you. Hochzeitsbitter *I am called and sent by the bridegroom and the bride. The groom is _____ , the bride _____ . The two greet you kindly and pray that the man-servant and the maid-servant, young and old, great and small, as they are found in this house, shall be kindly greeted by me. And if you wish to understand my invitation better, then you may come next Tuesday to the home of Mr._____ to attend the wedding. And after that you may refresh yourselves with cold beer and with brandy. I fancy there we shall begin to be merry. There you shall see the groom stand beside his bride and listen to the marriage ceremony, how the husband his wife and the wife her husband shall honor. And when all this is done, then the tables shall be set. And when you have satisfied your appetite, then the tables shall be cleared away. After that I'll provide room and space, fire and light, that each may see what he does. But to tell more is too hard for me. Give me something to drink. One glass of beer is not too much, two is my real capacity. Will you give me something to drink? Otherwise I desire to go a house farther. Now she who wishes to be a good girl let her decorate my hat with pretty ribbons. What I am not, I may yet become, and that which I do not know I may yet learn. If I have not made my speech well, I have at least made it short and have brought it to a close.*

The next poem plainly shows how imperfectly these things are remembered. The young farmer from whom these lines were obtained had served as *Brautbitter* some few years ago. The first part seems pretty well remembered. The close, however, suddenly comes to an abrupt stop.

Guten Tag! Guten Tag in diesem Haus!
Die Hochzeitsgäste bitt' ich heraus.
Hochzeitsbitter ist mein Begehr,
Und wenn es auch nicht gefällig wär'.
Es lassen Euch grüssen der Brautigam_____
*   und die Braut_____*
Ihr sollt am nächsten Donnerstag zur Hochzeit kommen.
Dazu lad' ich Euch alle ein,
Gross und klein,
Und wie sie hier im Hause sein.
Potztausend, bald hätt' ich noch eins vergessen —
Die Hausfrau oder die Jungfrau
Muss mir den Hut noch bekränzen.

Among the poems which came into my possession, there is one which is not used by the Concordia Germans any more. It was used some years ago, however, as I am assured by trustworthy persons. It is not an invitation to the wedding, as will be seen; but it shows the survival of another custom, namely that of some one going to fetch the bride to the place where the wedding is to take place. This person may have been a near kinsman or a good friend. Besides asking for the bride, the messenger admonishes the maid to observe certain things which will give her and those associated with her pleasure.

This is the poem: —

Guten Tag in diesem Haus,
Mit einem gewünschten Hochzeitsgruss!
Ich bin ausgesandt von dem Herrn Bräutigam,
Um die Jungfrau Braut zu holen.
Ist sie hier so wollen wir stille stehn,
Ist sie nicht hier so wollen wir weiter gehen.
Ist sie hier
So trete sie herfür.
Der Bräutigam wartet mit Verlangen,
Mit Freuden wird er dich empfangen,
An seinem Herd in seinem Haus.
Das Haus zier Du mit Reinlichkeit,
Dass Ordnung herrsche jederzeit.
Sei Du zu allem nütze.
O dann wird man stets Dich lieben,
Nie betrüben.
Deinem Stande
Mache Du Ehre und keine Schande.
Die Schwiegereltern liebe.
Sei Du ihnen stets von Herzen gut
Und sind sie traurig mach' ihnen Mut.
Tu' es aus Kindesliebe.
O dann ist die Ehe
Ohne Wehe.
Keine Leiden
Werden Dich vom Frieden scheiden.

The English of this poem is the following: —

Good day to all in this house, with a welcome wedding greet-ing! I am sent the groom to fetch the bride. If she is here, I will remain here; if she is not here, I will go on. If she is here, then let her step forth. The groom waits with longing, with joy to receive thee, at his hearth in his house. The house thou shalt adorn with cleanliness that order may reign at all times. Be thou useful in all things. Oh, then one will ever love thee, never grieve thee. To thy station lend thou honor and no dishonor. Thy parents-in-law do thou honor, be good to them from thy heart, and if they are sorrowful, give them courage. Do it in the love of a child. Oh, then is the married state without suffering. No discomfort will separate thee from peace.

This article originally appeared in the Journal of American Folklore *21 (1908), pp. 60-67 and is reprinted here with the permission of the American Folklore Society.*

Wesolego Alleluja = Happy Easter

Joann Bratkowski

In the following paper Ms. Bratkowski deals with what folklorists call a calendar custom, i. e. a custom linked to a specific annual event or celebration. In Europe there are many such celebrations, but relatively few have survived in America. The most prominent ones found in this country, along with the most common tradition associated with it, are: St. Patrick's Day *(wearing green);* April Fool's Day *(pulling pranks);* Easter *(dyeing eggs);* May Day *(giving "may baskets");* Independence Day *(shooting fireworks);* Halloween *(going "begging");* Christmas *(caroling);* New Year's Eve *(attending a "watch party" which ends in great noisemaking and general congratulations at the stroke of midnight). In some parts of the country* Valentine's Day, Groundhog Day, Mother's Day, Father's Day, *and* Labor Day *might also qualify, but generally the customs associated with these days are maintained not by folk tradition but by commercial or mass-media interests.*

For additional information on American calendar customs, see George William Douglas and Helen Douglas Compton, The American Book of Days *(New York: H. W. Wilson Co., 1948) and George R. Stewart's chapter on holidays (pp. 222-248) in his book* American Ways of Life *(Garden City, New York: Doubleday and Company, 1954). Kelsie B. Harder's "Just An April Fool,"* Tennessee Folklore Society Bulletin *27 (1961), pp. 5-7 is an entertaining paper on a specific calendar custom.*

If I ever tell people that I spend my Easter holiday pounding cottage cheese, eating Krakow and throwing water on my brother, they laugh. They ask why. I say it's because I'm Polish. Then they laugh harder.

Coping with the temptation of my friends to tell me every Polish joke they've ever heard has its own rewards. But being a 100% Polish-American is a special joy on holidays. My family celebrates Easter with a fierce pride that comes

169

from trying to maintain old-fashioned customs in a country where "holiday" means closing the bank on Monday.

The wealth of our Polish Easter traditions begins on Palm Sunday when we receive blessed palms at the Polish National Catholic Church in St. Louis. This is a family parish founded by my grandfather, who immigrated to the United States during World War I. The masses are still said in Polish and I am related to just about everyone there except the priest.

The palms are placed behind portraits hanging in the home or they are woven into flower shapes during the week preceding Easter Sunday.

My dad spends this week making his own hand-stuffed Polish sausage called "kielbasa" and a lean beef and pork sausage called "Krakow." He has a smoke-house fashioned from two metal barrels in the middle of the yard and I have yet to learn just what the neighbors think that thing is.

My official duty during Holy Week is making the "pisanki," or colored Easter eggs. Eggs are a major item in a Polish Easter, for they are regarded as a symbol of life. Ancient tradition holds that "pisanki" are endowed with magical properties thought to ensure both plentiful harvests and good health. Their decoration has become a folk-art form and different sections of Poland are noted for their distinctive designs.

We dye the eggs at our house not with White Rabbit-brand dye, but with onion peelings. We use white wax or crayons to make a design on the uncooked eggs and then boil them with purple or brown onion skins. The true Pole writes "Wesolego Alleluja" (Happy Easter) on each egg, but I never can get all that on an uncooked egg without having to scramble it the next morning.

Holy Thursday is a day of fasting in honor of the Last Supper, the last Passover dinner eaten by Christ. Pike is an indispensable food item on this day because the bones of the head have the shapes of all the implements used in crucifying Jesus. Polish legend holds that the fish was eaten at the Last Supper, and for that reason the various head bones resemble a ladder, cross and lance. Curiously, these are single, while the bones shaped like the "nails" come in pairs.

Pike is hard to find in St. Louis, however, and we usually end up eating the broken eggs from the last egg-dyeing session.

In Poland many years ago on Good Friday, the mirrors in every household were covered in black in mourning for Jesus. Parents awoke their children by tapping them with a rod in memory of the crucifixion, uttering the words, "The wounds of God" in Polish. My grandmother carried this custom to America with her and switched my older sister on Good Friday morning, but the practice has been abandoned over the years.

In the church, an empty closed coffin used to be displayed in the center aisle during the evening Good Friday services. This practice was forsaken in our family church after my uncle Raymond, as a mischievous youngster, crawled into the coffin before it was rolled into the church and made ghostly noises throughout the mass.

My family has dropped most of the restrictive Good Friday traditions but my dad is still strict about not singing or dancing and we still don't eat meat. I've always been hard-pressed to explain to my boyfriends why they can't take me to a show on that particular Friday night.

Last year, however, Dad sat in his huge easy chair Friday evening and yelled for me to turn on the television, a previously forbidden activity on such a religious occasion. He later confided that if anybody asked him in church if he has turned on the TV, he could say no. But he wouldn't tell them that he'd made me do it.

On the Saturday before Easter, food to be eaten on Sunday is taken to the parish priest to be blessed in a ceremony called "Swiecone." Since the Easter dinner consists only of cold foods, this isn't too much of a problem, but modern Polish housewives generally present only a sampling of their Easter fare to the priest.

Easter morning finds my mother in her spring finery down on her hands and knees washing our kitchen floor before the 6 a.m. resurrection services. Our church still holds a procession of all the parishioners around the sanctuary, the steeple bells tolling all the while. Children dressed in white always precede the priest, throwing rose petals in his path.

Until I was 12, my mental picture of the concept "Easter Sunday" was of a pair of new white patent leather shoes with slippery soles that gave way when they met with a rose petal. My mother would rehearse me every year, saying, "Now show me how you're going to walk so you don't fall this year," but I never could keep slippery shoe and dew-drenched petal from connecting.

Because everyone has been eating scrambled eggs for a week, the rush to the food after the worship is astounding. The Easter table is traditionally decorated with garlands of greenery and is spread with the food blessed the day before.

Custom calls for a roasted pig's head but we use a baked ham instead. My dad's Polish sausage is always there, served with horseradish that represents the bitterness of Christ's suffering.

Bread and salt must be served, representing the mainstay of life and wishes of good fortune and good health. The traditional loaf is a yellow egg bread called "babka" and is always made in two pieces, one for the "babcia," or grandmother, the other for the "gagia," or grandfather.

Always on the table is an oval of dried cottage cheese, which must be wrapped in cheesecloth and pounded with a wooden mallet for days until all the moisture drips out so that it can be shaped into a cross or oval for the table. Another necessity is a cake baked in the shape of a lamb, decorated with coconut and sugar and holding a Polish flag or a cross.

The chief feature of the Easter table, however, is the "pisanki." These boiled eggs are broken and shared among the guests with an exchange of good wishes.

The way my dad tells it, because the Poles had no television, they would play a game at Easter in which two players would hit the ends of their "pisanki" together. The player whose egg remains whole wins the cracked egg of his opponent.

I can never win this game when playing against my dad because his hands are big enough to completely encircle his egg, thus giving it boosted hitting power. My grandfather used to cheat by sneaking in a colored duck's egg, the shell of which is about three times harder than a chicken's egg.

The Polish Easter season ends on Monday, when the "Dyngus-Smigus" custom is oberved, the most humorous of the Easter traditions. The boys switch the girls with willow branches and then douse them with water. The victim is never supposed to fight back. On Tuesday, the girls are supposed to reciprocate.

In my family, it never really works that way. The men always forget that it's "Dyngus." Heaven forbid the women should ever remind them, because on Tuesday the men become open game. The girls can throw water to their hearts' content while the men have lost their chance at revenge.

My mother always told me the amount of water thrown on you indicated how much you were loved, but the origin of the custom is unknown. Some say it is a reminder of the belief that the sinner has been washed clean by the blood of the newly risen Christ. Others say that, according to legend, the Jews flung water at the early Christians to disperse them as they gathered in Jerusalem to talk about the resurrection of Christ.

Polish Easter customs are a mixture of worship and legend maintained through the generations by a people anxious to uphold their heritage and culture. It's distinctive to be Polish where I came from.

The colorful Polish holiday customs have always been a part of my life and my way of thinking. Those who haven't experienced them cannot possibly know the fun, togetherness, self-identity, love and sense of wholeness that exist within a family culture so richly endowed with tradition. I am only sorry that so many of the customs and much of the language have been lost over the years. I hope if I have children, they carry on what I will teach them.

This article originally appeared in the Columbia, Missouri Missourian, *March 30, 1975, pp. 3-5 and is reprinted here with the permission of the author.*

A Country Dance in the Ozarks in 1874

John Q. Wolf

John Quincy Wolf (1901-1972) is one of the most important names in the history of folksong scholarship in the Arkansas Ozarks. A native of Batesville, Wolf spent his teaching career at Arkansas College and Southwestern at Memphis. His Ph.D. was in English literature, and that was the subject he taught, but he also had a consuming passion for folk music, particularly that of his native Arkansas Ozarks. Beginning in the 1940s and continuing until shortly before his death, he recorded a huge body of songs from singers scattered throughout the Ozarks of northern Arkansas. Wolf was largely responsible for bringing Arkansas singers Almeda Riddle and James Morris (better known as Jimmie Driftwood) to national attention. He also produced a number of important publications, one of which is "Folksingers and the Re-Creation of Folksong," Western Folklore *(1967), pp. 101-111. In that article, based on examples from the White River Valley, Wolf concludes that traditional singers do not intentionally alter their material. Wolf's folksong collection is now being readied for publication by his widow, Bess.*

It is hardly surprising that Wolf developed strong and varied scholarly interests, for his father, John Quincy Wolf, Sr. (1864-1949), was a man of broad intellectual interests who developed one of the finest personal libraries in Arkansas. A banker by profession, he spent much of his retirement years writing short pieces for the Batesville/Guard-Record; *many of these were later edited by his son and published as* Life in the Leatherwoods *(Memphis: Memphis State University Press, 1974). The following paper represents a rarely encountered, and much needed, type of historical work on American folk dancing; it is reprinted on pp. 120-122 of the chapter "Big Doings in the Leatherwoods" in* Life in the Leatherwoods.

Unfortunately, there is no good, or even adequate, study of folk dancing in the United States. Richard Nevell's A Time to Dance: American Country Dancing from Hornpipes to Hot Hash *(New York: St. Martin's Press, 1977) is a recent attempt to provide a definitive volume on this subject but, except for some interesting sketches of people involved in country dancing, should not be taken too seriously. An early collection of data on one type of Missouri dancing is Goldie Hamilton's "The Play-Party in Northeast Missouri,"* Journal of American Folklore *27 (1914), pp. 289-303. Ruth Ann Musick also published a note on "A Missouri Dance Call" in* Journal of American Folklore *59 (1946), pp. 323-324. The "play-party" discussed in Hamilton's article was a special type of dance in which there was no instrumental accompaniment; instead, the dancers supplied the music by singing. This type of activity (it usually was not called a dance but rather a "play-party," "games," or some other euphemism) was once popular throughout most of the United States but, by World War II, was just about dead as a traditional form of entertainment.*

The sound of pianos, organs, and trumpets had never been heard in the Leatherwood spur of the Arkansas Ozarks, where I was growing up during the eighteen-sixties, -seventies and -eighties. Even violins were unknown — but everybody knew the sound of a fiddle. The country fiddler was an important personage, looked upon with almost as much respect and reverence as the country parson. His vocabulary in the way of tunes was rather limited, but he played the few he knew like a house afire. "Mandy Lockett," "Ole Dan Tucker," "Ryestraw," "Arkansas Traveler," "Old Molly Hare," "Fisher's Hornpipe," "The Devil's Dream," "Soldier's Joy," and "Turkey in the Straw" were his classics.

In the fall and winter there was an occasional dance at some home in the City Rock neighborhood, and everybody in the community who wanted to attend invited himself — it was free for all. The old-fashioned square dance was the only step the backwoods folk knew, and they threw themselves into it with fury. Fighting fire was a mild, conservative exercise compared to it.

The fiddler brought his fiddle and bow tied up in a pillow case to guard the delicate tone of the instrument against the weather. When he had tuned up the fiddle, rosined his bow and got all set, and when the dancing broke out, some obliging young man got two steel knitting needles and beat a tattoo on the strings as the fiddler played — a trick that was supposed to liven the music and to put mettle into the heels of the dancers. It was pretty! Girls with good looks and those nimble on their feet were in demand as partners and danced nearly every "set," while clumsy girls, if any, were neglected.

I recall a dance at the home of Charlie Benbrook, later in life Dr. C. E. Benbrook, in the City Rock neighborhood, that was full of interest and excitement. Major Reynolds was the fiddler, the only one within a radius of ten miles, and with him was his grown daughter Emma, who had had the misfortune years before of getting one of her hands cut off in a sorghum mill. She loved to dance, she always came to the dances with her father, and she was well liked; but the young men tended to shun her as a partner because they found it awkward or embarrassing to "swing on the corners and all promenade" with her because of her arm.

The dance had been in full swing only an hour or so when suddenly the fiddler quit playing, put his fiddle in the pillow case and began tying it up. The young men gathered about him in vigorous protest, calling his attention to the fact that it was still early in the night. They asked for an explanation and got none. In sullen silence he continued to tie up his fiddle in the pillow slip. Dow Harris quickly sensed the cause of his attitude and lost no time in trying a remedy. He walked over to the fiddler's daughter and asked her to dance with him. She promptly accepted, and they stepped out onto the floor. Then in a rather loud voice Harris begged the old man to "give us just one more tune, Major; we want to dance one more set." Mr. Reynolds looked up, and seeing his daughter, who had been neglected up to that time, standing beside Harris, promptly untied the pillow case, took out his fiddle, tuned up the instrument, rosined his bow, bit off a chew of tobacco, and lit into some of the liveliest dance music that ever rent the unoffending air in our neighborhood.

Before the set ended, other young men held a conference outside and bound themselves by solemn compact that they would thereafter take turns dancing with Emma, notwithstanding difficulties, for the rest of the night. They almost danced her to exhaustion, engaging her for every set thereafter; they also worked her father hard, for he gave them fast and furious music until the early morning hours, when the young people went home happy as birds and praising Harris for his more or less delicate diplomacy.

During the evening three young men from the north side of White River dropped in. One of them was a stranger, set off from the crowd by his broad-brimmed hat and light boots: none of us had ever seen him before. I speak of "us," but I do not know how I came to be at the dance. I was too young to dance, and besides I didn't know how. But I was there, and probably in the way. While the revelers were having a little resting-spell between sets, giving the fiddler and his now-popular daughter a recess, Dow Harris, the hero of the evening, who was the best dancer in our community, stepped out onto the floor and began to entertain us with a solo exhibition. He did not know very many steps, but he was fairly adept and a pleasing figure to watch. The stranger referred to must have sat and looked on for five minutes, when suddenly he fairly leaped out into the middle of the floor and began to dance beside Dow. He was a handsome young man, with glossy black curly hair and a complexion ruddy with health; he was unusually graceful, and as nimble as an acrobat. His dancing at first was restrained and easy. Harris soon took his seat as he realized he was no longer an attraction, and like the rest of us, he was entranced by the performance of this stranger, who was now warming up to his work and doing some unusual dancing. His performance was sometimes quiet, almost noiseless, his body nearly motionless, his legs and feet going like lightning; then he would suddenly break out into a veritable storm of activity, ending up in a breath-taking climax, backward and forward, here and there, this side then that, up and down, now almost still, now active in every muscle of his body, his feet all the while working in perfect rhythm and making quite a clatter against the floor; now he would execute a "double-shuffle," "cut the pigeon's wing," and finally whirl into astonishing leaps and spins, the like of which we had never seen before.

When he was about to end his exhibition, Mr. Reynolds seized his fiddle and played "The Devil's Dream" for him, putting every bit of fire and energy he had into it, and the dancer responded in kind. He danced the very life out of the lively

175

and inspiring old tune and won the admiration and praise of saint and sinner alike. When he quit the floor and sat down, all of us realized we had witnessed a rare and remarkable exhibition. I have seen a great many dancers perform on the stage and on the screen since that night, but no dancer has given me as thrilling an experience as did the romantic young man at Benbrook's. The stranger was Rufus P. Jones, just arrived from Texas. He became a citizen of Izard County, married a daughter of the late Capt. R. C. Matthews of Pineville, and died a few years ago at his home near Calico Rock.

This was the most memorable square dance I ever attended.

This article originally appeared in Southern Folklore Quarterly *29 (1965), pp. 319-321 and is reprinted here with the permission of the* Southern Folklore Quarterly.

The Interlude of Game: A Study of Washers

Robert Cochran

*They did everything that didn't
matter. It made them feel good.*
William Gass

*For various reasons, the study of folk games has been almost exclusively
confined to consideration of children's games. The first major American study,
William Wells Newell's* Games and Songs of American Children *(1883), initiated
this pattern of scholarship which persists to the present day in such works as
Paul G. Brewster's* American Non-Singing Games *(1953). But this emphasis is
misleading, for many folk games are not solely or even primarily maintained by
children. A number of possible explanations can be offered to account for the
one-sided nature of scholarship on folk games. Many nineteenth-century authorities, Newell included, subscribed to the idea that children's games were
one example of* gesunkenes kulturgut *(literally "sunken good culture"). In
other words, these items have their origin in an upper-class source but over
time have become debased and are now only practiced by groups such as
children. The games are, according to this view, dying out, and once children
discontinue using them, they will be gone forever. Thus, collectors who gather
them are rescuing the last remaining fragments of an ancient tradition.*

*Perhaps the main reason most writers concern themselves solely with
children's games is that children usually are excellent informants. They are
easy to find, generally eager to perform and, unlike many adults, are usually
not self-conscious or inhibited with their responses. What makes them even
more desirable is that there are certain places, such as schools, where large
crowds of children can be interviewed relatively quickly. Many collectors, such
as Brewster, have recorded much of their data from school collecting sessions.
Such material is, of course, useful but, as Professor Cochran demonstrates in*

the following essay, certainly does not represent the total possibilities available for the study of folk games. This is a model study of the genre that includes game rules, illustration of play area, and some historical and social aspects of the event, as well as an attempt to trace the geographic distribution of the tradition.

The game of washers, although occasionally mentioned on television or in popular magazines, and recently identified in *Newsweek* as the "town sport" of Luckenbach, Texas, has been almost completely ignored by folklorists.[1] This is unfortunate, since the game is noteworthy on several counts. In the first place, it seems clearly to be a folk game — it exists in many variant forms, with numberless differences in rules and scoring; it is almost invariably learned in face-to-face situations; its origins are anonymous and obscure; its distribution is regionally limited, and its very existence is mostly unrecorded. Secondly, washers is not exclusively or even primarily a game of children, so that its documentation may serve as a welcome addition to a body of scholarship still heavily weighted, for no good reason, on the side of juvenile games. Finally, washers is even today a widely known game, played by many people, and thus easily investigated.

Two versions of washers, both ascribed to Arkansas, are briefly described in Paul G. Brewster's study, *American Non-Singing Games*, but a fairly close survey of the folklore journals turns up virtually nothing about the game.[2] It seems probable that, like the craft of chairmaking studied so appreciatively by Michael Owen Jones, the game of washers has seemed to researchers "so rudimentary and unsophisticated as to offer no field for investigation."[3] Studied with care, however, washers reveals itself as a delicately calibrated instrument, a game of skill which includes elements of chance sufficient to its social contexts. The presentation of the game within these contexts is the purpose of this essay.

Washers is a pitching game, very likely deriving from horsehoes, and formally similar. It takes its name from the object pitched — a metal washer approximately two inches in diameter, which is thrown from varying distances (usually about fifteen feet) at one or more holes in the ground. Washers is played by groups as small as two, and games were observed where as many as eight played in turn, with all contestants giving more or less continuous attention to the play. It is played by children and by adults, by men and by women, by whites and by blacks. Children often play the game at school, during recess and lunch periods; but, among adults, washers is most frequently played at family centered gatherings — reunions, picnics, Sunday afternoon visits, and the like. People play washers with their friends and with their neighbors — play with strangers is very rare. Gambling, invariably for small stakes, is sometimes involved, but more often the game is played in a purely recreational context.[4]

THE SHAPES OF THE GAME

While washers is played according to widely various rules and in several different forms, it is clear that the two-hole version is by far the most common.

(Fig. 1) Two-hole washers: the holes are about 2½" in diameter. (Based on a drawing by Hugh Groom, Texarkana, Texas, August, 1977)

This is Brewster's (A) form, and his observation that the game is most often played by two teams of two persons each was supported by the present study.[5] Of sixty-eight players questioned in depth concerning their experiences, fifty-five described the two-hole version. Many were familiar with only this form. A similar pattern was observed among respondents interviewed more casually. The two-hole version, then, was reported by 80% of those questioned — no other version was reported by more than 25%.

Two holes are dug, most often to a depth of three to five inches, and separated most commonly by a distance of about fifteen feet (reports ranged from ten feet to thirty feet). Cans with the tops removed (and occasionally the bottoms also) are sometimes buried in the holes with their top edges flush with the surface.[6]

Players then position themselves behind or beside one hole and pitch to the opposite hole. If two-man teams are playing, one player from each team goes to each end. Three washers are usually thrown by each player in every round, with all throws pitched to the same hole and with the pitches alternating between players. If the game is being played by two people, both move to the opposite hole at the completion of the round, pick up the washers, and continue by pitching back to the hole where they stood for the first round. If two-man teams are playing, the second round is played by the teammates standing at the hole to which the first round was played. (Figure 1)

The usual scoring involves a five point score for a washer pitched into the hole and a one point score for each washer closer to the hole than the opponent's best throw. The distinction reported by Brewster between the scoring for washers lying flat in the hole and those leaning against the hole's sides was only rarely observed. Only one team may score in each round, and almost invariably the rules provide for the cancellation of all points if a successful pitch is duplicated or "covered" by an opponent. Thus, during a single round, if one player pitched two washers into the hole to his opponent's one and pitched his other washer closer to the hole than either of his opponent's, he would score a total of six points for that round.

Games in the two-hole version are customarily played to twenty-one points, and often there are penalties for "busting over," scoring more points than the number required for victory. It is not unusual for a player or team guilty of "busting over" to be required to start over again.

When more than four players are involved, the usual procedure calls for third and fourth two-man teams to be formed, and for the team losing the first game to be replaced for the next game by the third team. Games may thus continue indefinitely, with the winners of each continuing play, while the losers retire for one or more games, depending upon the number of teams involved.

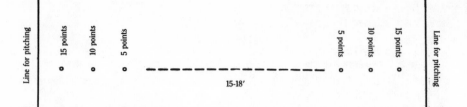

(Fig. 2) Six-hole washers: three holes, about 8" apart and 3½-4" in diameter, are placed at each end of the court in hard clay or sand; the washers are 2-2½" in diameter. (Based on a drawing by Leroy McJunkins, Saratoga, Arkansas, July, 1977)

Although at least six additional forms of washers were reported, only one of these was at all widespread. This was the six-hole version, which was reported by fourteen of the sixty-eight central respondents, or approximately 20% of the total. This version, too, is most often played by either two or four persons, and the number of washers pitched in each round, the positioning of players, and many of the rules governing scoring are also similar to the two-hole form. The significant differences are based on the more elaborate arrangement of holes, with the accompanying opportunity for higher point totals. Three holes, instead of one, are placed at each end in a straight line, separated from each other by six to eight inches, so that the finished "court" consists of six aligned holes — the ends separated, usually, by about fifteen feet, as in the two-hole form. Most often, the closest hole is worth five points, the intermediate hole ten points, and the most distant hole fifteen points. Games are usually played to higher point totals than the twenty-one points characteristic of the two-hole form, with games to one hundred points or more reported by several players. (Figure 2)

THE ORIGINS AND DISTRIBUTION OF THE GAME

Washers was connected with horseshoes by a number of respondents, who often mentioned it in explaining the form or scoring of the game. Several claimed that washers developed in areas where horseshoes were not available: "Land around here, people didn't shoe horses so much."[7]

Horseshoes is itself evidently derived from quoits, and "probably began at the time of the Roman occupation of Britain, when officers played quoits and the men copied them (without cost) by throwing horseshoes at stakes."[8] Both games were brought to this continent by the colonists, but it was horseshoes, of course, which prospered in this country. Also, in addition to the parallels with horseshoes, there are several games played with marbles which exhibit formal similarity to washers.[9] The obvious point is that formally washers is a simple game, easily adapted to create versions based upon other popular games and pastimes.

Several informants born in the 1890s reported learning the game as children, often from parents or grandparents. Georgia Lumpkin, born in 1894 in Cass County, Texas, was taught the game by her father and first played when she

180

was "five or six years old."[10] Monroe Lawrence, born in 1896 in Mountain View, Arkansas, learned the game from "friends and family" and first played when he was "eight or nine."[11] One younger player, Miller Williams, now a poet and professor at the University of Arkansas, learned the game as a boy near Hoxie, Arkansas, and still keeps the old set of wagon-wheel washers given to him by his father. It is clear, then, that washers was played, in several of its present shapes, in the years at the turn of the century.

The distribution of washers appears to be sharply defined, at least in its areas of greatest popularity. A core area in east Texas, southwest Arkansas, and northwest Louisiana is indicated, with a center close to Texarkana and a radius of approximately 200 miles.[12] Many people outside this area play washers, especially in the regions immediately to the east, in eastern Arkansas and in Mississippi. The game was also encountered in southern Indiana, in the Evansville area. There is a degree, too, to which the survey is skewed by the concentration of research in areas where positive responses were common — this because historic-geographic questions were of peripheral concern. It remains true, however, that people inside the indicated core area are more likely to know about washers than people in other places. When a preliminary report based on this study was presented to the annual meeting of the Missouri Folklore Society in November, 1977, only one person in attendance had prior familiarity with the game.[13]

In general, then, washers is a southern folk game and, more especially, a game of the lowland southwest. It is played in towns and in rural areas — with no marked tendency to be associated more commonly with either context — and its popularity is most often ascribed to the ease with which play can be arranged. "All you need is a yard," said one informant. The most commonly used washer can still be purchased in any hardware store for eleven or twelve cents, and no other equipment is required. "We used what was available," said another player, "but we preferred the big washers (probably 2" or so) used on the heel bolts (the bolts used to hold the plows on the cultivators and plow stocks)."[14]

Few respondents gave detailed attention to the social implications of the game, beyond stressing its play in family-centered situations. Several did say that the game was popular because "you could play it even if you were poor," and a very few reported parental disapproval of their youthful participation. Robert Anderson, who learned the game in 1959 as a young child in Wichita Falls, Texas, wrote: "My parents didn't approve. My father never associated with those who played."[15] Another young player whose parents were apprehensive was Coy Garbett, who played washers in Seagoville, Texas, in 1948:

> The kid who taught me the game was about four years older than I. His family was pushing poverty fairly hard, but they were well-scrubbed if foul-mouthed. My mother didn't want me playing with them because of their language and because the mother was divorced. But Bobby Young was like a Huck Finn to my Tom Sawyer and I loved being with him because of all the "neat" things he could do. It was with him that I caught my first fish.[16]

His counting and measuring completed, his data assembled, the scholar turns to the heart of his task. It is his favorite time. His mind has "facts" to juggle, steps for building the dance he strains to see. How deeply does he scan? How does the player move, according to the scholar's score? What tale is told by his gaming? What's learned of his loving, his manner of friending, his posture to time and to heaven?

By such criteria, finally, by the depth and precision of his imagining, the art of the scholar is judged. But more important even than countings and measurings (means, after all, not ends) is the portrait of the player. It is this portrait, poorly or finely drawn, which determines the worth of the scholar's work.

Consider then: washers is played by families. Men, women, children — the game must "fit" them all, must allow each to play on equal footing with the others. A horseshoe, for these ends, is too heavy. A washer is perfect. With very young children, some alterations may even yet be necessary: "the distance of the pitch was determined by the size of the pitcher."[17]

The accounts of players, repeated many times, outline a typical scene. It is summer. Sunday afternoon. Church and dinner over, the family drawn together in its day of rest. The game is slow, appropriate to the heat, punctuated by conversation. Children, eager to impress, are given extra turns. There are many games, many winners. The game is physically undemanding, relaxing and restful. Wives and husbands stand together comfortably, leaning against porches, their arms over shoulders and around waists. The hair of children is tousled. Lucky throws are frequent and provoke a laughter shared by all. The game, it begins to appear, is a perfect thing. It nourishes the occasion of its playing.

Consider further: washers is played among friends. It is a game for neighbors and co-workers. It must serve convivial ends — must open, develop, and close in fields unfired by animosity. Victory must fall short of triumph, defeat be too gentle for loss. The game must give to all and take inordinately from none.

In washers, no players are eliminated (except briefly in large, three or four team games), taken prisoner, or made "it." The game unfolds in regular turns, sedately, like bowling, and unlike baseball, where offensive success may allow one team to remain at bat indefinitely.

At every turn, the rules strive to conjoin, to bring victory and defeat into proximity. The rules for "covering" and "busting over" are important in this regard. One team may lead another by a large margin, eighteen to three, say, in a game to twenty-one. At this point, it is crucial that only one team may score in each round, so that the trailing team may yet, by improving their play, deny the leaders the few points they need. Also, should the leaders, in their attempt to gain the final points one at a time — the only way, since a five point throw would cause them to "bust over" — inadvertently throw the washer into the hole, well, the former trailers and apparent losers have only to avoid "covering" this unfortunate accident in order to gain the lead by a score of three to zero.

Another common rule makes clear the purpose of these arrangements. In many games, a player or team reaching the score needed to win is required ceremonially to shy from victory, to give all washers yet unthrown in that round to the apparent loser(s). A player with twenty points, then, who throws his first washer closer to the cup than his opponent's, must then stop throwing in his turn until the opponent cancels his point with either a pitch into the hole or a closer pitch. If the opponent throws both of his remaining washers unsuccessfully, the apparent winner must now give the opponent one of *his* remaining washers. If his initial throw is still closest to the hole, he must give the opponent his last washer. Every attempt, then, is directed to sustaining the game, to keeping it "close" in every sense of that fine word.

In this same context, it is important to understand the careful balance of skill and chance offered by washers. In a game where physical skills predominate, the danger is always present of a too great personal investment. To lose in such circumstances is to be demeaned, to appear generally inferior. That such a use of game may run counter to its deepest tendencies, may ignore its most profound lessons, is beside the point. Humans are imperfect beings, and partisan responses to games are not uncommon.

"Pick up your jock," is a taunt we may hear on the playground, after the hotshot basketball player has faked us out badly, gone past us for his showboat layup, left us flailing helplessly in his wake. The loss of very manhood is clearly suggested — our jock, by crude metonymy, made to stand for its contents. "In your face," he may scream at the other end, as he sails high to block our jump shot into the crowd of amused bystanders. It's face, in fact, we stand to lose in such a game, with such a player.

Washers, however, presents a very different picture. Physical skills, needed in the name of interest, are not overwhelmingly dominant. Chance, with its refuge of excuse, its power to depersonalize defeat, is more prominent. Very poor pitches will not infrequently roll into the hole — "dog ass" throws, according to the players studied most intensively.[18] The result is the appropriate one — washers is a low-key game. Players do not bicker or argue. Hard feelings are absent — only one of the sixty-eight central informants mentioned a less convivial situation: "The play was very skilled. The washers were usually on target and novices were pretty much scorned."[19] In the more usual setting, nobody is scorned. The game was played, as one player put it, because "it was good fun and created a lot of conversation as well as competition."[20] Again, in its design and in the details of its rules, the game unveils its perfections.

So much for the game itself. Consider now the men and women who play — these often unmonied, mostly white, mostly rural or small town southerners. What storied folks they are! What a horde of scholars, journalists, poets, novelists and the like have attempted their telling. From Beverley's Virginians and Byrd's Carolina Lubberlanders to Jimmy Carter and his siblings — from Sut Lovingood and James Dickey, Ellen Glasgow and Eudora Welty, Walker Evans and H. L. Mencken, W. J. Cash and C. Vann Woodward — from these and countless others our myths have taken shape.

The myths, first of all, present figures and codes of restraint. The sense is of a being suppressed, a smoldering essence held in check. The face to the world is a mask. Agee's people wear their skulls like helmets, and Annie Mae Gudger faces the camera gravely, with thin, locked lips, the lines of her face as rigid as the grain in the boards behind her.[21] When Henry Glassie looks at houses as statements of their makers, reads them with care and attempts to drive "deeper and deeper into mind," he arrives at last at that mind's most basic issue, "the opposition of chaos and control."[22]

If the drive to control, then, issues in austerity, in sober, Stoic dignity, in an ethic of sacrifice and endurance, the claims of chaos, says the myth, surface in periodic eruptions, the flaring of buried fire, when the "stolid" yeoman goes on a tear and ends up "whooping and singing, maybe bloody and goddamming, in the jailhouse."[23]

With these mythic poles in mind — the "fearful control" and the counterbalancing "thunderstorm" — picture again the man playing washers.[24] It is a good place to see him, for he is at home, and his guard may be lowered, his mask not in place. Look at him — the sight is incongruous and comic. This large fellow, his features drawn in concentration, a washer in his hand. He's far removed, this unsung figure, this cracker Dagwood Bumstead, from the famed male rituals — of gun, and horse, and dog — so central to his saga. The washer is the thing — it's too small. A horseshoe or a bowling ball would be better, for him. He's reduced to a mincing style, a bear in a tutu.

He knows full well he's silly, but that's what games are — silliness. Note here the southerner's marked penchant for games where the "silliness" is obvious and highlighted — contests in tobacco spitting, cowchip throwing, turkey calling and the like. A very sardonic element of parody is operative here, as well. If games are by definition silliness, unseriousness, it follows that only a comic demeanor is fully appropriate. To treat a game as a finally serious thing, as one sees done on television and by misguided high school coaches, is to lose touch with play, to make a work of game, and is in such a viewer's eye to be truly naive, truly unsophisticated. The "seriousness," then, of the expert tobacco spitter or washer player will typically be bounded by a fundamental levity which is at once a clue to his understanding of games and an implicit critique of the unrelieved earnestness he sees in the world of big-time athletics.

The game, for such a player, provides an escape, a gentle release from the codes of stern denial, from the postures of fierce pride. It offers a middle ground, a temperate zone between the poles of myth. Here, in play, the "fearful control" is relaxed — and not by a "thunderstorm" either. More like a cooling, vivifying shower. But a game, a slight thing after all, is not enough to answer Glassie's question about his house builder — how did he "treat his wife and children?" They are not exactly the same folks anyway, his builder and my player, and the pan-southern mythos is easily overstated. But given these qualifications, the man pitching washers yet offers a small, lovely antistrophe, a gentle addendum, to the "unpleasant scene" suggested by the evidence of the houses.[25]

In the shapes of the game, in the design that welcomes the child, in the context which allows moments of tenderness to a mightily constrained man — in all of this a happier possibility is advanced. The family, with friends perhaps, gathered in the yard on a Sunday afternoon, at play with this surprising and delicate game, its own creation — what is glimpsed here is an interlude, the interlude of game. It's a good word, interlude is, a resonant, complex word, encompassing in its etymologies and connotations many of this study's concerns. It will make a fine title.

184

To several people I am indebted too generally for adequate citation. Tom Cochran and his wife Debby (Debby Miller when she fired my interest in washers with a paper which introduced me to her husband) encouraged and aided this project at many points. Jerry Davis and his Mid-Valley Pipeline Company right-of-way crew — Gene Baker, Tommy Cadenhead, Jim Carmichael, Casey Clawson, Alan Sherman, Everett Speer, Red Thompson — invited me into their washer games and shared pizza and beer with me later. More than any others, they helped me appreciate the game's perfections. Charles Mazer, friend and folklore teacher at East Texas State University, put himself and his students helpfully to work in my behalf.

[1]On January 18, 1978, CBS Morning News aired a piece showing Hughes Rudd's visit to the Luckenbach washer pitchers. See also Pete Axthelm, "Outlaw Places," *Newsweek* 12 December 1977, 48. Washers is also mentioned on occasion by sportscaster Don Meredith, who played as a youth in Mount Vernon, Texas. (Don Meredith, letter to the author, September, 1977.) See also Chapter III of William Faulkner's *Soldiers' Pay*, where "a lawyer, a drug clerk and two nondescripts" play washers. The epigraph is from William Gass, *Omensetter's Luck* (New York: New American Library, 1972), 31.

[2]Paul G. Brewster, *American Non-Singing Games* (Norman: University of Oklahoma Press, 1953), 148-149. Other material was located in unpublished folklore collections — for example, Bill Carter, "Games I've Played," (Mary C. Parler Folklore Archive, Special Collections, University of Arkansas Library, F. 16, 6.38, 1959), 4.

[3]Michael Owen Jones, *The Hand Made Object and Its Maker* (Berkeley: University of California Press, 1975), vi.

[4]Seven of the sixty-eight central informants mentioned a form of the game involving the pitching of silver dollars. Most often, this game was played only by men, and when gambling was present the dollars pitched would be kept by the winner.

[5]Brewster, 148.

[6]The choice of cans is at times a matter of considerable debate and experimentation, as indicated by Tom Cochran, a Haynesville, Louisiana, washer pitcher: "When I first played we pitched into a bare hole in the clay. Then we went to a Lysol spray top, but it wasn't deep enough. Finally, we got to the Contadina tomato cans, which proved perfect for the game." (Tom Cochran, Fayetteville, Arkansas, July, 1977.)

[7]Jerry Davis, Bastrop, Louisiana, July, 1977.

[8]John Arlott, ed., *The Oxford Companion to World Sports and Games* (London: Oxford University Press, 1975), 506.

[9]See the references to Hundreds and Three Holes in Ruth Midgley, ed., *The Way To Play* (New York: Paddington Press, Ltd., 1975), 126.

[10]Georgia Lenola Lumpkin, Mount Pleasant, Texas, August, 1977.

[11]Monroe Lawrence, Mountain View, Arkansas, July, 1977.

[12]The area is of course not a circle, and seems in fact to be markedly elongated on the east/west axis. This is perhaps a good place to note that one "public washer court" was reported, said to be located in Pecan Gap, Texas, in the 1930s and 1940s. (Mike Luster, Fayetteville, Arkansas, May, 1977.)

[13]The one person was Donald M. Lance, who played washers as a child in Gainesville, Texas, in the 1930s. (Donald M. Lance, Columbia, Missouri, November, 1977.) The general impression suggested — that washers is not widely known north of the Arkansas/Missouri line — was corroborated by Vance Randolph. He was unaware of the game, and his intimate familiarity with the Missouri and Arkansas Ozarks makes it unlikely that the game could have been widely played without his knowledge. (Vance Randolph, Fayetteville, Arkansas, November, 1977.) Negative evidence for widespread distribution of washers in the southeastern United States was provided by Henry Glassie, who reported

that washers was not encountered during his researches in the region. (Henry Glassie, Winslow, Arkansas, February, 1978.)

[14]Mrs. Leister E. Presley. (Letter to the author, February, 1978.)

[15]Robert Anderson, Fayetteville, Arkansas, December, 1977.

[16]Coy Garbett, Fayetteville, Arkansas, December, 1977.

[17]Mrs. Leister E. Presley. (Letter to the author, February, 1978.)

[18]This term is credited by Jerry Davis and his right-of-way crew to Terry Don Perkins, recently of Houston, Texas, who evidently had a rare skill with this type of throw. (Jerry Davis, Bastrop, Louisiana, July, 1977).

[19]William Harrison, Fayetteville, Arkansas, December, 1977.

[20]Evelyn Pace, Texarkana, Texas, August, 1977.

[21]James Agee and Walker Evans, *Let Us Now Praise Famous Men* (New York: Ballantine, 1966). For references to helmets see pp. 32, 65. For the photograph described (I only guess that it is Mrs. Gudger) see the third in the unpaginated selection of photographs at the front of the volume.

[22]Henry Glassie, *Folk Housing in Middle Virginia: A Structural Analysis of Historic Artifacts* (Knoxville: University of Tennessee Press, 1975), 160.

[23]W. J. Cash, *The Mind of the South* (New York: Alfred Knopf, Inc., 1941), 296. For an extended treatment of American character(s) in terms of such polarities, see Michael Kammen, *People of Paradox: An Inquiry Concerning the Origins of American Civilization* (New York: Random House, 1973).

[24]Glassie, *Folk Housing in Middle Virginia,* 162; Cash, *The Mind of the South,* 48, 52.

[25]Glassie, *Folk Housing in Middle Virginia,* 162.

This article originally appeared in Western Folklore *XXXVIII: 2 (April, 1979), pp. 71-82 and is reprinted here with the permission of the author and publisher.*

John Arnold's Link Chains:
A Study in Folk Art

Frank Reuter

Few terms have been used in a more vague and inconsistent manner than that of folk art. To some, folk art is amateur art and, by implication, inferior art. Those who categorize folk art in this manner are primarily speaking from the viewpoint of academic art and are judging items from an aesthetic criteria foreign to the material. This stance is akin to judging the quality of comic books from the perspective of classical literature or judging classical literature from a comic book perspective. In other words, standards meant to apply to one type of material are often invalid as a means of judging other types of material. Anything that is the product of man's culture reveals much about that culture and is worthy of study, but said products should be evaluated on the basis of relevant value systems.

Actually, the folklorist's primary concern is not to make aesthetic judgments, although certainly he should be interested in his informants' aesthetic views. The folklorist's main emphasis is the study of traditional forms of art, their distribution, function, the context of production, etc. As Dr. Reuter demonstrates in the following essay, recording the folk artist's aesthetic opinions is worthwhile. Not only do these views reveal much about John Arnold's carvings and how and why they are created, they also indicate that a person can create an object that is beautiful and pleasurable to someone not sharing the same aesthetic ideas. Thus, while John Arnold is apparently unconcerned with elitist aesthetic concepts, his carvings are often pleasing to elitist audiences. Although not explicitly stated by Reuter, the maker's intent is one of the features that moves a craft, such as carving, into the realm of folk art.

For other accounts of various aspects of folk art in Arkansas and Missouri see Don Van Horn, Carved in Wood: Folk Sculpture in the Arkansas Ozarks *(Batesville: Arkansas College, 1979); Bonnie Lela Crump,* Arts and Crafts of the Ozarks *(Eureka Springs, Arkansas: Times-Echo Press, 1957); Ralph M. Hudson,*

187

"Art in Arkansas," Arkansas Historical Quarterly *3 (Winter, 1944), pp. 299-350; and several sections of Otto Rayburn's* Ozark Country *(New York: Duell, Sloan & Pearce, 1941). Jerry Poole's unpublished Ph.D. dissertation,* Folk Painters of the Arkansas Ozarks, *University of Arkansas, 1974, is an excellent survey of folk painting in northern Arkansas.*

Until rather recently, little attention has been paid to serious study of the folk arts of non-Indian peoples in the United States, a condition that gives any collector-researcher problems in classifying and analyzing folk art. In 1950 a symposium was held on the question "What is American Folk Art?" and the inconsistency of the responses to the question and the different perspectives that were taken clearly demonstrate that, at the time, there was no consensus of opinion in defining American folk art nor much agreement regarding what direction study should take.[1] One of the difficulties in dealing with folk art is that the term covers such a wide range of activity: from the whittling of wood, the subject of this essay, to painting, to the construction of practical implements, and to decorative flourishes on utilitarian materials. While some direction is now being offered in the work of scholars like Henry Glassie and Michael Owen Jones,[2] especially in treating folk art in terms of its traditions and its contextual setting — where have the styles come from and what is the artist doing in relationship to his whole life and culture? — much research still needs to be done, as both Glassie and Jones have pointed out. This paper is intended to serve two purposes: to record the styles and techniques of a particularly talented chain whittler, John Arnold, and to offer some comments on folk aesthetics by reporting John's attitudes toward his work.

THE ARTIST

John Arnold, who presently resides in Monticello, Arkansas, was born on 10 March 1897 at Otwell, Indiana. At the age of thirteen he moved to Arkansas where, except for a number of years spent working as a farmhand in Illinois, he has lived ever since. Although he began whittling at an early age, he only started carving chains when he was employed in Illinois where, he reports, he whittled to pass the time in the Winter when the temperature dipped below freezing and he needed something to fight boredom. John relates that the woman of the house at which he stayed allowed him to whittle inside only if he would be careful to sweep up all his shavings after he had done whittling, and to this day he seems to like to whittle for long periods of time in one place — normally on a chair in front of his garage-shed — so that he can easily remove all the leavings of his work. It was in Illinois that John first began to draw attention to his whittling; he reports that one of his link chains was pictured on the front page of the Peoria newspaper, and it was also in Illinois that he lent an unusual balls-in-cages chain to some "American Legion boys" who, John contends, took it to a World's Fair.[3]

John, who originally began whittling chains as a pastime in the Winter, now whittles all year round and sells his chains. So popular are his chains now that he is always faced with a backlog of orders. Although John does not know how many chains he has made, he reports having made "thousands of dollars worth before he ever sold any" and also having once had two hundred chains which he sold all at once. Normally John sells his link chains for fifteen or twenty dollars apiece depending on their length. Either price is very reasonable, for it takes John on the average about fifty-five hours to whittle a chain.[4]

MATERIALS

For his whittling, John keeps a large number of knives; he always has a pocketful ready for use, and he reports having had as many as sixty-five knives at once. John distinguishes his knives according to the type of blade they have: either spey blades, which are used for planing when there is no delicate work to be done, or spear blades, thinner and sharper, which are used in doing the fine whittling.[5] John's love of his whittling is reflected in his willingness to display his knives and to discuss their role in his work. His craftsman's attachment to his tools is evident in his ability to remember the year and place of purchase of his favorite knives. In recent years John has also come to use a Black and Decker drill to help him speed up the process of breaking the links, a practice that saves him a significant amount of time on any one chain.

For all the chains that John carves at present he uses one of two types of wood: linden or cedar. John prefers to carve the linden or basswood, which he calls "lin," because it is easier to work than the cedar, which is brittle and can shatter like glass if it is dropped. Though John contends that he has not dropped a chain in years, the threat of lost effort is a serious concern for him.[6] And though he prefers the linden wood because of its texture and the relative ease with which it may be carved, his customers seem to prefer the cedar chains, which unlike the white linden, generally have a two-tone color, making them especially attractive.

CHAINS

While all the chains that John presently carves are of a style that may be called Varied Chains, John once whittled several unusual chains that will be discussed first in order to demonstrate John's ability to conceptualize unusual patterns and designs. The pieces were whittled back in the late 1920s or early 1930s, yet John has kept them and displays them readily to anyone who is interested. The first such item is the World's Fair ball-in-cages chain, a series of three cages with respectively eight, two, and one ball nested in each cage (Fig. 1). John also keeps in his private collection a link chain which measures twenty-two feet, ten and a half inches. In order to whittle this chain, which holds John's personal if not a world's record for length, he began with a piece of wood about eight feet long and whittled two parallel rows of links which are connected at one end. He then broke the other end to separate the parallel rows which, together with the lengthening of the links after they were whittled, accounts for the remarkable overall length. John has also whittled a set of three interlinking

(Fig. 1) John Arnold and the World's Fair Chain

(Fig. 2) John Arnold's Interlocking Rings

rings, each ring passing through the other two (Fig. 2). His description of how he made this piece illustrates John's persistence in struggling with technical problems.[7] John, who decided to try this piece when he lived in Illinois, began with numerous freehand attempts in sweet potatoes, but nothing he tried worked out. He spent an entire Winter frustrated by the problem before he decided to make a copper wire model of what he was trying to carve. By carefully imitating the model, John was able to complete in wood the three interlocking rings.

The most common type of chain John whittles and the type he presently sells is the Varied Chain (Fig. 3). These chains, no two of which are exactly alike, vary in length from as short as thirty-three inches to as long as fifty-five inches. Moreover, John varies the organization of the designs according to the demands of the particular piece of wood that he is carving. The length of the wood and the possibility of a design being marred by a knot will cause John to modify the arrangement of the designs to make the medium and the end product mesh. For example, John often centers small surface scars that might reveal deeper knots on the interconnecting knobs of his chains, or if he can predict where a deep knot will appear, he will often center it in a section of the chain that is deeply carved away.

191

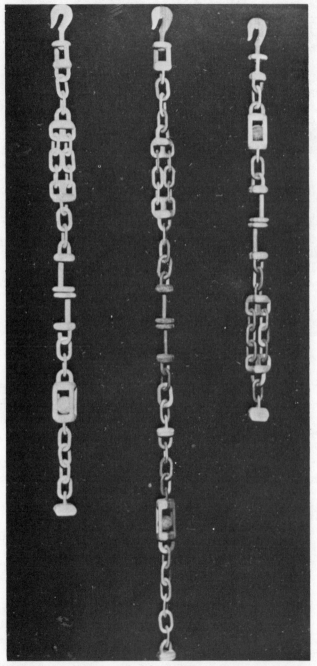

(Fig. 3) Varied chains: the chain on the left is carved out of basswood; the other two are cedar. Double Links, Slip Joints, Single Links, and Ball-in-Cages are illustrated.

John's technique in whittling these chains is very consistent. He begins with a piece of wood that looks about the size of a vertically quartered fence post, and he marks off with pencil on the wood the form he wants the chain to take. This requires estimating the length of the piece and fitting a number of designs into the allotted space in such a way as to fill up all the space and eliminate or disguise any flaws or knots in the wood. John contends that when he first started making chains he never marked off his designs the way he does now, but he must have found the pencil markings helpful in executing his chains because he reports that he has been marking off his chains for almost fifty years, or since shortly after he began whittling them. After he has set up his pattern, John will bore out and whittle an outline of his basic designs, usually by the use of a spey blade and wood chisel. After he has worked the wood into a skeletal outline of the finished product, he then uses a power drill to help break the links and to start the ball that will nest in a cage. He finishes his work with a spear blade and always does the hook and swivel at the top of the chain last so as not to get it caught in anything while he is still whittling the rest of the chain.

John uses a series of designs in his Varied Chains which I shall term Single Links, Double Links, Ball-in-Cage, Slip Joint, and Step Design. John has no name for any of these patterns; the terms have been borrowed from printed sources, except for the term Step Design, which I will use to describe a pattern possibly unique to John's craft.[8] When John carves any chain, he places these designs in whatever order is necessary to make the pattern fit the specific chain, but there do seem to be certain abstract patterns that are rigidly observed. If, for example, we allow the Single Link sections to be represented by an x and all the other designs by other letters — a, b, c, etc. — John always places an x or Single Link section between all the other designs: for example, xaxbxcx. He has carved some chains by beginning the top section under the hook and swivel with a Double Link, and he has finished some chains with a design other than a Single Link pattern. The result is that some chains might be represented by the following formulas: axbxcx or xaxbc; Single Links, though, are always used to set off the other designs. Even in a particularly short chain (see Fig. 3, chain on right) on which John had to cram a number of designs, he kept Single Link sections between all the other designs although there is only one full single link and two half links in each of the separating sections of the chain. And for a particularly long chain, when John has excess wood to carve, he has devised an extra knob that separates one of the Single Link sections in two (see Fig. 3, chain in center), but always the other designs are kept separate by the Single Link sections. This symmetrical pattern, which John does not seem to execute consciously, makes the chains appealing, at least in the eyes of the elitist critic, because it keeps the specialized and eye-catching designs from running together and producing a cluttered effect.

To whittle the Single Links, John makes incisions with a hand saw into the square piece of wood from opposite sides of the wood to close to the center, repeating the process at right angles to the first incisions about an inch apart. He repeats this process for as many links as he wishes and then gouges out with a

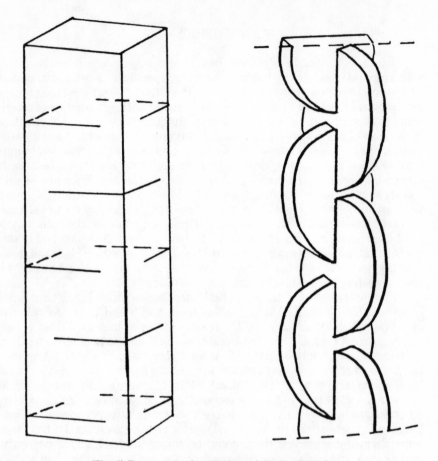

(Fig. 4) Two steps in the whittling of the Single Links

wood chisel all of the wood except two planes which intersect like a cross (Fig. 4). Then John uses a drill to break through the wood before he finishes the whittling that separates the links. The separation of the links contributes to the lengthening of the chain since there is a space of about an extra half-inch that falls free in every link that is whittled. For the Double Links John follows very much the same procedure, except that in this case he must gouge the wood differently so that he creates a double set of potential links set against a flat plane.

In whittling the Ball-in-Cage, John makes twenty drill marks, ten on each of two opposite faces of the wood. Of these ten, five are placed on the inside of what will be the roof of the cage, and five are placed on the inside of what will be the base of the cage (Fig. 5). John then drills through these holes, working his drill back and forth until he fuses all the drilled holes. He then takes a knife and digs incisions into the wood along vertical lines between the areas he has drilled, and these vertical lines will become the inside posts of the cage. In forming the

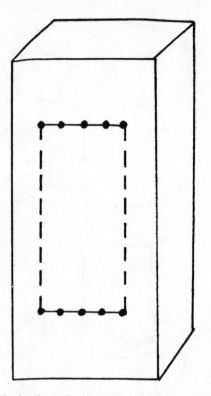

(Fig. 5) Drill marks for the Ball-in-Cage: the dotted line represents the vertical incision.

ball, John takes a spear blade and cuts grooves in the wood from the center of the design toward the sides where he has dug his incisions. He continues working this way, digging his knife deeper at the ends where the material must be cut away and rounded to form the ball.

The Slip Joint adds a bit of virtuosity to a non-utilitarian piece of art and a sense of tactile pleasure for anyone who picks up and handles John's chains. To allow the joints to slide freely, John whittles away all but four horizontal, circular sections and three groups of two short vertical posts that hold the four circular sections together (Fig. 6). Two of these posts on the opposite sides of the outer sections are then cut away, and incisions are made into the middle sections at the base of the four remaining posts, which allow the four posts to connect, become two, and slide freely.

John's Step Design (Fig. 7) is of special interest because it is the one pattern in his chains that I have been unable to find pictured or described in literature on whittling.[9] John contends that he originally used the design to remove a particularly deep knot from a piece of wood, the center section of the Step Design being the narrowest area John ever whittles in his chains. There are times that scars run so deep in a piece of wood that even this drastic method fails to remove the entire scar (as in Fig. 7). After developing this design to rid his chains of

195

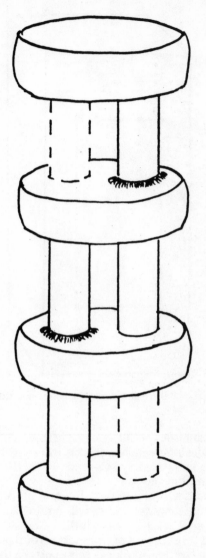

(Fig. 6) Slip Joint: the dotted posts are cut away completely.

knots, John indicates that he once used the pattern at the bottom of a chain just because it fit the amount of space that he needed. He eventually placed the design on some chains where there was no need for cleaning up knots or scars in the wood. Although this is the least commonly used of John's designs, he is of late using it more and more as part of his repertoire and not merely as a device for saving a piece of wood.

196

(Fig. 7) John Arnold's Step Design with remnant of a knot scar

AESTHETICS

John's attitude toward his work and his comments about it deserve discussion because they reveal a typical characteristic of the folk artist: the lack of an expressed aesthetic. It is interesting to note that John lacks a vocabulary of terms with which to discuss his chains, not only in dealing with aesthetics, but even in identifying the specific parts of the chains he whittles. For example, I asked John on several occasions what he calls the various parts of his chains (what I term Slip Joint, Step Design, etc.), and each time he indicated that he had no name for them. John's failure to offer names for these patterns cannot be ascribed to a reluctance to report such names because John always freely volunteered information. In fact, in proving to me that he had no names for his patterns and various pieces, he related a story that a man in Illinois, who had heard of his work, once called him on the phone and offered him a large sum of money for the World's Fair Chain. But never having seen the chain, the prospective buyer demanded a name and description of the object he would be buying. When John told him that he could not say exactly what it was and that he had no name for it, the man withdrew his offer.[10]

The absence of verbalized response to questions about his art is a fairly typical feature of the folk artist, and John's lack of terminology is paralleled by an inability to discuss aesthetics.[11] I once remarked to John, for example, that I preferred his cedar chains because the two-tone color of the wood set off the two halves of the Slip Joints and the Double Links so perfectly and because at times the two-toned whittled ball in a Ball-in-Cage would get spun out of line with the original two-tone pattern of the wood. John's response was not to respond; he seemed baffled by my comments. Though the chain is obviously attractive because of this effect, John's reaction seemed to indicate that he neither strived for it nor recognized it as a pleasing feature of his chains. Whenever he did discuss cedar chains, John would emphasize the difficulties he had in working with the medium; he favors the linden to the cedar for that reason. On another occasion, I asked John why he spaced all his designs with Single Link sections, and John again failed to respond. When the question was reasked, John, having looked carefully at the chain he was working on, said, yes, he did use Single Link sections on his chains between the other patterns. Then in qualifying that statement, he talked about the measurements of the Single Links down to a sixteenth of an inch, revealing that he was not so much aware of the abstract pattern as he was concerned with the measurements that he had to know to mark out his chains.

In one interview, however, John made a startling statement that may indicate that he does have an awareness of aesthetics. He reported that he once accidentally ran a Ball-in-Cage and a Slip Joint together because he was careless and failed to see his mistake before he began whittling his piece of marked wood. John knew that to run two such designs together was bad and he was angry with himself, but he had no real explanation as to why it was bad. One trained in art could produce an aesthetic explanation of the problem resulting from running two designs together: the effect would be cluttered and would not allow the eye sufficient time to separate and distinguish the various specialized designs on the chain, and, of course, the symmetry would be destroyed. Yet John knew only that he had made a mistake. It may be then that John separates all his special designs with Single Link sections, not because he is consciously aware of any theories regarding symmetry, but because he has developed intuitively, devoid of an aesthetic vocabulary, a recognition of what works.[12]

But I may be making a serious error in judgment if I assume that John responded to the mistake of running the Ball-in-Cage and the Slip Joint together by recognizing what I recognize — namely, that the resultant chain would be less attractive. There is another way of looking at the problem that may lend insight into the technique of the folk artist. A careful study of John's chains indicates that if John ran a Ball-in-Cage and a Slip Joint together, he would also run into a difficult technical problem: the base of the Ball-in-Cage would have to serve as the top of the Slip Joint, an impossible situation because the Ball-in-Cage invariably has a square base and the Slip Joint a round top. We might assume then that the aesthetically pleasing symmetrical effects in John's chains (xaxbxc) are the result of the technical requirement of separating the oddly shaped bases of the various designs.[13]

All this leads me to believe that the attractiveness of John's chains is either the result of a fortunate accident, as in the two-tone color of the cedar, or the result of John's need to solve a technical problem, as in the symmetry which develops from the need to space with Single Links the dissimilarly shaped bases of the other designs. The attractive Step Design, too, evolved from the need to overcome a technical problem: the possibility of a chain being made unattractive if a deep knot scar were not eliminated. The solution of technical problems, not aesthetic awareness, is the basis of the development of these beautiful chains.

There is one other significant recognition that tends to confirm the idea that John is not aware of or concerned with elitist concepts of aesthetics such as symmetry. The pleasure that John experiences in whittling derives from the challenge of overcoming the technical problems of manipulating the wood, and John is proud of his accomplishment in this area. He reported, for example, that several men have tried to imitate his chains but have had difficulty in executing them. John does not object to anyone imitating his chains — an obvious mark of a folk artist — partly because he realizes how difficult it is to do so. John brags that a man in Pine Bluff, Arkansas, "wasted enough lumber to build a bridge" in attempting to develop the skills that John has mastered. Scholars from Franz Boas to Michael Owen Jones have recognized that the pleasure derived from solving technical problems is one of the prime motivating forces of the folk artist.[14] Nor has John's fascination with technical challenges ceased, for John recently told me that if he can only get some white pine, he wants to try a new twisting link that he has had in his head for some time, but that he had not yet had the opportunity to try.

NOTES

[1] See "What is American Folk Art? A Symposium," *Antiques* 57 (1950), pp. 355-362.
[2] Michael Owen Jones has published numerous essays on folk art; the most important for this paper are "The Concept of 'Aesthetic' in the Traditional Arts," *Western Folklore* 30

(1971), pp. 77-104; "Two Directions for Folkloristics in the Study of American Arts," *Southern Folklore Quarterly* 32 (1968), pp. 249-259; "Violations of Standards of Excellence and Preference in Utilitarian Art," *Western Folklore* 32 (1973), pp. 19-32; and "The Useful and the Useless in Folk Art," *Journal of Popular Culture* 6 (1973), pp. 794-819. In *Pattern in the Material Folk Culture of the Eastern United States* (Philadelphia: University of Pennsylvania Press, 1968), Henry Glassie defines qualities that he feels are essential to folk art and traces historic and geographic connections for some specific traditions. See also Henry Glassie, "Folk Art," in *Folklore and Folklife, An Introduction*, ed. Richard M. Dorson (Chicago: University of Chicago Press, 1972), pp. 253-280.

[3]The fair was the Chicago Century of Progress Exposition of 1933-34, but I have been unable to determine if the chain was ever formally displayed. The printed guide to the fair only gives a broad description of the major exhibits, and thus no record exists of the chain. John only knows that the chain was brought to the fair; he does not know what happened to it while in Chicago. Perhaps it was exhibited, perhaps the individuals who brought it merely displayed it around by themselves.

[4]John is not consistent in reporting an average time for the whittling of his chains because the time required varies due largely to a variety in the quality of the wood and the length of the chain. He has reported that it takes him as little as thirty to thirty-five hours for a chain and as much as seventy. Fifty-five hours is a common answer.

[5]Illustrations of the various types of blades and knives are available in E. J. Tangerman, *Whittling and Woodcarving* (1936: reprint New York: Dover, 1962), pp. 28-29.

[6]John reports that he recently left a craft fair at Monticello's Pioneer Days because a number of children made him nervous by handling his chains carelessly.

[7]John's struggle with the problem of whittling interlocking rings is not unique. For example, see William Harvest, "How to Whittle Interlocked Rings," *Popular Science*, December 1932, p. 70. Tangerman (p. 81) offers a brief suggestion on how to whittle interlocked rings.

[8]The term Ball-in-Cage is taken from Tangerman; his term Simple Chain has been modified to Single Links to differentiate it from Double Links. The term Slip Joint derives from an article by Lynne Beeles entitled "Whittling is 65-Year Old Hobby for Monticello Man," which appeared in the *Advance Monticellonian*, 31 January 1974, p. 2, section 1, col. 3.

[9]Any information from anyone who knows of a design similar to this one would be appreciated. I have been unable to discover anything like it either in illustrations or at fairs and art and craft displays. A large number of chains and whittled artifacts are pictured in Tangerman (see especially pp. 74, 84, 108-109). These chains were part of a collection made for a national contest announced in *Popular Mechanics*, January 1932, pp. 7-8, and entitled "$1,000 in Cash Offered to Whittlers." An official of *Popular Mechanics* informed me that neither the collection nor the photographs were preserved. Illustrations of a few other chains are available in Grover Brinkman, "Artist With a Pocket Knife," *Relics*, June 1970, p. 9; and Joan Roberson, "Intricate Carving," *Relics*, June 1971, pp. 16-18.

[10]Lynne Beeles, who interviewed John for an article which appeared in a local newspaper, reports similar findings: "Arnold has never named his creations, though he has been urged to do so by various persons from time to time. He has read books in which identifications of some carvings are made, but to him the whittling is whittling and he knows the design he want [sic] to make."

[11]Numerous scholars have written about the folk artist's inability to discuss aesthetics. In "Folk Art," p. 266, Glassie comments, "With centuries of art criticism behind us, it is often surprising that the folk artist has no articulation for his aesthetic other than production." In "The Concept of 'Aesthetic,'" p. 80, Jones explains, "One of the most

difficult tasks in an investigation of folk aesthetics is how to ascertain what an individual's response to an object is when present evidence suggests that he does not usually verbalize his reactions." Although Jones is speaking as much of the audience as of the craftsman or artist, he criticizes scholars like Franz Boas for arriving at aesthetic principles *a posteriori* because, he feels, "we still do not know who within a group takes the objects aesthetically how much of the time, nor do we know the depth of the response of the individuals" (p. 81).

[12]An interesting analogy might be drawn between symmetrical patterns in folk art and the use of formulas in oral-formulaic verse. In *The Singer of Tales* (Cambridge: Harvard University Press, 1960), p. 32, Albert Lord comments on the acquisition of such a style: "If the singer is in the Yugoslav tradition, he obtains a sense of ten syllables followed by a syntactic pause, although he never counts out ten syllables, and if asked, might not be able to tell how many syllables there are between pauses."

[13]The Double Links have oval bases and thus also need to be separated by Single Link sections from the square-based Ball-in-Cage and the circular-based Slip Joint.

[14]In "The Useful and the Useless," p. 796, Jones contends that "one can empathize with the master craftsman who derived pleasure from overcoming diffiulties that initially baffled his cleverness, for one of the essential features of folk art is simply that it gives pleasure — to the creator as well as to the owner — whether the object be viewed or used." See also Franz Boas, *Primitive Art* (1927: reprint New York: Dover, 1955), p. 349.

Thanks are due to Diane Gilleland for technical assistance with the photographs, to Mary Reuter for the sketches, and to Wayne Viitanen for criticism of earlier stages of the paper.

This article originally appeared in Mid-South Folklore *5 (Summer, 1977), pp. 41-52 and is reprinted here with the permission of the author and the Ozark States Folklore Society.*